THE PERSONAL COMPUTER INVESTMENT HANDBOOK

THE PERSONAL COMPUTER INVESTMENT HANDBOOK

BY JON ZONDERMAN

TAB BOOKS Inc.
BLUE RIDGE SUMMIT, PA. 17214

FIRST EDITION

FIRST PRINTING

Printed in the United States of America

Library of Congress Cataloging in Publication Data

Zonderman, Jon.
The personal computer investment handbook.

Includes index.
1. Investment—Data processing. 2. Microcomputers-Programming. I. Title.
HG4515.5.Z66 1984 332.6'78'02854 84-8789
ISBN 0-8306-0807-9
ISBN 0-8306-1807-4 (pbk.)

Contents

Acknowledgments

I would like to acknowledge the assistance of all the people in both the securities and computer industries who gave their time for telephone and face-to-face interviews, demonstrations of their products, and their views of where we are going in the computerized investing world.

Most of all, I would like to thank my wife, Laurel Shader, for taking time out from her busy schedule as a medical student to read, critique, and proofread successive drafts of the manuscript, and for her unending patience with a new author.

Introduction

In the past five years, the phrase "personal computing" has taken on new meaning. With the introduction of desktop computers available at prices most middle-class consumers can afford, the power of the computer is available to all.

When Apple Computer Company and other innovators in the personal computer world began introducing desktop computers in 1977 and 1978, their advertising and marketing people tried to convince Americans that personal computers would soon be used to perform a myriad of household functions.

This proved not to be, and by 1979 personal computers were being marketed as business-oriented tools. Today, while the majority of PCs are still being sold to business users, we are seeing a re-emergence of activity in the household market. Yet the list of household chores computers can perform remains paltry and is mostly limited to game playing, running education programs for reinforcement of what children learn in school, some data-base management tasks such as organizing the recipe book or cataloging the library, and some simple home financial management. The computer still cannot—or at least cannot *effectively* and *inexpensively*—control the heat, turn on the coffeepot in the morning, run the security and fire alarm systems, and do an ongoing energy audit.

One area of home use in which the computer *has* gained a prominent place is investment decisions. *The Personal Computer Investment Handbook* is designed to help you understand how the personal computer can be employed in investing and the history of the computer-investing movement.

This book is for the individual investor, regardless of how much money he or she has invested. The theories—both of investing and of computing—are the same regardless of your stake in the financial markets. The way you apply those theories and the amount of time, effort, and money you spend in the attempt to maximize your investments will depend on how you view your investing: as hobby, avocation in the hopes of making enough to make it a vocation, or merely computer game. Because you will have to make an initial investment in computer hardware and additional investments in software to become a computerized investor, you may find the money necessary to get involved in computer-aided investing is more than you can ever hope to make on investment returns.

You may decide that scratch paper and calculator will continue to suffice. There are some other ways around the cost issue. You can write your own programs or copy some of the "public domain" software that exists through computer user and investment groups. In the future, given changes in current copyright laws, there is even the possibility of software sharing.

This book will not attempt to teach you how to program computers to do investment decision programs. Nor will it attempt to teach you all there is to know about investment theory. It will give you a rudimentary understanding of the various types of investments that can be entered into by an individual and of how to analyze possible investments. There are many good books on investment theory and an increasing number of information sources becoming available for those who would like to learn about programming simple investment-oriented programs. Some of these are listed in Appendix B.

I will concentrate on software that is commercially available. At the end of many of the chapters will be lists of software to perform the tasks described in the chapter: fundamental analysis of stocks, technical analysis, bond analysis, analysis of stock options and financial futures, and analysis of commodities. There is also a list of programs to help manage and analyze your portfolio. These lists are as comprehensive as possible, although new programs are being marketed all the time. The prices listed as well as the types of computers each program runs on are current to December 1983. I have not personally tested all of the programs listed, and much of the material about them comes from the companies' promotional literature.

This book will deal only with financial investments, not with hard assets such as gold, art, and collectibles. So far, the only hard asset that computer programs have been designed to analyze is real estate. Although there are many programs for analyzing the real estate market, it is so different from "paper" investments that it falls far beyond the scope of this book.

This book will not deal with the increasing number of personal computer programs that assist in tax record-keeping and tax preparation or with home financial management programs. Although many of the portfolio management programs discussed take into account the tax consequences of various investment decisions, they are not primarily concerned with taxes.

In addition to the discussion of how personal computers are used for individual investors to analyze various markets and to manage their portfolios, the final two chapters of this book deal with how the personal computer has affected and will affect the broader investment world. Chapter 12 discusses the brokerage industry and how the personal computer is turning it upside down. Chapter 13 takes a brief look at some of the new technological breakthroughs of Artificial Intelligence and Local Area Networks that could add other dimensions to the personal computer and the investing field in the next decade or two.

In short, this book is a primer for the

personal investor who wants—in fact, *needs*—to understand how his or her life will be changed as we approach the 21st century.

This book will incorporate some of my own biases with regard to both investing and computing. I will always endeavor to present all possible approaches to a problem. There will, no doubt, be many who will disagree with my notions of computers, investments, and where we are going in the future.

Chapter 1

In the Beginning

"As time goes on we are going to rely less and less on our feelings. We will instead feed data into computers and the computers will analyze it. The catch is, what data will we put into the computers?"

Isaac Asimov, the noted scientist, science fiction author, historian, and man-of-letters asked this not-so-rhetorical question on December 8, 1983, at Impact 84, a meeting and exposition for investment professionals sponsored by *Wall Street Computer Review*. In his glib way, Asimov, in his luncheon address to the members of the audience—investment software makers and dealers, brokers, bank trust officers, private money managers, and a few individual investors—captured the central irony about the computer age and the aspect of computers most misunderstood by the public at large. Computers neither think nor create the data they use. They are only as good as the data stored in their memory and the ways they have been programmed to manipulate that data.

Asimov recounted to his listeners the idea behind one of his masterpieces of science fiction, the *Foundation* trilogy. *Foundation's* premise is this: A prior civilization has destroyed itself. The computers that have been developed over the years by the three major powers that make up the civilization—computers that have been programmed to determine what each major power should do in the economic realm—begin collaborating, taking the human element out of international—indeed intergalactic—decision-making. Now the new civilization is spawning, and Harry Seldon tries to devise a system of analyzing past and present human experience so that the rulers of the new civilization will be more efficient. All human behavior is averaged so that neither a saint nor an abomination can skew the overall chart. No one is allowed to know that he or she is being watched and analyzed, for fear that he would then behave unnaturally—like a person who senses his picture is about to be taken at a party or people who are at an event where there are television cameras. After conducting his analysis of billions of bits of historical and contemporary human behavior, Seldon devices the study of "psychohistory." Given any hypothetical situation, Seldon could predict the response of individuals, nations, worlds, and even galaxies.

Just as he was in danger of losing his audience of hard-driving, bottom-line-oriented money people, Asimov made the connection between his nearly 40-year-old literary triumph and the topic at hand. "What information is necessary for computers to analyze Wall Street?" he asked. Then, answering his own question, he stated:

"They have to know everything about human beings. There isn't anything human beings can do that doesn't affect the markets. It is impossible to do a proper job of computerizing the investing without computerizing humanity. We're going to end up not just with a program to analyze the stock market, but we're going to end up with psychohistory. Anything that can reduce Wall Street to calculations and logical analysis will reduce humanity and its emotions to calculations and logical analysis."

While psychohistory and perfect analysis are, most likely, going to remain forever in the imaginations of men like Asimov and on the pages of books such as the *Foundation* trilogy, it is obvious that since the dawning of the computer age—roughly 30 years ago—quantification of the behavior of markets, if not people, has become more refined. This has led us to a new age for investors—an age that is both exciting and frought with peril, a field loaded with creative tension and mined with apprehension. New methods of gambling on the financial and economic future of the world are being devised every day; new sources of information are becoming available. Deregulation of the financial services industry is diversifying the information sources open to individual investors, and the downward trend in prices of computers is making them increasingly more accessible to all.

But there is also an increasing danger that the investor will lose sight of the forest for the trees—lose sight of his or her investment goals and be devoured by the myriad of opportunities to make (and lose) money playing what is increasingly becoming one gigantic crapshoot.

Of Markets and Micros: Markets

Investing has long been one of America's favorite pastimes. Companies looking to put their spare cash to work for a short while, pension funds seeking to parlay worker contributions into more money for future retirees, and individuals—those who seek to establish a nest egg for later life and those who like the gambling aspect of investing—each year trade billions of shares in America's corporate wealth.

They do this investing in a number of different ways, through a number of different vehicles, and there are probably only a few of us alive who do not own—however indirectly—some corporate wealth. Our banks invest in short-term commercial paper; our insurance companies own massive portfolios, as do our pension funds.

There is, to be sure, no way to make your money grow without investing it. From the first person who realized that he could lend spare cash to someone else and get more back at a later date, to the world's first bankers, to those who began a business and sold stock in it, through the bubbles and pyramids and runups and pools of history, past the Medecis, the Rothchilds, the Rockefellers, and the Ponzis, people have been trying to increase their wealth by investing it in businesses, governments, banks, insurance, and a variety of other schemes, scams, and games.

Your checking account—if you have a NOW account—is an investment, as is your house, the silverware you use at holiday dinners, and the art that hangs on your walls. But for the sake of this book, we will discuss only *financial* investments—paper investments that represent shares of businesses, governments, or future production and refinement of natural resources. The markets we will discuss at greatest length are the *stock* market, the *bond* market, the market for *options* on stocks and stock indexes, and the *commodities* markets, where contracts for future delivery of raw materials are made.

These markets offer different risks and rewards. Bonds pay a fixed rate of interest—sometimes without federal and/or state tax on the return—and hence have modest swings in open-market price. Stocks often have a dividend payment as well as the opportunity to appreciate or depreciate more wildly on the open market. Options are used as a tool by both speculators in search of fast money and hedgers who want to protect an investment. Commodities provide much the same type of market as stock options.

The market most people know the most about is, no doubt, the stock market. At a certain point in the life of many companies, they get so big that family or "closely-held" ownership cannot provide the money needed to keep the business going. A company may find its market increasing so fast that it needs more manufacturing space and component parts than private financing—through individual investors and loans—can accommodate. At this point the company engages in an "initial public offering," selling stock either held by the company or by original investors to the public to provide capital for future expansion. Pressure to "go public" also comes from those who put up the original capital to begin the business, who often do so with the idea that the company will eventually sell stock to the public and the value of their percentage of the company will be increased dramatically. Stock, therefore, is a small piece of ownership in the company issuing it, and is also known as *equity*.

After this initial public offering, investors are no longer buying stock from the company or from the original investors and owners, but instead from one another on the open market. This occurs either through a central exchange such as the New York Stock Exchange or American Stock Exchange, or through the so-called "Over-the-Counter" markets. Once the stock is on the open market, changes in price have as much to do with what people think the market will do in the future as it does with what people think the company will do in the future. The stock market also fluctuates with the fortunes of other investment markets and with rumor and speculation about the economy and world events. Since the options market is predicated on the underlying stock values in the stock market, these two markets move somewhat in tandem.

The bond market is affected by a more narrow range of factors, since bondholders are creditors—a bond is actually an IOU for the face value, payable at a certain date in the future, with the promise that interest on the loan will be paid regularly. Bondholders, therefore, are not equity owners but merely creditors. In the case of the financial failure of a company, bondholders would be paid before stockholders. In a similar way, short-term fluctuations in a company's fortunes do not send the price of bonds in that company nosediving like stocks, because the bondholders are more confident that the money will continue to be in the company coffers to meet the bond obligations.

The bond market is more significantly affected by the interest rate, the rate that must be paid to borrow funds. Bonds that pay lower interest are considered inferior investments if there are bonds issued—either in the same company or in different companies—that pay higher interest.

Commodity markets are affected by all sorts of vagaries such as the weather in regions of the world where resources are, as well as other matters that influence supply and demand.

But let's get back to the stock market for a moment, because that is where the majority of trading action is, especially among small investors. It is also the market that the majority of computer software is designed to deal with, although there is some software that can be used to analyze more than one market.

Investors and Speculators

When investors work to determine how to invest their money, a number of factors come into play. But when these factors are reduced to the lowest common denominator, the name of the game is *risk versus reward.* How much risk do I want to incur in an effort for great reward versus how much steady reward do I want for as little risk as possible? Is $5,000 in a bank account earning nine percent better than the same $5,000 in stocks, or a tax-free bond, or a contract to buy winter wheat? Is $5,000 in the stock market better off in AT&T or spread out over five growth stocks?

The decision has a lot to do with your basic theory of investing. *Investing* in its most narrow meaning is the preservation of capital and the accumulation of added wealth—making your money grow—at a steady, if not great, rate. This is the conservative definition, and conservatives define all the fast-paced, high risk/reward methods of investing as *speculation*.

Many people get into investing in the conservative sense only to be caught up in what many experts see as the gamesmanship of investing; they gradually broaden their definition to include things that, only a short time before, they may have considered purely speculative forms of gambling—buying soybean contracts, high-technology stocks, etc. This happens to investors who do their own decision-making as well as to those who have their investments managed by a money manager, by putting them into a *mutual fund* (otherwise known as an *investment company*) with a stated investment goal, or by giving their brokers discretion to manage their accounts.

As "Adam Smith" (the pseudonym for George Goodman, a long-time Wall Street honcho) wrote in his 1967 *The Money Game*:

"If you are a player in the Game, or are thinking of becoming one, there is one irony of which you should be aware. The object of the Game is to make money, hopefully a lot of it. And the players in the Game are getting rapidly more professional; the amount of sheer information poured out on what is going on has become almost too much to absorb. The true professionals in the Game—the professional money managers—grow more skilled all the time. They are human and they make mistakes, but if you have your money managed by a truly alert mutual fund or even by one of the better banks, you will probably have a better job done for you than at any time in the past."

One of the reasons for this increase in the amount of information available and the increase in professionalism on the part of money managers, Smith theorized, was the growth in use of large computers to both store data and crunch numbers as part of the money manager's analysis.

In addition to increasing the ability of money managers to do detailed, careful analysis and accumulate more information more quickly, Smith also argues that the rise of the mainframe computer changed the complexion of investing—along with other factors in the post-Word War II economy of the United States.

In the 1960s, partially because of the computer and the confidence it gave money managers in following more stocks, getting more information about each company, and doing faster analysis, the name of the Game changed. Prudence gave way to performance. Mutual funds were rated each year for their performance, and money managers were chosen by individual clients on the basis of how "go-go" they had been, not how steady. A 50 percent increase in the value of one's holdings in one year was better than five consecutive 10 percent increases, many investors felt. As Smith writes:

"For years, it didn't matter that the managers had taken over. The portfolio was not yet an Instrument of Personality. The Portfolio Manager was instructed to leave speculation to the speculators; he was participating in the Long-Term Growth of the American Economy. His portfolio had two hundred stocks, and they were the two hundred biggest companies in America. The two hundred stocks were only two-thirds of the portfolio; the other third was bonds. The portfolio manager's charter came from an ancient case, Amory vs. Harvard College, 1831, which ruled that a fiduciary act 'as would any Prudent Man.' To be a Prudent Man, one preserved capital, one was conservative, one ate breakfast, lunched at the Club, and died with an estate that won the admiration of the lawyers for its order and efficiency. The Prudent Man managing securities did his business with his classmates who happened to be brokers, and in a radical move he might reduce Steels from 3.3 percent to 2.9 percent of the portfolio, and buy a little more telephone."

Smith's glibness hides a very important point: As computers entered the fray and computing power—both in terms of information storage and numbers crunching—became worth money, the Game changed from one of steady growth with a little on the side for a speculative venture to one of trying to find something that was, in the words of the brokerage profession, "going to pop" and finding out about it before everyone else did. Money managers and mutual fund managers tripped over each other trying to get at "good things," and as the tools of the trade—computers and the analysis tool that they used—became more widely disseminated in the money management community, it became harder and harder to beat the other players to the real deals.

Of Markets and Micros: Micros

Whatever the strategy, the key to investment management is *information*. And until recently, large investment houses and financial institutions, with bullpens of researchers and powerful mainframe computers, were able to keep track of and determine the quality of far more investment possibilities than any individual or small shop—usually working with pencil and paper, or at best constrained to the financial limitations of timesharing on a large computer system—could ever dream of.

But the microcomputer—or personal computer, as individuals are wont to call it—is rapidly diminishing the large company's advantage. With increasingly sophisticated software packages and access to electronic databases replete with the latest financial news, prices, required filings to the Securities and Exchange Commission, and macroeconomic forecasting, microcomputer users are rapidly becoming serious players in the Game. Personal computers are, in short, democratizing the Game.

Personal computer users from both major schools of investment analysis—technical analysis and fundamental analysis—now have a full line of software to increase the information they receive and allow them to characterize that information in ways they are most accustomed to dealing with.

Adherents of *technical analysis* believe that an investment's past performance with regard to volume and price will determine how it will move in the future. Disciples of the *fundamental analysis* school believe the markets react to outside influences that are often found in the miniscule headlines on the back pages of newspapers or lost in the news processing business altogether—items that tell of a drop in earnings at the company, a shakeup in management, or such positive news as a new product or that the company has taken a larger market share against a major competitor. While many hard-core technical analysts—often called *chartists*—concern themselves only with the statistical information, some limit themselves to following the charts of companies they find fundamentally sound. Many fundamental analyists, once they have decided what company to invest in, then chart the stock's past performance, looking for a soft spot to make a purchase below the point where the investor thinks the stock's intrinsic value lies.

There is also a third theory of investing, the "Random Walk" or "Efficient Market." Adherents to this theory believe that if you pick stocks by sticking a pin in the New York Stock Exchange chart in the daily newspapers every three months and buying that stock, then hold the stocks for a few years each, your portfolio will perform as well as an actively managed one—either a technical or fundamental analyst's—over the long haul. These people obviously have no need for computer software to help them in their decision-making.

What takes a computer seconds would take an investor working by hand hours. Gathering statistical data on a potential investment's past performance and putting those statistics into a manageable form—usually a graphic representation—is only the first step. Keeping files on companies, including these charts, newspaper clippings, prospectuses, and other pertinent data is a nearly impossible task for an individual. Even the most diligent investor is missing information. Under the rules of the Securities and Exchange Commission and other federal government agencies, companies are compelled to disclose enormous amounts of information. The Dow Jones News Service collects this information, but only a fraction gets into the *Wall Street Journal*, much less metropolitan newspapers or wire services. It does, however, stay in the news service files long enough to be read by a personal computer user who has access to the Dow Jones News/Retrieval Service.

The current investment software for personal computers falls into a number of categories. There is software to do fundamental analysis—to screen possible investments for a broad array of fundamental criteria. There is software (an abundance of it) for technical analysis, charting based on the most sophisticated and most obscure notions of important market indicators. There is software to analyze options, commodities, bonds, and convertible bonds (bonds that have a value if converted to stock as well as bonds). There are programs to keep track of your portfolio, including your sales, purchases, gains, losses and all the associated tax consequences. There are also programs that allow you to turn your personal computer into a tickertape and keep track of the moment-to-moment activities of the market.

Hardware

Before we delve into the world of software, let's take a look at the computer hardware you will need to become a 21st-century investor.

What hardware is necessary for the home investor? As we will see later when we discuss software, that depends on exactly *what you want to do*.

The basics of a personal computer are a *central processing unit*, at least one *disk drive* (there is no investment software on tape cassette or cartridge), and a *monitor.* Two disk drives are more useful than one, since a number of the programs call for data to be stored on diskettes, and for ease of making backup copies of data diskettes.

If you want to use programs that produce graphics, you will need to make sure that your central processing unit will accommodate graphics software and that your monitor will reproduce the graphics.

If you want to be able to get hard copy of the data you work with on your screen, you will need a *printer.* A *letter-quality* printer is not necessary; in fact, to do graphics you will want a good quality *dot-matrix* printer.

Finally, more and more investment-oriented software is predicated on the ability to communicate with remote databases over telephone lines. To do this, you need a *modem* (modulator/demodulator), which allows your computer to get information from other computers, store it, display it, or print it out. Investors who want to get prices on a daily basis will probably want to get an auto-dialer so the computer can be programmed to call the Dow/Jones News Retrieval Service each evening during the off-peak hours.

Very few new investment programs are being written that do not necessitate the use of a modem. For the investor who has a lot of different holdings and wants to update them constantly, the modem is almost an indispensable tool. After all, why have a computer if you have to spend hours each day—or even each week—keying in information from the stock pages?

The Apple and IBM Market

Although there is investment software available for a number of different personal computers, the vast majority of the software runs on Apple II, *II*e, and II+ systems, and the IBM Personal Computer.

These computers provide the power and versatility to do sophisticated investment-oriented tasks. When investment software first came on the scene (about 1980), the Apple II was the top-of-the-line personal computer and the one for which most writers of "serious" software were writing. Since then, the IBM PC has become the *de facto* industry standard, but the Apple is still on the desks of enough investors to make it worthwhile to write software for both machines.

A number of good packages are also becoming available for the Digital Equipment Corporation's Personal Computer line, most notably the Rainbow. Some of the less expensive, less sophisticated programs are also available for the Radio Shack TRS-80 computers, the ATARI 400 and 800, and CP/M-based computers such as the Osborne and KAYPRO. There are even a few programs (though none I know of are available commercially) for some of the new pad-of-paper-sized computers such as the Radio Shack TRS-80 Model 100.

One note of caution: Many computer purchasers are cajoled into buying a cheaper "IBM-compatible" model, known to the less charitable as an "IBM clone." There are more than 25 machines that are considered "compatible," at least by their manufacturers. They are advertised as being compatible because they use the same operating system as the IBM—so called MS-DOS operating system—and the same Intel 8088 16-bit microprocessor chip. The compatibles are often portable, with screens and disk drives built into the basic central processing unit housing and weighing in at less than 30 pounds.

But in many instances they are not *truly* compatible. Compatability is based on how the particular software you want to use is programmed. While some use the generic MS-DOS, some are more deeply programmed, especially to do graphics, depending on the special IBM PC ROM (read only memory), and therefore are hardware-dependent.

If you are considering buying an IBM-compatible, it is especially important that you do some shopping for software before purchasing the hardware to determine if the software you want will run on the machine you are going to buy.

The Economics of Computer-Aided Investing

Those who write software for computer-aided investing like to tell their customers that it's simple and inexpensive, that information about what stocks, bonds, and other investments to buy will be falling into their hands faster than ever before for only a few pennies.

Is this true?

If you already own a computer, you can probably add investing assistance to your repertoire of computer activities for a few hundred dollars up front, depending on how sophisticated you want to get. But let us, for an exercise, build a system from the ground up.

An IBM PC (two disk drives included), with monitor, a decent dot-matrix printer, modem, and auto-dialer will run somewhat over $4,000. An Apple II+ or *II*e comparably equipped, or one of the truly IBM-compatible machines, will be somewhat less, but still over $3,000 with graphics capability.

If you use the computer solely as a tool for investing there is some precedent for Uncle Sam giving you a break on your federal income taxes, but that takes five years to depreciate and if you use your computer only part-time for investing, only the portion of time you use it for that purpose is deductible.

So before you have bought one piece of software or hooked up to a database for one minute (most charge by the minute), you are more than $3,500 in the hole. Add software, time to get connected to a few databases and rummage through them to find out what kind of information is available, and time to figure out how to get the information you want from the databases into your machine, and you have probably spent $5,000 before you make an investment.

This may sound silly. After all, very few people who have never invested before are going to run out and buy computer equipment to begin. If you're reading this book, you're probably already a computer owner and/or an investor—probably both. The point is this: Once you buy the computer you must figure it into your per-trade costs, just as you would commissions to your brokers and taxes. Authors of books that begin "How I Made One Million . . ." often use glib prose in their stories of parlaying a few thousand dollars into the big time to cover the fact that you pay a broker's commission and taxes on each and every trade you make.

A stock bought at $10 and sold at $15 does not make a pure $5 profit. You pay someone to make the purchase and to make the sale. Then you have to pay taxes on the profit. Of course, the taxable profit is calculated after the commissions have been taken into account, so if you bought 100 shares at $10 and sold them for $15, your $500 profit would be reduced by the commissions—probably about $80 to buy and sell through a full-service broker—before you determine your taxable profit.

On the other hand, the time you spend hooked into databases to do your analysis before the purchase, the computer software you buy to help do the analysis, and all the time you are "on-line" getting your daily quotes instead of looking them up in the newspaper the next morning are off-the-top expenses, and cannot be figured into the cost of your transactions (as can your brokers' fees) before you figure your taxable gain or loss. But they are actual expenses and must be figured into your pure profit-from-investing figures to see if you made or lost money. It's similar to determining if you made or lost money at the track—do you include admission, the price of the program, and the *Daily Racing Form* or not? This is a $5 up-front expense these days before you even place a bet—$5 you have to win before you can truly consider that you "broke even." On top of the daily charges you must amortize the computer hardware.

However, the computer can be much more than a toy that siphons off your profits from good trades and makes your bad trades look even worse. Used wisely, the computer can make information gathering that much faster, help keep your records organized, and, indeed, help you make better trades. It can give you time to make money at your primary vocation or spend more time in leisure activities to keep your mind and body fresh for the daily playing of the Game.

One tiny example is called *tax-lot accounting.* If you buy 100 shares of XYZ stock on Jan. 1, 1984, for $10 per share and 100 more shares of XYZ on May 1, 1984, for $9 per share (buying on weakness a company you feel is fundamentally sound), then sell some of it in April 1985 at $7 per share, it is important to determine which lot you want to sell. The reason is taxes.

As tax laws stand right now, a long-term capital gain or loss is a gain or loss from the sale of stock (or any other capital investment) held for more than one year and one day. A short-term capital gain or loss is a gain or loss on a sale of an investment held less than one year and one day. Forty percent of the profit from a long-term capital gain is taxed at your income tax rate, but only 50 percent of a long-term capital loss may be taken off your taxes. In other words, you are taxed for two dollars of every five you make on a long-term capital gain and can write off one dollar for every two you lose on a long-term capital loss. In a short-term situation, any gain is taxed at your regular tax rate, but you are also allowed to write off each dollar you lose.

In the example here, we have a long-term capital loss of $3 per share on the 100 shares purchased in January and a short-term loss of $2 per share on the 100 shares purchased in May. Which is more advantageous to sell? The May purchase, since it will afford us a short-term capital loss writeoff, worth $400, as opposed to a long-term writeoff good for only $300.

But to get the short-term loss benefit, you must declare at the time of the sale which "tax lot" you are selling, or else the IRS will consider that you sold the first block you bought—first in/first out, or FIFO, tax accounting.

If this is your only stock holding, you will have a pretty good idea of when you made your purchase and, consequently, the need to make a decision before your short-term loss runs out. But if you make 100 or 200 trades a year, you can't keep all the short-term/long-term dates in mind.

Your computer can. There are portfolio management programs that warn you when your short-term holding is about to go long-term, and help you keep proper tax-lot records for the IRS each year.

It would take a lot of tax-lot accounting for a computer system to pay for itself. Let's go back to our example of the new investor who shells out $5,000 for a system. How much does he have to use it to get his money's worth?

That depends.

It depends on how long he intends to use the computer—and thus amortize it—as well as how much time he will spend with the computer doing his investments. If he has been saving his pennies for five years and wants to make one stock trade, the computer is going to be a bust. If he has inherited $10,000, spent $5,000 on the computer, and will put the other $5,000 into the market, he's going to have to do some awfully fast footwork or be very lucky to make the investment pay off. If, on the other hand, he inherited $100,000 and will get $95,000 into the market, the computer should pay for itself. (This does not take into account that for the novice investor, without benefit of prior understanding of markets, a computer could grossly mask the complexity of investing and the human element involved.)

Money, Time, and Services

The computer will be far more useful for an investor who has done it by hand—keeping records, charting, clipping, noting, dialing a broker—and has an appreciation for how much time he or she will be saving when using the computer.

I like to frame the question this way: How much time do you spend each week analyzing possible investments, tracking, charting, and maintaining your portfolio? Are you months behind in clipping your copies of the *Wall Street Journal*, causing a fire hazard in your den or office? Do you constantly run out of graph paper in the middle of an important chart? Do you dread tax time not so much for the check you will have to write to Uncle Sam but for the hours it will take you to sort through your piles of confirmation slips and brokerage statements to figure out investment gains and losses?

If the answers to these questions are: "More than 10, yes, yes, and you-betcha," your best investment for this year could turn out to be a personal computer.

Ultimately, the question of whether or not a computer is worthwhile depends not only on how much money you have tied up in the markets, but on how much time you spend each week, what other work or leisure activities you are displacing with the time spent working on your portfolio, and what investment services you could displace with your computer.

The first service you could dispense with if you were a serious computer user and a serious investor would be a full-service broker. With all the available information on databases, you would no longer have to depend on your broker for research—unless of course you trust his or her "tips," unlike many investors. With a computer to help you structure your own research, you could trade through a discount broker, saving between 50 and 75 percent of your commissions.

My guess is that in the next few years we will not see the end of full-service brokerage houses. In the first place, I don't expect computers to invade the home of every small investor. But, in addition, I expect to see changes in the way brokerage houses market services. This will be discussed at greater length later, but some brokerages are currently allowing clients to hook into research "on-line" via computer rather than in paper form, and there are independent research companies putting their information on-line. In the future it seems reasonable to assume that what are presently full-service brokerages will charge customers on a per-service basis.

The second service you can get rid of is your yearly subscription to the *Wall Street Journal.* All price information, and all news information, will be available to you via the computer. Once you become adroit at handling the menu on the screen, you should be able to download the few news stories you want to read in a matter of seconds and store them in your computer's memory until your printer prints them out. Your prices can be downloaded automatically in the late evening with your autodialer. In the future, your autodialer may even work on a keyword basis whereby it can scan the News/Retrieval Service for all articles that interest you, download, and print overnight.

If you are an adherent to technical analysis—a chartist—but don't do your own charts, you can get rid of your chartmaking service. You can also do away with your subscription to the Value Line or Standard and Poor's investors' surveys.

You can get rid of all your subscriptions to newsletters and investors' magazines, since all the information they deal with will be available to you—and, indeed, many of these newsletters will eventually be available online for a fraction of the price you pay for paper copy. Some already are.

Harry Seldon and the Market

Isaac Asimov wrote the *Foundation* trilogy as a series of short stories during the 1940s and early 1950s, when he was considered somewhat of a Utopian thinker—if not a socialist. He gave Seldon, his protagonist, the goal of making a more perfect universe, where governments would not fight if possible and where he could tinker with human events.

Given 40 years of experience in the real world and a more mature—some might say jaded—view of the world, would Asimov, if he were to write the *Foundation* trilogy today, have Harry Seldon corner the market? He only laughed at the question and said he would have to think about it.

There is little chance that Seldon or anyone will ever corner the market. As more and more people have access to greater stores of information—via personal computers—and greater ability to analyze data, what we may see is markets becoming more efficient. Rather than a few dozen money managers chomping at the bit, trying to outguess each other not so much on what they will buy but *when* they will buy it, we may have thousands of investors doing the same thing.

The personal computer gives investors much power, but also adds much temptation to the Game. The goals should remain the same, and the investor whose personal computer does the most for him will be the one who learns how to control the computer—to make it do what he wants it to do—not the one who gets caught up in what the computer can do that he could never do himself.

The successful 21st century investor will be the same type of investor who was successful in the 20th century and the 19th century: the one who does not lose sight of his investment goals. It can only be hoped that the personal computer, with its ability to communicate with data bases and put great amounts of data formerly not available to individual investors at their fingertips in seconds, will democratize the Game, limiting the insiders' ability to rule the markets.

Chapter 2

Going On-Line

Before we look at software for doing specific types of analysis, let's take a brief poke through the world of on-line computing.

As has been mentioned, most new software coming out these days has what is known as "communications capability," the ability to draw prices from on-line databases—usually the Dow Jones News/Retrieval Service—and use that information to update the records of your holdings. This is done using a modem and communications software that allows your computer to communicate with other computers over telephone lines. Dow Jones is by far the most widely used on-line service for individual investors. There is a $50 initial fee to receive a password, and then time charges. The service is on-line from 6 A.M. to 4 A.M. seven days a week, and off-peak charges are as low as $9 per hour.

In addition to downloading prices to update your portfolio management software, you can get information from a number of the databases Dow Jones maintains (on-line information services maintain anywhere from a few to dozens of databases.) This service, known as the Dow Jones Quotes, is available on a 15-minute delay, and includes price information on stocks, options, and corporate bonds. It also gives daily updates of U.S. Treasury bonds and notes, mutual funds, national Over-the-Counter (OTC) quotes, and other foreign and domestic securities.

Dow Jones Databases

Other Dow Jones databases include news from the *Wall Street Journal, Barron's* and the Dow Jones News Service. Rather than waiting for the next morning's *Wall Street Journal* you can receive the news only 90 seconds after it is entered into the news service by the editors.

If you don't want to plow your way through the menu until you find what you want, you can turn to the *Wall Street Journal* Highlights Online, which includes the headlines from major news and summaries of the front and back page stories, descriptions of the editorials, and summaries of the markets page. This is updated each morning at 7:00.

The free text search includes over 150,000 articles from the *Wall Street Journal*, *Barron's* and the Dow Jones News Service dating back to 1979. You can conduct word or date searches. This can be useful to build a back-file on companies or industries you are interested in analyzing.

To delve more deeply into individual companies you can use the Media General Financial Services database, which provides detailed financial data on about 3,200 companies and 170 industries. Information includes revenues, earnings, dividends, price/earnings ratios, and other information. You can also find Disclosure II database on Dow Jones. Disclosure II includes summaries of mandatory Securities and Exchange Commission filings from all New York Stock Exchange, American Stock Exchange, and 6,000 OTC stocks. Information includes balance sheets, income statements, and business segment data, as well as five-year trends for sales, income, and earnings per share. The database also provides names of officers, directors, and subsidiaries. The information is drawn from the 10K and 10Q statements filed with the SEC.

The Corporate Earnings Estimator has per-share earnings forecasts for 2,400 widely followed companies made by analysts at 45 brokerage houses.

For those who want to look at the macroeconomic and national financial outlook, Dow Jones provides two databases. The Weekly Economic Update is a compilation of economic information from the *Wall Street Journal*, *Barron's* and the Dow Jones News Service. Money Market Services provides weekly money supply forecasts as well as forecasts on other leading indicators made by economists and money market dealers at more than 40 financial institutions.

Louis Rukeyser fans will enjoy *Wall Street Week* Online, electronic transcripts of the more recent episodes of the true-life soap opera called Wall Street.

If you get tired poring over all that financial information you can turn to the weather report or sports report, the last two News/Retrieval data bases.

The Dow Jones News/Retrieval Service (P.O. Box 300, Princeton N.J. 08540, toll-free 800-257-5114; in New Jersey 609-452-1511) is considered one of the "Big Three" on-line services available (in terms of number of customers). The other two are The Source (Source Telecomputing Corporation, 1616 Anderson Road, McLean, Va., 22102) and CompuServe (CompuServe Inc., 500 Arlington Center Blvd., Columbus Ohio, 43220).

The Dow Jones system contains far more business and investment information than do The Source and CompuServe, but those two services provide a number of other services, such as airline schedules, news from the major wire services—Associated Press on CompuServe and United Press International on The Source—home banking services and on-line free-for-all discussions on The Source.

For the serious investor there are a number of other on-line data services available. Here are just a few:

Data Resources (Data Resources Inc., Data Products Division Headquarters, 1750 K. St., N.W., Washington D.C. 20006, 202-862-3760): Data Resources headquarters are located in Lexington, Mass. The company has been known for a number of years as a provider of econometric and macroeconomic information and models. Former DRI Senior Economist Alan Sinai has been frequently in-

Rep. to checks Sept. 2 '86

terviewed on the state of the economy, and DRI's founder, Otto Eckstein, is a well-known and well-respected professor of economics. DRI's founder, the late Otto Eckstein, was a well-known and well-respected professor of economics. DRI produces some databases itself and distributes some databases produced by third parties. The DRI databases include DRI Current Economic Indicators, which has statistical information on 20 developed and seven developing countries from 1960 to the present, and Commodities Data Bank, which gives opening, closing, high, and low prices, as well as other information on commodities futures contracts for each trading day. Data from every major exchange in the United States, Canada, and London are offered on such commodities as grains, livestock, foreign currency, financial instruments, energy, and metal.

DRI also has databases that have information on United States economic data, interest rates, stock and bond prices, and a number of other areas.

Recently, DRI has developed two software programs to link personal computers to mainframes.

Chase Econometrics/Interactive Data (486 Totten Pond Road, Waltham MA 02154, 617-890-1234). IDC, as it is still known (Interactive Data Corp. was purchased by Chase Manhattan Bank), boasts the largest data service (over 100 separate databases) of financial and corporate statistics in the world. Among them are Financial, which offers broad coverage of economic indicators including member bank reserves, interest rates, bond and stock activity, and commercial and industrial loans. U.S. Macroeconomics provides figures relating to the nation's economy from weekly, monthly, quarterly and annual statistics from the mid-1940s to the present. Financial Forecast ties this information together and provides two-year forecasts with alternatives using interest rates as the variable. This database draws on information from 1961 to the present. All three databases are produced by Chase.

Compustat, produced by Standard and Poor's Compustat Services Inc., offers financial data for more than 6,000 American companies and quarterly data on 2,800 of them. The data is derived from 10K and 10Q filings with the SEC, updated weekly. (Compustat is also available through DRI and at least seven other on-line information services.)

IDC's commodity database is International Commodities, which has more than 5,500 daily, monthly, quarterly, and annual supply and demand figures going back to 1950 for tin, copper, rubber, coffee, and sugar.

The most useful Chase database is probably Securities Market Data, which covers American and Canadian securities. Over 45,000 securities are updated periodically. Thirty-three descriptive and statistical breakdowns are given. Daily price and volume information dating back to 1968 is provided for over 12,000 equity and fixed-income securities, while weekly bid prices are maintained for over 15,000 unlisted corporate bonds and 7,000 OTC stocks.

Chase/IDC, like DRI, has recently been designing and manufacturing software to link personal computers to their mainframe and databases.

Merlin is a financial database that contains information going back to 1970 on 12,000 stocks, warrants, rights, bonds and government financial instruments; options traded on the American and other exchanges; and commodities information from major exchanges in the United States, Canada, and London. Merlin is distributed by Remote Computing Corporation (1076 East Meadow Circle, Palo Alto

CA 94304, 800-645-3120).

In addition to DRI, other information services provide access to Disclosure II. Warner Communications announced such a link in Dec. 1983, and recently the Disclosure company (5161 River Road, Bethesda MD 20816, 800-638-8076) has produced microDISCLOSURE, a special software package that links users to Disclosure II without having to go through a service.

Research On-Line

In addition to raw information, you can now receive research on-line through a number of brokerage firms and from independent research services.

Argus Research Group (42 Broadway, New York NY 10004, 212-425-7500) in late 1983 introduced Argus On-Line to provide research reports on about 500 stock plus daily updates of news and information impinging on markets. The service provides daily "hot pages" of how the latest news will affect specific equities and bonds, daily options recommendations, daily market comments and economic forecasts (in narrative form rather than numeric charts), and risk arbitrage strategies.

Brokers are also getting into the act, although so far they have limited access to their computers to customers. At the very end of 1983, E.F. Hutton announced Huttonline, a service for its customers to use their home computers to get up-to-the-minute information about their personal accounts (for extra security and privacy, access to the system requires not only a password but the customer's account number to log on) as well as research information and market values.

A number of other information services have databases that are useful to investors if not essential. There are databases of financial periodicals and newsletters, as well as periodicals and newsletters covering a number of specific industries (trade journals), medicine, law, the social sciences, and public affairs, all of which impinge on the economy and individual investments.

The *Directory of On-line Data Bases* (published twice a year by Cuadra Associates Inc., 2001 Wilshire Blvd., Suite 305, Santa Monica, CA 90403) lists 270 on-line services that together offer about 1,800 databases (fall 1983 issue). The number is growing all the time.

Ready to Roll

Once you have plugged into the databases you desire and have learned how to get the information you need to conduct your own analysis, you are ready to roll. It may be as simple as learning how to download stock information from Dow Jones or as complicated as getting trade journal articles, research reports, econometric information, and constant prices.

Now comes the difficult part—determining which software fits your needs and desires. In the chapters to come we'll discuss the various financial investment options and briefly outline some applicable software for each.

Chapter 3

Stocks

One of the strongest bull markets in the history of the American stock market occurred from August 1982 through about June 1983—and it couldn't have come at a better time for the manufacturers of investment-oriented personal computer software.

Large investors, small investors, and would-be investors gobbled up programs to help them analyze, manage, and account for their investment portfolios. During the bull market a new generation of software was developed that integrates different methods of investment analysis and a number of investment functions and allows individuals to monitor the stock, bond, options, and commodities markets with one package. However, there are still a number of packages that are dedicated to analyzing the stock market, and most people use the integrated packages primarily for this same purpose.

In the next few chapters we will take a systematic look at the software that is used for evaluating different types of markets. We will start with the stock market since it is the most widely understood by the general public, and since many of the theoretical principles (at least in the realm of technical analysis) used to analyze the stock market can also be applied to the other markets.

In order to understand the software, one must understand the theory, so this section of the book will be broken into chapters describing the theories behind—and the software used for—fundamental analysis, technical analysis, and financial/economic analysis. In addition to looking at software in these areas, at the end of the section there will be a brief discussion of software that allows you to get on-line with the stock market without the 15-minute delay of the Dow Jones News/Retrieval Service so you can keep track of the market and conduct active trading.

What Is a Stock?

A *stock* is a piece of paper that says an owner has paid money in exchange for an equity ownership in a company.

When a company wants to raise money to finance continued growth and payment for operating expenses, it sells part of the company to the public. If a founder put up $100,000 to start a company and had $1,000,000 in debt (probably through a bank) but needed another $1,000,000, he probably would find it hard to borrow. His debt-to-equity ratio would already be 10/1 ($1 million/$100,000). So he might decide to sell part of the company to the public. If he offered 100,000 shares of stock at $10 per share, he could raise the $1 million necessary. Depending on how much stock the company had issued (and given to him when he founded the corporation) and how much the board of directors and shareholders had approved to be issued, his own financial position in the company will change after the sale of stock to the public. The value of his stock (and the value of his percentage of ownership in the company) would go up in cash terms after a sale of stock to the public, but his percentage of ownership would go down; it would be diluted. For instance:

Owner's position before stock sale: 100,000 shares at $1 per share, $100,000 equity, 100 percent ownership of the company.

Owner's position after stock sale: 100,000 shares at $10 per share, $1,000,000 equity. Public owns 100,000 shares at $10 per share ($1 million equity).

Owner now owns 50 percent of equity.

There are now 200,000 shares of stock outstanding. The company, overnight, has gone from an equity value of $100,000 to an equity value of $2 million. The debt-to-equity ratio has gone from 10/1 to 1/2. Each share of stock is now worth 1/200,000 of the company, or 1/2000 of one percent.

As a publicly-owned company, the owners, and potential owners, must be informed of how the company is doing. The company must make yearly and quarterly reports to the Securities and Exchange Commission (SEC) about the financial well-being of the company, its past actions, and future plans and goals. A careful reading of these reports is important in the fundamental analysis of a stock's value, probability of continued health, and potential for growth.

The stock would now be traded publicly, fluctuating in price as the market value put on it by all the investors who buy and sell the stock are concerned changes—as they respond to the company's development.

As the company grows, it may issue more stock. It may "split" the stock, giving two, three, or maybe even four shares for each share held. This would increase the number of shares of stock outstanding and lower the price per share, since each new share would be worth ½, ⅓, or ¼ as much as it had been. This would make the stock available to shareholders who could not afford a higher-priced stock. As the number of shares in a company increases, the base of the shareholders increases and institutions find there is enough stock on the market for them to take a meaningful position in dollar value without taking such a big percentage chunk that the stock does not trade actively and the price stagnates. This sets the stage for a vibrant market, with institutions seeking out opportunities for buying large chunks of companies and influencing management's policies while small investors seek to ride the waves of "hot stocks," the trends of "hot industries," and the coattails of institutional "smart money."

As the equity base increases and the stockholder base broadens, the company may also issue public debt—bonds and convertible bonds. The stock price may increase dramatically if the company shows production and earning growth, and when the company becomes more mature it may decide to slow its growth and pay some earnings to investors in the form of dividends rather than retain the earnings for investment in other projects.

You Can't Tell the Players Without a Scorecard

Just as there are two basic ways of analyzing the stock market—fundamentally and technically—there are two different types of stock market players. There are *investors* and there are *traders*. To be perfectly arbitrary, investors are those who generally expect to hold stocks long enough to make them long-term capital gains or losses (one year and one day), although they can also obviously take short-term profits if they are great, as well as sell at losses short-term if they are great or as part of an overall tax strategy. Traders, on the other hand, are strictly short-term players, often buying and selling the same stock in a matter of days or on a movement of a couple of points. Investors are more inclined to have some bonds included in their portfolio, while traders are more likely to gamble on the commodities markets when not playing the stock markets.

To generalize, investors are more inclined toward fundamental and economic analysis—if not completely devoid of analytical thought and adherents of the Random Walk Theory—while traders tend to think in technical terms.

In addition, I am inclined to say that there are very few "small investors," in the generic sense, who are traders rather than investors. At least, there are very few *smart* small investors who are traders. The reason for this should be obvious: the economics of fixed costs in playing the market.

Back to the horse-racing analogy from Chapter 1: When you place a bet at the track, the state, the horsemen, and the owners of the track take about 20 percent off the top for taxes, purse money, and operating the track, distributing the remaining 80 percent to the winners. A bettor, therefore, has to win back the 20 percent "breakage" before he can consider himself even. Given a perfect market at the track (which we know is not the case), if a bettor plays long enough, collects on longshots and favorites and loses on longshots and favorites at the ratios longshots and favorites are supposed to produce, statistics tell us that he should win back about 80 percent of the money he bets. The breakage must be considered a gambling overhead, just like admission, a program, and the *Daily Racing Form.*

For an even more dramatic example of how breakage can affect you, consider the roulette wheel in Las Vegas or Atlantic City. The wheel has 36 numbers on which you can bet either odd-or-even or red-or-black, plus two numbers—0 and 00—which the house "owns" and on which you cannot bet. When 0 or 00 come up, the house wins all bets. This constitutes a 5.26 percent edge for the house (2/38).

Thus, if the wheel operates as a "perfect market"—if all 38 numbers appear with equal frequency—in a series of 38 spins you can expect to win 18 times and lose 20. If you amortize those two extra losses in every 38 spins over an entire gambling session, you might as well consider that the house has skimmed 5.26 percent right off the top of every bet you've made.

Pay attention to those last few words. The house takes a percentage of *every* bet—every transaction. Thus it is incorrect to think that since the house has a 5.26 percent advantage at the wheel, you can expect to leave the casino with 94.74 percent of the money you came in with. The 5.26 tariff applied to every transaction will eventually eat you alive. In fact, mathematically, the house will have 90 percent of your money after just 40 spins. Now you know why they call it "breakage."

There are people who won't go to Las Vegas because the house has a five percent breakage built into the wheel and there is, statistically, a perfect market on the wheel. But many of these same people will play the markets, because, they argue, there is no such thing as a perfect, or "efficient," market.

In his book *The Money Game,* Adam Smith asked "What the Hell is a Random Walk?" He cites *The Random Character of Stock Market Prices,* published by the Massachusetts Institute of Technology, as the best source on Random Walk theory.

The Random Walk theory is based on complex theorems of Boolean algebra, but its basic tenet is that prices do not have any relationship to prices in the past. Picking horses by putting hatpins through the eye of the horse on the cover of the racing program (a favorite little-old-lady image) and picking stocks by throwing darts at a dartboard with the stock market page tacked to it (as Senator Thomas McIntyre once did at a Senate Banking Committee hearing) will, over time, produce just as many winners and just as many losers as analyzing a balance sheet or the past performances—or so the idea goes. Stocks, like horses, don't have any memories.

It's like the joke about the two men who go to the movie and see a three-minute film clip of the Kentucky Derby before the start of the feature film. The number three horse beats the number two horse. Two weeks later they go back to see the film again. One friend turns to the other and bets the number two horse will win. The friend, of course, accepts the bet. When the three horse wins, he asks why his friend bet the two horse when he had already seen the film. "He had two weeks to improve," the friend replies.

Each day the market has a 50-50 chance of going up or down, as does each individual security, according to Random Walkers. Stocks have a 50-50 chance of moving with or against a trend. If the last five trades have all been upticks (the price of the stock moving up), the odds of the next trade following the trend and being an uptick are—50-50, no more and no less, argue the Random Walk theorists. This is the same as the statistical odds of throwing a sixth "head" after a silver dollar has come up heads five times in a row. Each flip, or each stock trade, is an independent variable, with no history and no memory of past performance.

The Random Walkers don't discount market psychology or value, but say that because of all the competing interests at work on the market and all the competing ideas about value, the best one can expect of a security is for it to wander randomly around its "intrinsic value," which ends up being no more than the aggregate value placed on it by all the different competing parties with competing ideas about value.

This is really what Asimov contended in *Foundation.* The Random Walkers argue that as more people have more information, all the competing interests and competing ideas of value combine to produce a more efficient, if not a more true, notion of intrinsic value. This works both for fundamental and technical analysts. The more sophisticated the fundamental analysts are about determining a stock's long-term potential from all the variables they use, the more efficient the market becomes. The more technical analysts can pinpoint minute trading patterns—and beat the psychology that is such a big part of determining trends—the more efficient the market will become.

I will add a third efficient-market-maker: the computer. The more people use computers to gather, analyze, and act on large volumes of data and the more small investors are "playing like the big boys," the more efficient the market will become in the long run. We will, at some point—if everyone is using computers—create a market where no one will have more information than anyone else and no one will have a jump on the psychology of the market.

Of course, I don't believe this will ever happen. Human nature is to get a jump on everyone else. Just as it is currently the investor—more likely the investment manager—who thinks one step ahead of the market makes the most money, the more efficient the market becomes, the more it will be a case of who is two steps, or three steps, or four steps, ahead of the market. The desire to beat the other players at the game will always be there, and there is not a possibility of setting up a perfectly efficient market.

In the long run, the birth of computer power for the masses and the intensification of computer power for the elite could hurt the economy more than it helps it as it causes the functioning of the investment markets to drift further and further from the realities of the underlying economic circumstances of the world.

The Inefficient Market

What factors make the market inefficient?

Tax considerations, for one thing, cause the market to be imperfect. Because of the tax laws, investors often sell against the market simply because their stock is about to change from short-term to long-term investment and they are either selling a losing stock before it turns long-term (selling a short-term loss is tax-advantageous) or selling a winner that has just gone long-term (selling a long-term winner is tax-advantageous). In addition, as the end of the year draws near, a lot of market players are trading winners or losers to offset previous winners or losers and even out their tax position for the year. (This will be discussed more fully later.)

Another aspect of an imperfect market is the retail market—the individual investor. The share of trading conducted on behalf of individual investors has been steadily declining over the past two decades. The vast majority of trading each day is done for institutions—mutual funds, pension plans, and endowed institutions—and the market is handling five or six times the daily volume it did two decades ago. Days of 100 million shares traded are not uncommon, and many observers believe that days of 150 million shares traded will become routine within the next couple of years.

As we shall see in the future, larger investors are closer to the "inside" information than smaller investors, and a number of larger investors try to gauge market sentiment by what smaller investors are doing.

As Milton Weiler Jr. (a former brokerage house executive and now chairman of Computer Aided Decisions, a firm that sells software to brokerage houses, money managers, and banks) says of the small investor, "Stocks aren't bought by anyone. You didn't really want to buy that stock. You were really talked into it—by a friend or by a broker or somebody."

Given that on every trade you will pay about three percent to buy and three percent to sell (an estimate of full-service brokerage prices for a transaction of about $1,500), your investments have to average a six-percent gain *just to break even.* If you can make six percent on a fast-paced trade, you are doing extremely well.

Larger traders, however, only have to play for three or four percent. How do they do it? Well, it's just like the old gag about the five-piece living-room set for $99.99—*volume.* Traders trade volume and get discounts from their full-service broker—or use discount brokers since they do their own analysis.

The price of full-service brokerage goes down as a percentage of the total transaction price as the price goes up. Institutions—pension funds, university endowments, mutual funds and the like—can get their commissions as low as two-tenths of one percent on very high-volume trades. A round-trip ride for these institutions (and a few of the largest private investors) can run to less than one-half percent. While the small investor pays about $90 round-trip to buy and sell $1,500 worth of stock, the person who buys and sells blocks of the same stock worth $20,000 at a clip does not pay $1,200. He may pay $800, but will probably pay even less—maybe as little as $400 (one percent each way) for these transactions. Institutional and ultra-large personal investors, who may buy 20,000 *shares* ($300,000), may get in for commissions of only about $600 (one-tenth of one percent each way.) See Table 3-1.

The $15 stock only has to go up three eighths of a point (37 cents) per share for the large investors to break even (the actual break-even point is 30 cents) and make seven cents per share profit above commission. The ultra-large investor must only see the stock go up one eighth of a point (12 ½ cents) per share to make back his commissions (the actual break-even point is three cents) and make nine and one-half cents per share profit above commission.

The small investor, on the other hand, must see the stock rise by one full point (one dollar) per share before he is even. His actual break-even point is 90 cents, which gives him 10 cents per share profit above commission.

Let's play out the scenario one step further (Table 3-2). Say the stock rose one full point in a short period of time and everyone decided to sell out their holdings. The small investor would get back $1,650 for his $1,500 investment (100 shares) and would have paid $90 in commissions. His total profit on the transaction would be $60. The large investor, who purchased 1,333 shares with his $20,000, will get back $21,333 and would have paid commissions of $400. His profit would be $933. The ultra-large investor would get back $330,000 for an investment of $300,000 (20,000 shares), and would have paid commissions of $600 for a profit of $29,400.

It may not be as neat a proof as those Descartes did, but it does show that a small investor cannot be a successful trader, because he cannot expect—even given access to all information and a perfect market—to make six percent on each transaction rapidly.

Indeed, small investors are considered such poor risks to be involved in frequent trading that when it occurs there is *prima facia* evidence for a charge of *churning,* which is

	Small Investor	Large Investor	Extra-Large Investor
Approximate	100 shares	1,333 shares	20,000 shares
Investment	$1,500	$20,000	$300,000
Commission	$90	$400	$600

Table 3-1. A comparison of the commissions paid for purchasing a $15 stock by a small investor (100 shares), a large investor ($20,000) and an extra-large investor (20,000 shares). These figures are for commissions for a "round-trip" investment, both purchase and sale of the stock.

	Small 100 shares	Large 1333 shares	Extra-Large 20,000 shares
Value of invest	$1,600	$21,333	$320,000
Profit	$100	$1,333	20,000
Profit after commis	$10	$933	$19,900

Table 3-2. A comparison of the investment profit, both before and after paying commission, for the same three investors if the stock increases in value by $1 per share.

defined in the Securities Act of 1933 and the Securities Exchange Act of 1934 (the federal laws that established the Securities and Exchange Commission and regulate brokerage activities) as excessive trading by a broker of a customer's account without economic merit in the hope of generating extensive commissions. There are cases on file in Federal District Court in Boston where accounts of from $30,000 to $500,000 and more (not insignificant by individual—or retail—account standards) have incurred losses of anywhere from 30 to 80 percent in value while generating commissions for brokers of up to $80,000 in a single year (a case involving a $600,000 account, which was settled out of court in March of 1984).

My own bias, as a miniscule investor, is to think long-term and analyze companies—to the degree that I do systematic analysis—in terms of fundamentals. I think technical indicators can give a general picture of the trend of the market, but unless you are in for the very short haul, my feeling is that trying to pick individual stocks on a technical basis is just too dangerous. To the long-term minded investor, the technical indicators might show a downtrend in the market during which some of his or her target stocks may go lower with the market and may reach the level he or she considers a bargain based on their chances of appreciating in value over the next year or two or five. This may cause the investor to wait a few weeks and see if he or she can pick the stocks up cheaper. On the other hand, strong technical indicators that the market will turn up may cause the small investor to buy now.

Information Everywhere, but Who Knows What to Do?

Adherents to all three investing theories believe they are right because of the flow of information. No matter what the underlying basis for one's stock market analysis, the thought is that the market has discounted information—some people even believe the market discounts rumors just in case. Given that the market has discounted all the information that is available, both the technical and the fundamental school of analysis think the tools they use give some systematic way to find bargains.

Technical analysts believe the market has discounted all the information there is available to the public and therefore the value of a stock is, *de facto,* fair value. At that point it becomes a matter of psychology—how each technical analyst believes the market will move given how it has moved in the past when similar situations have occurred. This is the closest notion to Asimov's speculation of psychohistory.

Random Walk believers think the market has discounted all the information there is about each stock and therefore there is no such thing as a good deal. Given the machinations of a complex mathematical formula they use and the movement of time—and the changes in psychology over time—a passive portfolio will do as well as an active portfolio, they argue, with a lot less hassle and worry, and a lot less time consumed in managing it. This, they might argue further, would give one more time to be productive and earn more money to invest. Since there are no computer investing programs that adhere to the Random Walk theory, we won't discuss it much further.

Fundamental analysts believe that the information available and the public's perception of stocks at any moment in time combine to create situations where certain stocks become undervalued. The market is viewed not merely as a market, but as a compilation of individual companies and diverse industries that make up an interlocking economy. Stocks are seen as pieces of paper that represent equity ownership in the means of economic production, not merely as pieces of paper that represent a cash equivalent, as some technical analysists see them.

In the next three chapters we'll take a closer look at fundamental and technical analysis of the stock markets and how the macroeconomic situation in the world economy can influence those markets.

Chapter 4

The Fundamentals of Fundamental Analysis

Fundamental analysts, since they are often playing for the long-term gain, are primarily interested in preserving the capital they put into an investment, then gaining as high a return as possible given the level of risk they would like to assume in the overall portfolio. In addition, long-term investing is often done with the thought of getting some income from the investment by means of dividends paid each year. Many long-term fundamental analysis-oriented investors look for stocks that will outperform the market over the next year and give the highest rate of return possible based on a sell-every-stock-the-day-it-turns-long-term strategy. Others look even further out—three to five years—for the industry and the stock that will be on the wave of the future; this is often seen in terms of "trawling for the next IBM." Some fundamental investment computer software packages, as we shall see in a little while, are beginning to look for shorter-term gain, but the theory is still based on a year-and-a-day hold.

When constructing a portfolio, the long-term investor will want to diversify it, buying stocks in a number of different industry groupings to guard against sudden shifts in the economy. For instance, a person who invested heavily in the auto industry in the early 1960s would have done well for 12 or 13 years, but would have been devastated over the last seven or eight years.

Diversifying also helps many investors search for the next important industry. For instance, biotechnology, after its initial market strength two or three years ago, became an industry on the outs with a lot of investors who hoped it would skyrocket them into the millionaire bracket in no time at all—*a la* the computer industry over the last decade. A person who believes biotechnology will have a place in the future of the country's medical and pharmaceutical industries may want to buy stock in one or two companies now that it is "cheap," some companies selling at only 50 or 60 percent of their initial public offering price, and hold it for a number of years.

A few speculative issues such as those of biotechnology companies and personal computer companies may be mixed in with some "growth stocks" that pay low dividends but are expected to grow at a rate of 15 to 20 percent each year on average, and the stocks of some "mature" companies that have stopped financing growth with profits and are distributing more of those profits to shareholders in the form of dividends. These dividends can often be used to reinvest in the company's stock without having to pay commissions. In addition, at least through 1985, when dividends of many electric utility companies are reinvested, the owner does not have to pay any income taxes on the dividends (up to $750 worth for an individual and $1,500 for couples filing joint returns). This measure, part of a tax package enacted in 1981, was meant as a boon to the electric utility industry, but it has really been more helpful to small investors than anyone else.

What Fundamental Analysts Look For

Fundamental analysts try to determine from past records of earnings, sales, dividends, and a number of other statistics having to do with the underlying or *fundamental* strength of a company, how that company will perform in the future as an economic entity. The belief is that companies that perform better as economic entities will have stocks that perform better as stocks because more people will see the fundamental strength of the company.

The devil's advocate could argue, "But what if so many people adhere to technical analysis that the general public believes the market will be bad and the stock goes down?" To this, the fundamental analyst would, I believe, answer: "That will only be in the short run. Over the long run, given all the long-term, intermediate-term, and short-term trends technical analysts play with, this stock will grow more than the market in general because the company is fundamentally sound." In short, all information being discounted, fundamental facts about companies stick in people's heads—even technical analysts'—and there will always be enough people who are strictly fundamental analysts to keep the price of a fundamentally sound stock (in a fundamentally sound industry) beating the general market.

To get the most up-to-date raw data on a company's financial position, the filings the company must make with the Securities and Exchange Commission are the best source. These 10K yearly statements and 10Q quarterly statements tell the SEC what the company has been up to in the last year in both narrative and numerical form—income statements, balance sheets, etc.—as well as an honest appraisal of what the company's projections are in the next year—a much more honest appraisal than you will find in any company report. Although much of the same information as is in the 10K and 10Q can be found in the company's annual and quarterly reports to stockholders, the information to stockholders is not as complete and the narrative parts often paint a quite rosy picture when the truth is somewhat different. Remember, in an annual report, the company can decide what to disclose to its investors. The SEC *demands* full disclosure. The most well-informed investor will read both documents carefully and will compare them for differences in tone and nuance, and for how much is left out of the annual report. In addition, some analysts believe a close reading of the narrative portions of the annual report can tell an investor better than anything else what the company hopes to do in the future; by comparing the narratives from past annual reports to the numbers in the present report and the present 10K, an investor can get an idea about how well a company is meeting its stated goals.

Let's take a look for a moment at a comparison of the annual report and the 10K forms for 1983 for the Gulf States Utilities Co. (I will use Gulf States Utilities and Dayton Power and Light Co. as examples throughout this chapter to illustrate different fundamental analysis techniques and software.)

The 1983 GSU annual report is 46 pages, on heavy stock, with four-color charts and color photography. The table of contents lists a report to the shareholders, sales figures, construction figures, a description of rates and regulation (utilities are heavily regulated by each state they serve, in this case Texas and Louisiana, as well as the federal government), statistics about financing, general operations, "GSU Weathers 1983," and finally, at the back of the report, all of the financial statements.

GSU's Form 10K runs to 68 pages and includes a number of items that are not in the annual report. While the bottom line numbers are the same in the financial statements in both the report and the 10K much of the narrative is different, with the 10K being much more explicit about a number of items.

The annual report uses a series of bar charts to give the reader a quick look at what

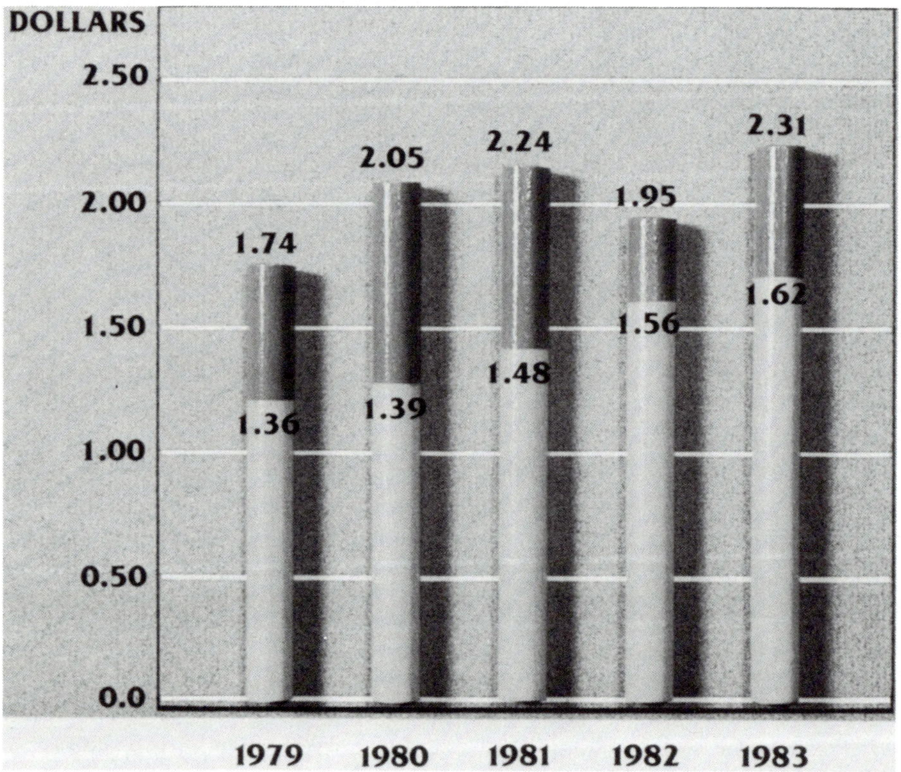

Fig. 4-1. Five year history of dividends (smaller figure) and earnings per share (larger figure) for Gulf States Utilities (reproduced from 1983 annual report).

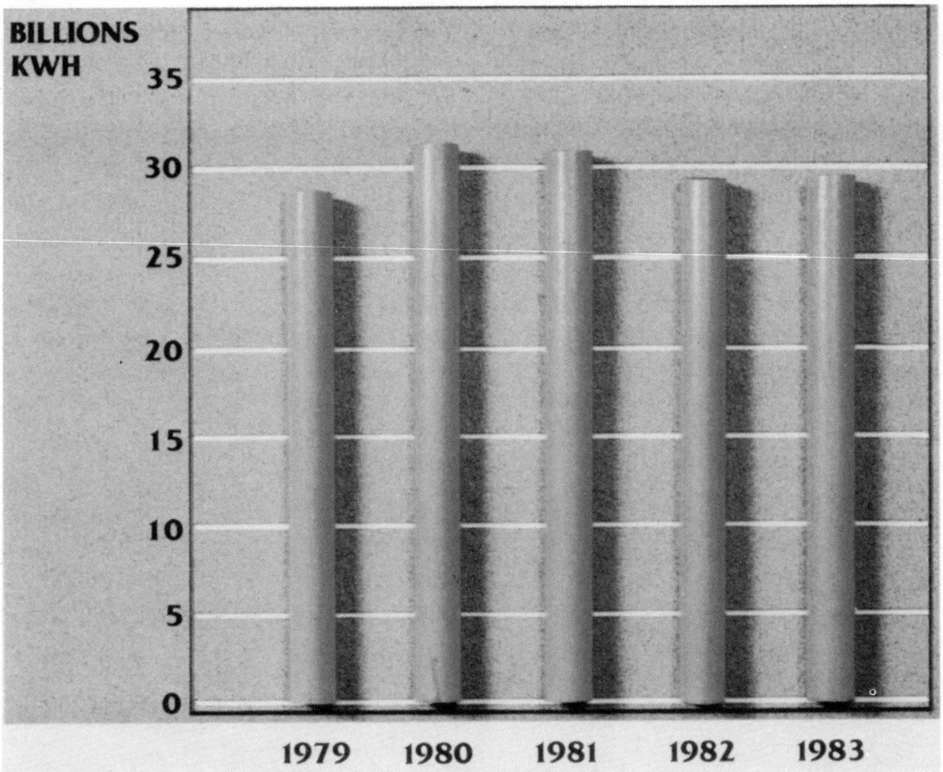

Fig. 4-2. Five year history of electric sales for Gulf States Utilities (reproduced from 1983 annual report).

the company feels are the most important statistics. These charts are at the front of the report and are probably what the reader will see first. They are sometimes conflicting, and a closer look at the financial figures, as well as a reading of the narrative portions of the 10K, is really necessary to determine why the company is behaving as it is. Notice the figures in Figs. 4-1 through 4-3.

Figure 4-1 is, to those who write the report, the most important; it appears on page four of the annual report right after the letter to shareholders from the president and chairman of the board of directors. It shows the earnings and dividends paid out per share of common stock held.

This truly looks impressive. After earnings slipped from $2.24 to $1.95 from 1981 to 1982, they rebounded to $2.31 in 1983. Dividends continued their steady climb, going up six cents per share. How were these increases achieved?

Annual sales of electricity were flat (Fig. 4-2) while the number of customers increased slightly to about 540,000. Construction expenditures increased to about $675 million (Fig. 4-3), reflecting the company's coming into the final stages of development of the 940-megawatt River Bend 1 nuclear power plant (82 percent complete and expected to be online in December 1985.)

For its discussion of rates, GSU says only that the Federal Energy Regulatory Commission (FERC) granted a rate increase, the Louisiana Public Service Commission (LPSC) denied a major rate increase, and the company has filed a two-step rate increase request with the Public Utility Commission of Texas(PUCT) in early 1984. These rate issues are mentioned both in the letter to shareholders and the more explicit narrative about company business. The issue of rates is described in more detail in the Form 10K.

Let's now turn to the financial statements (Figs. 4-4 through 4-8) which, as I have said, can be found in both the annual report and the form 10K.

Figures 4-4 through 4-8 (and the ten pages of notes about those statements that follow) distill all of the pertinent data about the company's performance over the previous year. Comparison figures for 1982 and 1981 are also given. Here is the raw data that brokerage house and bank analysts use to determine the financial wherewithall of a company. By combining these figures in a number of ways, ratios are devised (the most well-known being price-to-earnings) that give some way to measure one stock against another in a quick and dirty way. Many of the fundamental analytical tools devised for the personal computer attempt to use objective criteria to set parameters for stocks that investors will then take a closer look at, poring over the financial statements.

Let's take a quick look at what this all means.

First the income statement (Fig. 4-4). The statement gives us the total revenues from operations ($1,436,188 [thousand] or one billion, four hundred and thirty-six million, one hundred and eighty-eight thousand and some

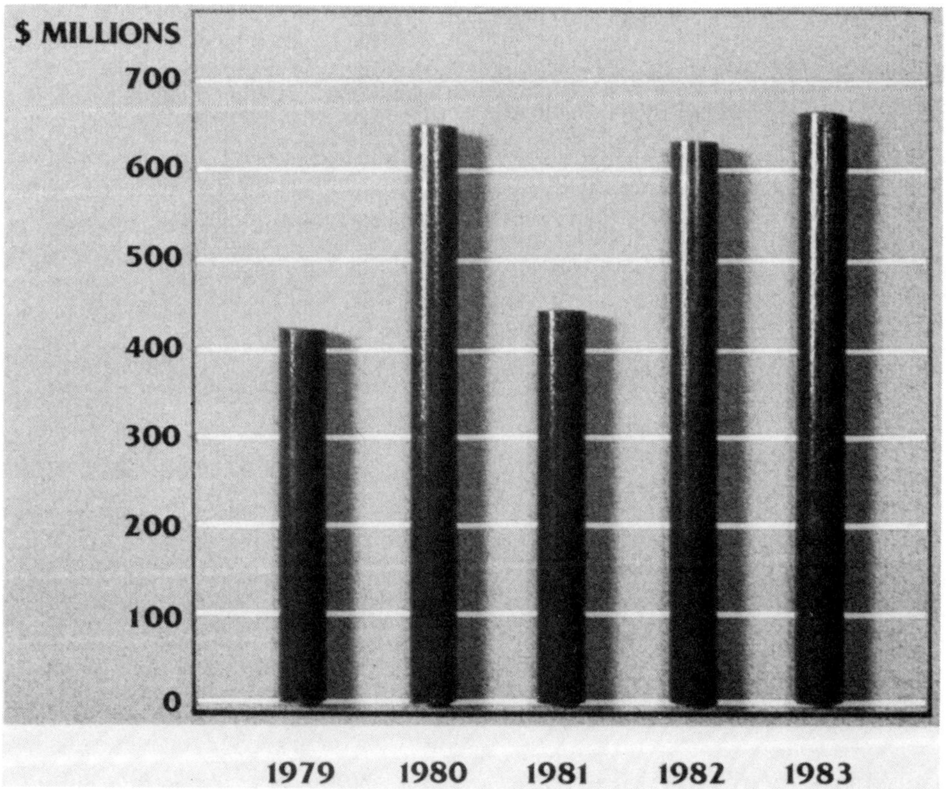

Fig. 4-3. Five year history of construction expenditures for Gulf States Utilities (reproduced from 1983 annual report).

Item 8. ***Financial Statements and Supplementary Data***

Statement of Income

For the years ended December 31
(in thousands except per share amounts)

	1983	1982	1981
Operating Revenue			
Electric	**$1,305,449**	$1,188,944	$1,106,522
Steam	**83,646**	75,213	77,624
Gas	**47,093**	43,102	37,568
	1,436,188	1,307,259	1,221,714
Operating Expenses and Taxes			
Fuel	**438,154**	446,521	481,285
Purchased power (Note 5)	**201,325**	182,106	150,463
Other operations	**173,151**	151,660	133,647
Maintenance	**78,971**	65,321	70,867
Depreciation and amortization	**103,251**	89,291	78,194
Income Taxes			
Federal (Note 2)	**70,538**	52,847	32,187
State	**4,236**	3,314	2,933
Other taxes	**53,269**	45,790	41,845
	1,122,895	1,036,850	991,421
Operating Income	**313,293**	270,409	230,293
Other Income and Deductions			
Allowance for equity funds used during construction	**88,172**	56,141	40,741
Non-utility subsidiary operations	**(2,228)**	(206)	11,498
Other — net	**(1,172)**	2,581	1,996
Income Before Interest Charges	**398,065**	328,925	284,528
Interest Charges			
Long-term debt (Note 8)	**196,502**	181,985	151,427
Short-term debt and other	**10,577**	14,398	17,698
Allowance for borrowed funds used during construction	**(38,813)**	(33,437)	(35,528)
	168,266	162,946	133,597
Net Income	**229,799**	165,979	150,931
Dividends on Preferred and Preference Stock	**49,052**	38,949	30,381
Income Applicable to Common Stock	**$ 180,747**	$ 127,030	$ 120,550
Average Shares of Common Stock Outstanding	**78,233**	65,056	53,851
Earnings Per Average Share of Common Stock Outstanding	**$ 2.31**	$ 1.95	$ 2.24

The accompanying notes are an integral part of the financial statements.

Fig. 4-4. 1983 Income statement for Gulf States Utilities (reproduced from 1983 Form 10K, Securities and Exchange Commission).

Statement of Sources of Funds Invested in Utility and Other Plant

For the years ended December 31
(in thousands)

	1983	1982	1981
Provided From Operations			
Net income	**$ 229,799**	$ 165,979	$ 150,931
Principal income items not requiring current funds			
Depreciation and amortization	**103,251**	89,291	78,194
Deferred income taxes — net	**37,246**	32,684	(6,252)
Investment tax credits — net	**24,670**	14,020	32,029
Equity component of allowance for funds used during construction	**(88,172)**	(56,141)	(40,741)
Non-utility subsidiary operations	**2,228**	206	(11,498)
Total provided from operations	**309,022**	246,039	202,663
Dividends			
Preferred and preference	**(49,052)**	(38,949)	(30,381)
Common	**(127,263)**	(101,223)	(79,379)
Reinvested funds provided from operations	**132,707**	105,867	92,903
Provided from Financing			
Sales of securities			
Common stock	**136,481**	164,820	132,762
Preferred stock subject to mandatory redemption	**30,000**	—	—
Preference stock	**—**	100,000	—
First mortgage bonds (principal amount)	**200,000**	167,000	168,000
Guaranteed debentures	**—**	60,000	60,000
Change in escrow deposit	**(11,048)**	(24,000)	—
Pollution control bonds	**17,450**	48,285	—
Net change in short-term borrowings	**3,093**	52,162	(20,433)
Retirement of first mortgage bonds and convertible debentures	**(11,049)**	(26,507)	(41,970)
Equipment purchase obligations	**—**	(53,691)	(16,181)
Nuclear fuel lease transaction	**—**	108,969	—
Net change in revolving credit agreement	**40,000**	(120,000)	30,000
Term loan agreement	**—**	24,000	—
Total provided from financing	**404,927**	501,038	312,178
Other Sources and Uses			
Investments in and advances to subsidiary companies	**(13,973)**	(11,582)	(1,123)
Retirement of Uranox Trust	**—**	(27,216)	—
Other — net (including changes in working capital)	**31,253**	5,246	(8,014)
Total other sources and uses	**17,280**	(33,552)	(9,137)
Expenditures for Utility and Other Plant	**554,914**	573,353	395,944
Equity component of allowance for funds used during construction	**88,172**	56,141	40,741
Invested in Utility and Other Plant	**$ 643,086**	$ 629,494	$ 436,685

The accompanying notes are an integral part of the financial statements.

Fig. 4-5. 1983 Statement of sources of funds invested in utility and other plant for Gulf States Utilities (reproduced from 1983 Form 10K, SEC).

Balance Sheet

December 31
(in thousands)

	1983	1982
Assets		
Utility and Other Plant, at original cost (Note 5)		
Plant in service	**$3,106,834**	$2,760,434
Less: Accumulated provision for depreciation	**904,919**	811,853
	2,201,915	1,948,581
Construction work in progress (Notes 10 and 11)	**1,844,163**	1,574,925
	4,046,078	3,523,506
Other Property and Investments		
Non-utility subsidiary companies	**55,595**	43,850
Other	**6,791**	7,035
	62,386	50,885
Current Assets		
Cash and temporary cash investments	**3,026**	6,230
Receivables		
Customers	**94,532**	102,188
Other	**20,780**	11,563
Materials and supplies	**13,224**	16,111
Fuel stock	**42,330**	42,526
Prepayments and other	**16,574**	6,560
	190,466	185,178
Deferred Charges		
Unamortized debt expense	**16,777**	14,567
Unamortized project cancellation costs	**9,594**	13,451
Accumulated deferred income taxes	**10,831**	8,378
Other	**17,266**	10,146
	54,468	46,542
	$4,353,398	$3,806,111
Capitalization and Liabilities		
Capitalization (See Statement of Capitalization)		
Common shareholders' equity	**$1,316,599**	$1,128,991
Preference stock	**100,000**	100,000
Preferred stock		
Not subject to mandatory redemption	**136,444**	136,444
Subject to mandatory redemption	**204,336**	175,553
Long-term debt	**1,839,833**	1,595,525
	3,597,212	3,136,513
Current Liabilities		
Long-term debt due within one year	**—**	10,000
Preferred stock sinking fund requirements (Note 7)	**1,217**	—
Notes payable (Note 9)		
Banks	**90,000**	69,000
Commercial paper	**—**	17,907
Accounts payable		
Trade	**98,955**	88,456
Subsidiaries	**3,819**	2,350
Customer deposits	**12,212**	9,599
Taxes accrued	**12,011**	15,073
Interest accrued	**61,695**	55,221
Other	**49,917**	40,855
	329,826	308,461
Deferred Credits		
Investment tax credits	**176,399**	151,696
Accumulated deferred income taxes	**239,296**	199,842
Other	**10,665**	9,599
	426,360	361,137
Commitments and Contingencies (Notes 5, 10 and 11)	**—**	—
	$4,353,398	$3,806,111

The accompanying notes are an integral part of the financial statements.

Fig. 4-6. 1983 Balance sheet for Gulf States Utilities (reproduced from 1983 Form 10K, SEC).

Statement of Capitalization

December 31
(in thousands)

			1983	1982
Common Shareholders' Equity (Note 6)				
Common stock				
Authorized 200,000,000 shares without par value				
Outstanding 83,687,644 and 74,049,921 shares, respectively			**$ 903,606**	$ 767,125
Premium and expense on capital stock			**3,601**	4,501
Other paid-in capital			**25,876**	25,876
Retained earnings			**383,516**	331,489
			1,316,599	1,128,991
Preference Stock (Note 6)				
Authorized 20,000,000 shares without par value, cumulative				
Outstanding 4,000,000 shares				
Dividend Series	**Shares Outstanding**	**Current Redemption Price**		
$4.40	2,000,000	$31.90	**50,000**	50,000
3.85	2,000,000	31.35	**50,000**	50,000
			100,000	100,000
Preferred Stock (Notes 6 and 7)				
Authorized 6,000,000 shares, $100 par value, cumulative				
Outstanding 3,419,970 and 3,119,970 shares, respectively				
Dividend Series	**Shares Outstanding**	**Current Redemption Price**		
Not subject to mandatory redemption				
$4.40	51,173	$ 108.00	**5,117**	5,117
4.50	5,830	105.00	**583**	583
4.40-1949	1,655	103.00	**166**	166
4.20	9,745	102.818	**975**	975
4.44	14,804	103.75	**1,480**	1,480
5.00	10,993	104.25	**1,099**	1,099
5.08	26,845	104.63	**2,685**	2,685
4.52	10,564	103.57	**1,056**	1,056
6.08	32,829	103.34	**3,283**	3,283
7.56	350,000	103.80	**35,000**	35,000
8.52	500,000	106.43	**50,000**	50,000
9.96	350,000	111.60	**35,000**	35,000
			136,444	136,444
Subject to mandatory redemption				
8.80	371,835	105.00	**37,183**	37,183
9.75	33,697	105.00	**3,370**	3,370
8.64	350,000	108.64	**35,000**	35,000
11.48	500,000	111.48	**50,000**	50,000
13.64	500,000	113.64	**50,000**	50,000
Adjustable Rate	300,000	111.50	**30,000**	—
			205,553	175,553
Preferred stock sinking fund requirement			**(1,217)**	—
			204,336	175,553

	1983	1982
Long-Term Debt (Note 8)		
First mortgage bonds		
Maturing 1984 through 1988 —		
4¼% due September 1, 1986	**15,000**	15,000
14¾% due March 1, 1987	**100,000**	100,000
4⅞% due October 1, 1987	**17,000**	17,000
4% due May 1, 1988	**20,000**	20,000
Maturing 1989 through 1993 — 4⅜% through 17½%	**295,000**	295,000
Maturing 1994 through 1998 — 5% through 6¾%	**120,000**	120,000
Maturing 1999 through 2003 — 7¼% through 8½%	**195,000**	195,000
Maturing 2004 through 2008 — 8⅜% through 10.15%	**220,000**	220,000
Maturing 2009 through 2013 — 10⅛% through 15%	**525,000**	325,000
	1,507,000	1,307,000
Pollution control and industrial development bonds		
7% due 2006	**25,000**	25,000
5.9% due 2007	**23,000**	23,000
10⅜% due 2012	**48,285**	48,285
9½% due 2013	**17,450**	—
Debentures		
Guaranteed debentures		
17½% due 1988	**60,000**	60,000
16% due 1990	**60,000**	60,000
Escrow deposit	**(35,048)**	(24,000)
Convertible debentures — 7¼% due 1992	**2,927**	3,976
Term loan agreement		
Variable rates (11% at December 31, 1983) due 1987	**24,000**	24,000
Revolving credit agreement	**110,000**	70,000
	1,842,614	1,597,261
Unamortized premium and discount on debt — net	**(2,781)**	(1,736)
	1,839,833	1,595,525
	$3,597,212	$3,136,513

First mortgage bond and preferred stock sinking fund requirements and long-term debt maturities for each of the next five years are as follows:

	Sinking Fund Requirements			
	First Mortgage Bonds		Preferred Stock	Long-Term Debt Maturities
	Cash	Other		
1984	$ —	$14,064	$ 1,217	$ —
1985	—	14,064	2,617	—
1986	—	14,064	6,617	15,000
1987	8,570	13,680	6,617	141,000
1988	27,320	13,440	6,617	80,000

The accompanying notes are an integral part of the financial statements.

Fig. 4-7. 1983 Statement of Capitalization for Gulf States Utilities (reproduced from 1983 Form 10K, SEC).

hundreds). The next major figure is the total expenses and taxes ($1,122,895 [thousand]), for a total operating income after expenses and taxes of $313,293,000. The company shows about $88 million in extra income from the allowance for owner equity used in construction, a loss of about $2 million from subsidiaries—a gas drilling company, a finance company, and a company that owns leases on lignite reserves in Texas—and a loss of about $1 million from "other" sources (maybe investments—after all, everybody lost money in the stock market in 1983). The company had total interest payments on debt of about $168 million for "net income" of about $230 million. It paid out $50 million in dividends for preferred and preference stock, leaving about $180 million in income applicable to common stock. With 78 million shares outstanding, that came out to $2.31 pershare in income (or earnings per share, EPS). Of these earnings, $1.64 per share was paid out to common shareholders in the form of dividends (although much actually never was paid, but was transferred into more common stock through the dividend reinvestment plan).

Where did GSU get all of the money to run its company, to invest in the continuation of the company and growth of the physical plant? The answers can be found on the next statement, that of sources of funds invested in utility and other plant (Fig. 4-5). The company invested $643 million in the plant and only had a net income of $229 million, of which about $127 million was paid out in the form of dividends.

Part of the extra investment occurred in the form of tax writeoffs, which don't involve the actual transfer of cash, only bookkeeping notations. These come under the heading "Principal Income Items Not Requiring Current Funds," and include depreciation of physical assets, investment tax credits, deferred taxes, and other items.

Principally the extra money came from financing—$136 million in sales of new common stock, $200 million in first mortgage bonds, and smaller amounts from the sales of other securities. By looking at this statement, you can see how the company has financed itself for the past three years. You can see that while the company invested $14 million more in utility and plant in 1983 than in 1982, it raised more from operations and nearly $100 million less from financing. It invested $107 million more than in 1981, but raised only $92 million more by financing.

The next statement, the balance sheet (Fig. 4-6), tells us what the company has and what it owes. The bottom lines of the two halves of a balance sheet, the "assets" and the "liabilities and capitalization," must balance, hence the name.

Take a quick look at the assets. It is amazing that a company with a total value of nearly four and one-half billion dollars has exactly $3,026,000 in cash on hand. The vast majority of the company's assets, as would be expected, are in physical plant.

On the capitalization and liabilities side of the ledger, the common stockholders equity is about $1.3 billion (about 35 percent) of total, while the long-term debt is about $1.85 billion (about 45 percent). The debt/equity ratio is about 9/7.

The next statement, capitalization (Fig. 4-7), gives you a more minutely detailed picture of the bottom half of the balance sheet, showing you what the dividend payout is for each of the groupings of preference and preferred stock and what the maturity dates and percentage rate of interest are for all of the debt issues.

The last statement, the statement of changes in capital stock and retained earnings (Fig. 4-8), gives a three-year history of the

Statement of Changes in Capital Stock and Retained Earnings

For the years ended December 31
(in thousands)

	Preferred Stock Subject to Mandatory Redemption	Preference Stock	Common Stock	Premium (Less Expense)	Other Paid-In Capital	Retained Earnings
Balance: January 1, 1981	$175,553	$ —	$469,543	$ (2,169)	$25,847	$269,975
Net income — 1981						150,931
Common stock sold:						
Public offerings (8,000,000 shares)			92,375			
Conversion of debentures (1,625,572 shares)			23,791			
Dividend reinvestment and stock purchase plan (570,428 shares)			6,648			
Employee benefit plans (883,053 shares)			9,936			
Acquisition of subsidiary (588,000 shares)			12		29	
Dividends declared:						
Preferred						(30,381)
Common						(79,379)
Capital stock expense				81		(3,856)
Balance: December 31, 1981	175,553	—	602,305	(2,088)	25,876	307,290
Net income — 1982						165,979
Preference stock sold (4,000,000 shares)		100,000		5,840		
Common stock sold:						
Public offerings (10,000,000 shares)			121,250			
Conversion of debentures (1,245,746 shares)			16,291			
Dividend reinvestment and stock purchase plan (1,636,481 shares)			20,056			
Employee benefit plans (592,817 shares)			7,223			
Dividends declared:						
Preferred and preference						(38,949)
Common						(101,223)
Capital stock expense				749		(1,608)
Balance: December 31, 1982	175,553	100,000	767,125	4,501	25,876	331,489
Net income — 1983						229,799
Preferred stock:						
Public offering (300,000 shares)	30,000					
Sinking fund requirements	(1,217)					
Common stock sold:						
Public offerings (6,000,000 shares)			85,500			
Conversion of debentures (79,141 shares)			1,036			
Dividend reinvestment and stock purchase plan (2,534,689 shares)			35,025			
Employee benefit plans (1,023,893 shares)			14,920			
Dividends declared:						
Preferred and preference						(49,052)
Common						(127,263)
Capital stock expense				(900)		(1,457)
Balance: December 31, 1983	**$204,336**	**$100,000**	**$903,606**	**$ 3,601**	**$25,876**	**$383,516**

The accompanying notes are an integral part of the financial statements.

Fig. 4-8. 1983 Statement of Changes in Capital Stock and Retained Earnings for Gulf States Utilities (reprinted from 1983 Form 10K, SEC).

first page of the capitalization statement, so you can get a picture of the pattern of how the company has acquired its funds.

This discussion has been, of necessity, quick. In order to really read a consolidated financial statement closely, you need to look at all the notes, which tell about one-time charges and all of the judgement calls that the company's accountants and auditors made.

To get a better idea about the business as an entity performing a service and providing a commodity (energy), you have to look beyond the financial numbers to the company's statistical records. This statement is also presented in both the annual report and the Form 10K (Fig. 4-9).

From this statistical summary of the company's last five years, you can see the growth in the customer base and how that customer base has changed in terms of residential, commercial, and industrial components. You can see that while average usage has dropped, revenue per unit of usage has increased. You can see that over the past five years of relationship between steam and gas as a portion of the company's revenue has changed dramatically, from about a 5/2 steam/gas ratio in 1979 to less than a 2/1 ratio in 1983.

Let's talk about nuclear power for a minute. GSU, like many utility companies, is involved in the building of a nuclear-powered electricity-generating facility. In the company's 1983 annual report, it states that the plant—River Bend 1—is about 82 percent complete, but that the most difficult stages lie ahead. It does not talk to any great degree about its projections for construction costs in the future, how the construction will affect its future need for funding from outside sources, or how the construction will affect its future needs for rate increases. These discussions, however, are undertaken in the Form 10K.

In the annual report, the company states that "Throughout its construction history, River Bend has made above-average progress when compared to 15 other nuclear plants . . . For example, the average nuclear construction project takes 50 months to reach the halfway mark. River Bend reached its halfway mark at 34 months. In fact, each of the first 19 construction milestones was reached on or ahead of schedule." That's a very rosy picture, and one that the company is rightly proud of considering the fate of many other nuclear plants over the last ten years.

But what is the fate of the River Bend and the company in the future? The Form 10K states: "Assuming River Bend Unit 1 goes on-line in 1985, construction expenditures for 1986 are expected to decline to approximately $260 million (from $643 million in 1983) . . . Actual expenditures in the past have been, and estimates of future expenditures may be, affected by greater-than-anticipated escalations in costs, additional expenditures for environmental, safety and other factors, and further delays in portions of the construction program."

With respect to construction financing, the 10K states: "The Company's ability to obtain necessary financing is being adversely affected by (i) inadequate cash earnings resulting from insufficient and untimely rate relief, (ii) high costs of capital, (iii) unstable securities markets, and (iv) negative market attitudes towards nuclear power."

In the 10K, the company spends three entire pages discussing rate structures in Texas, Louisiana, and through the FERC. In a very real way, this background about the regulatory conditions in these two states is important for the prospective investor to know so he or she can gauge in some way how rates may be affected in the future.

Another major item in the 10K that is hardly mentioned at all in the annual report is

Statistical Summary

For the years ended December 31

	1983	1982	1981	1980	1979
ELECTRIC					
Number of customers at year end:					
Residential	**475,782**	465,162	455,160	438,560	423,850
Commercial	**57,446**	55,265	52,955	52,731	50,807
Industrial	**4,146**	4,165	3,852	3,414	3,386
Temporary construction	**3,624**	3,132	2,871	3,354	3,279
Other	**2,101**	1,985	1,974	1,984	1,873
Total	**543,099**	529,709	516,812	500,043	483,195
Sales — Kilowatt-hours (thousands):					
Residential	**5,686,436**	5,991,578	5,717,715	5,682,016	5,147,436
Commercial	**4,341,093**	4,359,739	4,178,126	3,969,390	3,759,289
Industrial	**14,257,141**	13,728,469	15,066,330	14,870,419	14,961,211
Temporary construction	**55,927**	48,170	50,306	37,691	44,059
Other	**2,109,974**	2,261,350	2,797,761	3,098,910	2,638,490
Total Sales	**26,450,571**	26,389,306	27,810,238	27,658,426	26,550,485
Revenue — (thousands):					
Residential	**$ 396,026**	$ 362,223	$ 315,625	$ 249,603	$ 203,029
Commercial	**255,147**	226,104	198,676	157,616	133,988
Industrial	**534,066**	495,461	494,388	413,265	364,797
Temporary construction	**3,699**	2,786	2,723	1,728	1,673
Other	**116,511**	102,370	95,110	82,659	65,928
Total Electric Revenue	**$1,305,449**	$1,188,944	$1,106,522	$ 904,871	$ 769,415
Average Annual KWH Use Per Customer					
Residential	**12,097**	13,015	12,786	13,173	12,374
Commercial	**77,138**	80,814	79,558	76,529	75,291
Industrial	**3,431,322**	3,451,098	4,095,224	4,340,461	4,402,946
Revenue Per KWH — (cents):					
Residential	**6.96**	6.05	5.52	4.39	3.94
Commercial	**5.88**	5.19	4.76	3.97	3.56
Industrial	**3.75**	3.61	3.28	2.78	2.44
Electric Energy Output — Thousands of KWH					
Net Generated	**25,846,238**	25,523,512	28,115,700	27,775,374	25,381,996
Net Purchased and Interchanged	**4,987,292**	5,160,731	4,411,795	4,507,245	5,871,615
	30,833,530	30,684,243	32,527,495	32,282,619	31,253,611
System Peak Load — Including Interruptible Load — (MW)	**5,348**	5,164	5,542	5,604	5,229
Total Capability, Including Contract Purchases at Time of System Peak Load (MW)	**7,152**	7,208	6,745	6,602	6,169
Load Factor	**65.8%**	67.8%	67.0%	65.2%	68.2%
STEAM					
Steam Revenue (thousands)	**$ 83,646**	$ 75,213	$ 77,624	$ 69,346	$ 68,278
Steam Sales — KWH (millions)	**2,555**	2,579	2,887	2,927	3,191
Steam Sales — millions of pounds	**8,559**	9,447	12,209	14,906	14,796
GAS					
Gas Revenue (thousands)	**$ 47,093**	$ 43,102	$ 37,568	$ 31,009	$ 26,645
Number of Customers	**85,737**	85,394	85,664	85,218	83,910
Output — MM cu. ft. of natural gas purchased	**9,149**	8,229	8,738	9,148	10,333
Sales — MM cu. ft.	**8,498**	8,535	8,599	9,097	9,892
WEATHER DATA:					
Cooling degree days (Normal 2,732)	**2,418**	2,883	2,775	2,910	2,502
Percentage change from normal	**(11.5)**	5.8	1.8	6.7	(8.2)
Heating degree days (Normal 1,570)	**1,647**	1,588	1,620	1,637	1,885
Percentage change from normal	**4.9**	1.9	4.0	5.1	21.0

Fig. 4-9. 1983 Statistical summary for Gulf States Utilities (reprinted from 1983 Form 10K, SEC).

legal proceedings. GSU is a party in 14 legal proceedings. Most of them are administrative proceedings before regulatory agencies routinely involved in monitoring public utilities, but there are a couple that are more serious. Among them are a class action suit on behalf of blacks and women, a federal civil rights charge made by a dismissed female worker, and a proceeding before the Texas State Department of Water Resources over the responsibility to clean up a 14-acre tract of land owned by the company. These proceedings could all have an adverse affect on the company's finances.

In the annual report, the company mentions that employees and shareholders have contributed nearly $250,000 to a program called Project CARE, which helps over 3,000 elderly pay their utility bills. The company has also appointed consumer affairs coordinators and begun a public education drive about energy issues. These costs are absorbed without mention in the financial statements of a multibillion dollar company, and must be determined by reading the annual report's narrative.

In short, getting just the annual report of a company and not the *real* poop—the 10K, or the previous 10Qs for recently issued stocks, or at least a prospectus—does not complete one's research. However, one cannot read only the negative in a 10K or 10Q statement and dismiss the company's presentation in its annual report. After all, the annual report's role is to communicate the company's continued successes to its shareholders and will, of course, accentuate the positive for public relations value. On the other hand, the 10K is a document through which a company must make full disclosure to the Securities and Exchange Commission and must, of necessity, present a "worst case" scenario, often in overly-complex legalese. But 10 Ks *are* good reading.

The Value Line

Most investors look at distillations of company data provided by investment services. These services rank stocks by a number of variables. Probably the best known of these services is the Value Line Investment Survey, which has some proprietary ways of ranking both individual stocks and industries. Others are Moody's, Standard and Poor's, the Ford Investor's Survices Data Base, Merrill Lynch Equity Research Data Base, Lynch, Jones & Ryan I/B/E/S, and Financial Post Data Base. All have differing size data bases of stock information and differing variables for how to rate the stocks. A number of variables are common to these and other stock selection databases.

The one-page Value Line report on each company (each report is updated quarterly) is packed with information (Figs. 4-10, 4-11).

Let's take the Value Line report for Gulf States Utilities issued in January 1983 apart. You will notice that it presents all of the information from the consolidated financial statements and then some. But, as I said when we looked at the financial statements, Value Line and the other investor surveys don't give you the raw numbers. Instead, they give you ratios and per-unit numbers, such as revenues per share and capital spending per share. To come up with these ratios, you have to divide the total money figures by the number of outstanding shares.

A Value Line report is divided into a number of different parts, each of which tells a story. Along the first line is the stock's name, ticker symbol, and the exchange it trades on, along with its most recent price, most recent price/earning ratio, the earning yield, and the dividend yield. Below this is a graph that traces price for the past 12 years, along with a numerical chart of the high and low for each of those 12 years, the target price range for the

DAYTON P. & L. NYSE-DPL

RECENT PRICE	P/E RATIO		EARN'S YLD	DIV'D YLD	
18	7.0	(Trailing: 8.7 Median: 8.5)	14.3 %	11.1%	709

High	32.6	38.2	37.2	26.5	27.6	26.8	25.0	21.4	18.1	20.0	22.4	18.8	17.3	15.4	15.0	19.0
Low	26.5	27.6	23.5	21.0	22.6	21.8	17.8	10.6	12.0	17.0	18.0	14.6	13.9	11.1	12.0	14.1

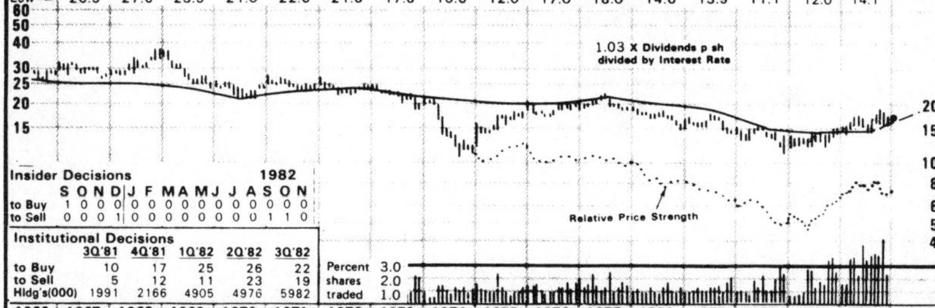

Insider Decisions

	S	O	N	D	J	F	M	A	M	J	J	A	S	O	N
					1982										
to Buy	1	0	0	0	0	0	0	0	0	0	0	0	0	0	0
to Sell	0	0	0	1	0	0	0	0	0	0	0	0	1	1	0

Institutional Decisions

	3Q'81	4Q'81	1Q'82	2Q'82	3Q'82
to Buy	10	17	25	26	22
to Sell	5	12	11	23	19
Hldg's(000)	1991	2166	4905	4976	5982

Jan. 28, 1983 Value Line

1984	1985	1986	1987
			50
			40
Target Price Range			30
			20
			15

TIMELINESS (Relative Price Performance Next 12 Mos.) **3** Average

SAFETY **2** Above Average (Scale: 1 Highest to 5 Lowest)

BETA .65 (1.00 = Market)

1985-87 PROJECTIONS

	Price	Gain	Ann'l Total Return
High	35	(+95%)	25%
Low	25	(+40%)	17%

1966	1967	1968	1969	1970	1971	1972	1973	1974	1975	1976	1977	1978	1979	1980	1981	1982	1983	© Arnold Bernhard & Co., Inc.	85-87E
14.53	15.33	16.08	17.29	17.29	19.32	18.50	19.13	21.79	23.17	22.55	21.87	22.94	24.22	23.63	24.83	*24.85*	*27.55*	Revenues per sh	*33.75*
3.02	3.29	3.44	3.64	3.49	3.81	3.57	3.57	3.34	3.70	3.43	2.85	2.80	3.25	2.89	3.64	*3.55*	*3.85*	"Cash Flow" per sh	*4.80*
1.91	2.15	2.22	2.28	2.15	2.07	2.15	1.87	1.89	2.24	2.05	1.70	1.73	2.01	1.85	2.51	*2.65*	*2.75*	Earnings per sh (A)	*3.10*
1.28	1.36	1.49	1.58	1.60	1.65	1.66	1.66	1.66	1.66	1.66	1.66	1.66	1.72	1.74	1.82	1.90	*2.00*	Div'd Decl'd per sh ■ (B)	*2.35*
2.99	4.75	6.72	7.45	6.90	6.53	5.54	6.45	6.84	6.02	5.68	5.81	7.30	9.14	8.08	7.93	*6.15*	*4.20*	Cap'l Spending per sh	*4.00*
13.43	14.27	15.07	15.80	17.02	17.45	18.44	18.65	17.89	18.15	18.39	18.60	18.39	18.60	18.06	18.01	*18.10*	*18.80*	Book Value per sh (C)	*20.60*
9.26	9.31	9.37	9.40	10.45	10.54	11.90	11.99	13.77	15.43	17.64	20.42	23.36	23.84	27.50	31.40	*36.60*	*37.40*	Common Shs Outst'g	*40.00*
15.1	13.7	14.1	12.6	10.8	11.9	10.9	11.5	7.8	7.0	9.0	11.6	9.8	7.8	7.4	5.3	*6.1*		Avg Ann'l P/E Ratio	*9.5*
6.6%	7.3%	7.1%	7.9%	9.3%	8.4%	9.2%	8.7%	12.8%	14.3%	11.1%	8.6%	10.2%	12.8%	13.5%	18.9%	*16.4%*		Avg Ann'l Earn's Yield	*10.5%*
4.4%	4.6%	4.8%	5.5%	6.9%	6.7%	7.1%	7.7%	11.3%	10.5%	9.0%	8.4%	9.8%	11.0%	12.7%	13.6%	11.8%		Avg Ann'l Div'd Yield	*8.1%*
						220.2	229.4	300.0	357.6	397.9	446.5	535.8	577.2	650.0	779.6	*910*	*1030*	Revenues ($mill)	*1350*
						27.1	27.0	29.7	41.2	43.4	40.2	47.6	61.5	64.8	94.0	*110*	*120*	Net Profit ($mill)	*140*
						16.6%	5.1%	- -	24.0%	23.8%	11.6%	20.5%	17.9%	18.0%	28.0%	*28.0%*	*28.0%*	Income Tax Rate	*30.0%*
						12.3%	11.8%	9.9%	11.5%	10.9%	9.0%	8.9%	10.7%	10.0%	12.1%	*12.1%*	*11.7%*	Net Profit Margin	*10.4%*
						52.6%	53.1%	50.9%	51.4%	51.6%	49.6%	48.3%	51.3%	48.4%	49.9%	*50.0%*	*50.0%*	Long-Term Debt Ratio	*48.5%*
						37.5%	34.2%	34.4%	35.1%	36.3%	39.2%	38.5%	34.1%	35.8%	36.2%	*37.5%*	*38.5%*	Common Equity Ratio	*40.0%*
						584.6	653.8	716.7	798.9	893.2	968.3	1114.5	1301.0	1387.6	1563.0	*1755*	*1825*	Total Capital ($mill)	*2060*
						603.9	656.5	724.7	791.0	860.3	951.5	1091.4	1278.5	1465.3	1676.6	*1840*	*1950*	Net Plant ($mill)	*2290*
						6.2%	5.5%	5.7%	6.9%	6.6%	6.0%	5.9%	6.4%	6.8%	8.4%	*9.0%*	*9.0%*	% Earned Total Cap'l	*9.5%*
						9.8%	8.8%	8.4%	10.6%	10.1%	8.3%	8.3%	9.7%	9.1%	12.0%	*12.5%*	*13.0%*	% Earned Net Worth	*13.0%*
						10.7%	10.0%	9.7%	11.7%	10.8%	8.4%	8.6%	10.7%	9.5%	13.2%	*13.5%*	*14.5%*	% Earned Comm Equity (D)	*14.5%*
						2.5%	1.1%	1.3%	3.1%	2.1%	.3%	.4%	1.5%	.5%	3.5%	*4.0%*	*4.0%*	% Retained to Comm Eq	*3.5%*
						80%	91%	89%	79%	85%	97%	97%	89%	96%	79%	*77%*	*77%*	% All Div'ds to Net Prof	*79%*

CAPITAL STRUCTURE as of 9/30/82
Total Debt $840.1 mill. **Due in 5 Yrs.** $77.5 mill.
LT Debt $838.0 mill. **LT Interest** $80.2 mill.
Incl. $4.0 mill. capitalized leases (LT interest earned: 2.7x;

Pension Liability None in '81 vs None in '80
Pfd Stock $215.9 mill. **Pfd Div'd** $19.2 mill.
2,170,000 shs. 3.75% to 12.5%; all $100 par and cum.; callable $101 to $112 per share. Incl. 1,362,500 shs. 8⅝%-12.50%, call. 100 to 112, sinking fund ends 5/15/2004.
Common Stock 36,504,080 shs. **as of 10/31/82**

ELECTRIC OPERATING STATISTICS

	1979	1980	1981
% Change Sales (KWH)	+.5	−.6	+1.2
Avg. Resid'l Use (KWH)	9794	10042	9600
Avg. Revs. per KWH (¢)	3.90	4.4	5.35
Capacity at Peak (Mw)	2537	2625	2659
Peak Load, Summer (Mw)	2105	2045	2122
Annual Load Factor (%)	59.6	59.5	59.1
% Change Customers (yr.-end)	+1.5	+.4	+.3
Fixed Charge Cov. (%)	105	103	155

ANNUAL RATES of change (per sh)	Past 10 Yrs	Past 5 Yrs	Est '79-'81 to '85-'87
Revenues	3.0%	1.5%	*5.5%*
"Cash Flow"	−1.0%	−1.5%	*6.5%*
Earnings	Nil	0.5%	*6.5%*
Dividends	1.0%	1.0%	*5.0%*
Book Value	1.0%	Nil	*2.0%*

Calendar	QUARTERLY REVENUES ($ mill.) Mar. 31	June 30	Sept. 30	Dec. 31	Full Year
1979	185.3	130.4	114.9	146.6	577.2
1980	195.0	145.0	160.0	150.0	650.0
1981	238.9	167.3	169.5	203.9	779.6
1982	293.0	199.2	184.1	*233.7*	*910*
1983	*310*	*240*	*230*	*250*	*1030*

Calendar	EARNINGS PER SHARE Mar. 31	June 30	Sept. 30	Dec. 31	(A) Full Year
1979	.70	.48	.43	.40	2.01
1980	.62	.45	.42	.36	1.85
1981	1.01	.44	.65	.41	2.51
1982	1.12	.60	.57	*.36*	*2.65*
1983	*1.05*	*.60*	*.60*	*.50*	*2.75*

Calendar	QUARTERLY DIVIDENDS PAID Mar. 31	June 30	Sept. 30	Dec. 31	(B) Full ■ Year
1979	.415	.435	.435	.435	1.72
1980	.435	.435	.435	.435	1.74
1981	.455	.455	.455	.455	1.82
1982	.475	.475	.475	.475	1.90
1983	.50				

BUSINESS: Dayton Power & Light sells elec., 69% of revenues; natural gas, 30%; and steam, 1%, in Dayton and west-central Ohio. Electric rev. breakdown: residential, 47%; comm'l, 19%; indus'l, 23%; other, 11%. Six generating units are owned with other Ohio utilities. The electrical and electronic machinery industry is the largest industrial customer. Power costs: 45% of revs.; labor costs, 11%. '81 rep't deprec. rate: 3.0%. Est'd plant age: 10 yrs. Prime fuels: coal, 98%; oil, 2%. Has 3,827 employees, 76,485 common shareholders. Chairman: Robert E. Frazer. President: Peter H. Forster. Incorporated: Ohio. Address: Courthouse Plaza S.W., Dayton, Ohio 45401.

Dayton's service area is depressed. DP&L's economy is heavily dependent on Detroit for its livelihood. As the auto industry slumped, so did Dayton. Through the first nine months of 1982, industrial sales declined 7%, year to year. Management projects annual electric sales growth of under 2% through mid-decade. The company has consequently postponed plans for the construction of the East-Bend coal-fired generator scheduled for 1988 operation.

Lower construction needs are easing financing requirements. With the Killen coal-fired generator on-stream in mid-1982, Dayton's only plant under construction is the 807-megawatt, 31.5%-owned Zimmer nuclear facility. (Please turn to page 705 for a review of Cincinnati Gas and Electric, the plant's construction manager.) Capital expenditures for 1983 and 1984 will average $160 million annually, down from $225 million in 1982. Internally generated funds will probably provide 30%-40% of necessary financing. But no public offering of common stock will be required till after mid-decade. This will reduce prospects that earnings gains will be diluted.

The recent rate order was near expectations. In December, the Public Utility Commission of Ohio granted the company a $33.9 million rate increase on a request for $63 million. The allowed return on common was boosted fractionally to 16.58% from 16.44%. The award will benefit earnings comparisons through 1983.

Another large rate application is pending. In July, DP&L filed for an annual $128 million rate hike and a 19% permitted return on common for its $400 million Killen generator. The commission's ruling is expected in April. Whatever increase is granted will contribute to higher profitability in the final three quarters of the year and, in our opinion, produce a third consecutive annual share earnings record in 1983.

We expect the dividend to increase at a 5% annual rate to mid-decade. Reduced construction costs and less dilution of common should provide higher share earnings, which, in turn, will probably be translated into higher dividends. *A.H.M./M.S.*

Restated Revenues (and Pretax Margins) by Business Line

	1979	1980	1981	1982
Electric	398.5(20.2%)	454.0(20.0%)	549.3(28.9%)	*642(27.9%)*
Gas	171.8 (3.6%)	188.5 (3.6%)	223.0 (1.9%)	*260(3.0%)*
Steam	6.9(d7.2%)	7.5(d6.7%)	7.3(d15.1%)	*8.0(d1.0%)*
Company Total	577.2(14.9%)	650.0(15.0%)	779.6(20.7%)	*910(20.5%)*

(A) Based on avg. shs. outst'g. Next egs. rep't due late Apr. Est'd constant-dollar egs./sh.: '81, 85¢. (B) Next div'd meet'g about Apr. 15. Goes ex about Feb. 2. Div'd paym't dates; Mar. 1, May 31, Sept. 1, Dec. 1. 12.4% tax-free in '81, est'd 15% in '82. ■ Div'd reinvest. plan av'ble. (C) Incl. intangibles. In '81: $1.90/sh. (D) Rate base: net orig. cost. Rate all'd com. eq. in '82: 16.58%; earn. avg. com. eq.: 13.8%. Reg. Climate: Avg.

Company's Financial Strength	B++
Stock's Price Stability	90
Price Growth Persistence	10
Earnings Predictability	80

Fig. 4-10. Value Line sheet from Jan. 1983 for Dayton Power and Light Co. (Reprinted from value Line Investment Survey, © 1983 Value Line, Inc. Reprinted with permission.)

GULF ST. UTILS. NYSE-GSU

RECENT PRICE	14	P/E RATIO	6.9 (Trailing: 7.9 Median: 7.5)	EARN'S YLD	14.6%	DIV'D YLD	11.6%	713

	1966	1967	1968	1969	1970	1971	1972	1973	1974	1975	1976	1977	1978	1979	1980	1981	1982
High	28.9	28.8	27.9	25.2	26.8	24.3	22.4	16.0	14.8	15.4	14.9	14.3	13.6	12.6	12.9	14.0	
Low	20.5	20.9	19.5	18.0	19.4	17.1	13.0	8.8	10.6	11.8	12.9	11.6	10.1	9.0	10.4	11.1	

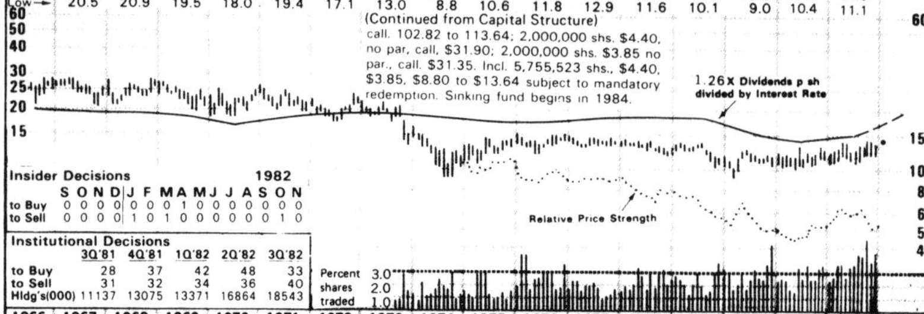

(Continued from Capital Structure) call. 102.82 to 113.64; 2,000,000 shs. $4.40, no par, call. $31.90; 2,000,000 shs. $3.85 no par., call. $31.35. Incl. 5,755,523 shs., $4.40, $3.85, $8.80 to $13.64 subject to mandatory redemption. Sinking fund begins in 1984.

Jan. 28, 1983 Value Line

1984	1985	1986	1987

Target Price Range: 30 / 20

TIMELINESS 4 Below Average (Relative Price Performance Next 12 Mos.)

SAFETY 2 Above Average (Scale: 1 Highest to 5 Lowest)

BETA .70 (1.00 = Market)

1985-87 PROJECTIONS

	Price	Gain	Ann'l Total Return
High	30	(+115%)	28%
Low	20	(+ 45%)	18%

Insider Decisions 1982

	S	O	N	D	J	F	M	A	M	J	J	A	S	O	N
to Buy	0	0	0	0	0	0	0	1	0	0	0	0	0	0	0
to Sell	0	0	0	0	1	0	1	0	0	0	0	0	0	1	0

Institutional Decisions

	3Q'81	4Q'81	1Q'82	2Q'82	3Q'82
to Buy	28	37	42	48	33
to Sell	31	32	34	36	40
Hldg's(000)	11137	13075	13371	16864	18543

1966	1967	1968	1969	1970	1971	1972	1973	1974	1975	1976	1977	1978	1979	1980	1981	1982	1983	© Arnold Bernhard & Co., Inc.	(E) 85-87E
6.55	7.12	7.47	8.27	8.26	8.23	9.39	11.30	14.47	12.80	13.76	17.92	18.74	20.23	20.55	20.17	***17.55***	***19.35***	**Revenues per sh**	***31.50***
1.98	2.10	2.20	2.43	2.58	2.54	2.90	3.10	3.44	3.32	3.18	3.51	3.18	3.08	3.39	3.28	***3.00***	***3.55***	**"Cash Flow" per sh**	***5.00***
1.15	1.19	1.30	1.38	1.49	1.46	1.59	1.70	1.69	1.62	1.54	1.69	1.73	1.74	2.05	2.24	***1.95***	***2.30***	**Earnings per sh** (A)	***2.75***
.78	.82	.88	.94	.98	1.04	1.04	1.10	1.12	1.12	1.12	1.15	1.24	1.30	1.39	1.48	1.58	***1.82***	**Div'd Decl'd per sh** ■ (B)	***1.95***
2.83	3.74	5.54	5.57	4.70	3.60	4.36	4.20	6.57	6.06	6.47	6.86	8.20	9.77	13.17	7.21	***8.60***	***7.50***	**Cap'l Spending per sh**	***3.60***
7.96	8.32	9.60	10.04	11.19	12.27	12.82	13.39	13.96	14.08	14.36	14.89	15.50	15.53	15.61	15.41	***15.15***	***15.75***	**Book Value per sh** (C)	***18.50***
20.75	20.75	22.15	22.15	23.55	25.55	25.55	25.55	25.55	28.55	32.55	32.80	38.30	42.72	48.91	60.57	***74.00***	***82.75***	**Common Shs Outst'g**	***88.00***
22.5	21.5	18.8	17.1	14.6	15.1	12.6	10.9	7.1	7.8	8.8	8.1	7.5	7.2	5.5	5.1	***6.3***		**Avg Ann'l P/E Ratio**	***8.5***
4.4%	4.7%	5.3%	5.9%	6.9%	6.6%	7.9%	9.2%	14.1%	12.8%	11.4%	12.4%	13.3%	13.9%	18.2%	19.6%	***15.8%***		**Avg Ann'l Earn's Yield**	***11.5%***
3.0%	3.2%	3.6%	4.0%	4.5%	4.7%	5.2%	6.0%	9.4%	8.9%	8.2%	8.4%	9.5%	10.9%	12.4%	12.9%	12.6%		**Avg Ann'l Div'd Yield**	***8.1%***

1972	1973	1974	1975	1976	1977	1978	1979	1980	1981	1982	1983		85-87E
240.0	288.6	369.6	365.3	447.7	587.8	718.0	864.3	1005.2	1221.7	***1300***	***1600***	**Revenues ($mill)**	***2775***
45.2	50.2	49.9	51.4	56.4	65.7	70.2	84.2	117.2	150.9	***165***	***235***	**Net Profit ($mill)**	***300***
40.6%	37.0%	41.7%	36.7%	36.2%	38.9%	39.7%	31.2%	27.4%	18.9%	***25.0%***	***25.0%***	**Income Tax Rate**	***23.0%***
18.8%	17.4%	13.5%	14.1%	12.6%	11.2%	9.8%	9.7%	11.7%	12.4%	***12.7%***	***14.7%***	**Net Profit Margin**	***10.8%***
51.9%	53.5%	56.2%	54.5%	54.7%	55.1%	53.3%	53.1%	54.1%	54.1%	***53.0%***	***52.0%***	**Long-Term Debt Ratio**	***50.0%***
35.4%	34.6%	32.9%	35.3%	36.2%	33.4%	37.4%	35.6%	32.6%	34.4%	***34.5%***	***35.5%***	**Common Equity Ratio**	***36.5%***
924.6	989.4	1083.6	1140.5	1290.3	1461.5	1588.7	1867.0	2344.2	2712.7	***3250***	***3700***	**Total Capital ($mill)**	***4400***
1017.4	1087.7	1206.2	1327.8	1483.3	1615.7	1846.0	2201.0	2727.3	3089.7	***3650***	***4235***	**Net Plant ($mill)**	***5550***
6.3%	6.6%	6.2%	6.3%	6.2%	6.3%	6.3%	6.4%	7.1%	8.4%	***8.0%***	***9.5%***	**% Earned Total Cap'l**	***10.0%***
10.2%	10.9%	10.5%	9.9%	9.7%	10.0%	9.5%	9.6%	10.9%	12.1%	***11.0%***	***13.0%***	**% Earned Net Worth**	***14.0%***
12.4%	12.7%	12.1%	11.1%	10.6%	11.3%	10.0%	10.3%	12.1%	12.9%	***11.5%***	***14.0%***	**% Earned Comm Equity** (D)	***14.5%***
4.3%	4.5%	4.1%	3.4%	2.8%	3.6%	2.8%	2.2%	3.9%	4.4%	***2.0%***	***4.0%***	**% Retained to Comm Eq**	***4.0%***
69%	69%	71%	74%	77%	73%	76%	83%	74%	73%	***85%***	***77%***	**% All Div'ds to Net Prof**	***78%***

CAPITAL STRUCTURE as of 9/30/82

Total Debt $1666.0 mill. **Due in 5 Yrs.** $82.7 mill.
LT Debt $1608.3 mill. **LT Interest** $192.0 mill.
Incl. $10.9 mill. capitalized leases.
(LT int. earned: 1.6x)
Incl. debt discount of $9.9 mill. Incl. $6.0 mill. 7¼% debs. (92) call. at 106.80 cv. into 75.47 com. shs. at $13.25 a com. sh.

Leases, Uncapitalized Annual rentals $1.0 mill.
Pension Liability None in '81 vs None in 1980
Pfd Stock $412.0 mill. **Pfd Div'd** $46.6 mill.
3,119,970 shs. $4.20 to $13.64, $100 par,
(Continued on Chart)
Common Stock 68,326,705 shs.
(68.8 mill. fully diluted shs.)

ELECTRIC OPERATING STATISTICS

	1979	1980	1981
% Change Sales (KWH)	+2.6	+4.23	+.5
Avg. Resid'l Use (KWH)	12374	13137	12786
Avg. Revs. per KWH (¢)	2.90	3.27	3.98
Capacity at Peak (Mw)	6169	6602	6745
Peak Load, Summer (Mw)	5229	5604	5542
Annual Load Factor (%)	68.2	65.2	67.0
% Change Customers (yr.-end)	+3.7	+3.5	+3.4
Fixed Charge Cov. (%)	131	125	115

ANNUAL RATES of change (per sh)	Past 10 Yrs	Past 5 Yrs	Est '79-'81 (E) to '85-'87
Revenues	9.5%	8.0%	7.5%
"Cash Flow"	2.5%	-0.5%	7.5%
Earnings	3.5%	4.5%	5.5%
Dividends	3.5%	4.5%	5.5%
Book Value	3.5%	2.0%	3.0%

Cal-endar	QUARTERLY REVENUES ($ mill.) Mar. 31	June 30	Sept. 30	Dec. 31	Full Year
1979	185.3	211.2	250.9	216.9	864.3
1970	227.9	242.5	297.5	237.3	1005.2
1981	266.1	320.6	373.1	261.9	1221.7
1982	285.7	309.8	375.3	***329.2***	***1300***
1983	***340***	***375***	***475***	***410***	***1600***

Cal-endar	EARNINGS PER SHARE Mar. 31	June 30	Sept. 30	Dec. 31	(A) Full Year
1979	.26	.24	.72	.52	1.74
1980	.34	.54	.85	.32	2.05
1981	.40	.50	.97	.37	2.24
1982	.31	.40	.69	***.55***	***1.95***
1983	***.35***	***.45***	***.90***	***.60***	***2.30***

Cal-endar	QUARTERLY DIVIDENDS PAID Mar. 31	June 30	Sept. 30	Dec. 31	(B) Full ■ Year
1979	.34	.34	.34	.34	1.36
1980	.34	.34	.34	.37	1.39
1981	.37	.37	.37	.37	1.48
1982	.39	.39	.39	.39	1.56
1983					

BUSINESS: Gulf States Utilities Co. supplies electricity (91% of revs.), steam (6%), and gas (3%) in south-central La. (54% of revs.) and southeastern Texas (46%). Elec. rev. sources: resid'l, 28%; indus'l, 45%; comm'l, 18%; other, 9%. The industrial revenue contribution is greater than the 30% for the average electricity utility. Chemicals and allied products industry is the largest (62% of ind'l revs). Prime fuels: gas, 98%; oil, 2%. Fuel costs: 57% of revs.; labor costs, 8%. '81 rep't deprec. rate: 3.7%. Est'd plant age: 10 yrs. Has 4,600 empls., 61,623 stkhldrs. Chrmn. & C.E.O.: P.W. Murrill. Pres.: N.R. Lee. Inc.: Texas. Address: 285 Liberty Ave., Beaumont, TX 77701.

GSU shares provide an above average yield. Assuming that the annual payout is boosted 8¢ a share (5%) next May, the 1983 yield would be a point higher than the industry norm. The generous yield, in our opinion, reflects the company's exposure in the River Bend nuclear facility (70% of its $2.5 billion cost). Currently, approximately 60% of the facility's construction has been completed, with the in-service date scheduled for late 1985. The investment in River Bend will require a significant amount of external financing, including common stock, until the nuclear facility is completed. As a result, the total annual return to 1985-87 is projected only about in line with that envisioned for the average electric utility equity.

Higher rates are needed to raise most of the capital to finance River Bend. In mid-December, the company applied to the Louisiana commission for $123.7 million of higher tariffs. Most of any allowed increase will be collected in 1984 since we expect a decision in late 1983. The requested return on common equity is the same 16.25% awarded in last September's rate order. We estimate that about 50%-60% of the request will be awarded in the final quarter. About that time, management also expects to put into effect higher rates for its Texas ratepayers. The company probably will file an application for higher rates in Texas this spring. No details of the expected filing were available at press time.

Inadequate rates and reduced electricity sales pulled 1982 share earnings about 13% below year-earlier results. About $200 million of higher tariffs annually received in the September 1982 quarter were insufficient over the balance of 1982 to offset about a 6% decline in sales and higher financing and operating expenses.

Prospects for this year are more favorable. Last year's rate increase will be in effect for the full year and electricity sales are expected to climb 3%, given some improvement in the economy of the company's services area after midyear. Share earnings may climb about 20%, we estimate, more than offsetting last year's earnings attrition. *W.M./M.S.*

Restated Revenues (and Pretax Operating Margins) by Business Line

	1979	1980	1981	1982
Electric	789.4(20.0%)	904.9(21.4%)	1106.5(21.7%)	*1170(26.5%)*
Steam	68.3(28.6%)	69.3(26.6%)	77.6(14.2%)	*85.0(18.0%)*
Gas	26.6(3.8%)	31.0(1.6%)	37.6(6.8%)	*45.0(7.5%)*
Company Total	864.3(20.1%)	1005.2(21.2%)	1221.7(20.7%)	*1300(25.5%)*

(A) Next egs. rep't: mid-Apr. Est'd constant-dollar egs./sh.: '81, 50¢. (B) Next div'd meet'g about Feb. 3. Goes ex about Feb. 10. Div'd paym't dates: Mar. 15, June 15, Sept. 15, Dec. 15. ■ Div'd reinvest. plan av'ble. (C) Incl. intangibles. In '81: 74¢/sh. (D) Rate base: La. and Tex.: Net orig. cost. Rates all'd on com. eq. in '82: La., 16.25%; Tex. 17.15%; earn. on '81 sys. avg. com. eq.: 14.2%. Reg. Climate: Tex., Above Avg.; La., Avg. (E) Fully diluted 3-5 yrs. hence.

Company's Financial Strength	B·
Stock's Price Stability	100
Price Growth Persistence	5
Earnings Predictability	85

Fig. 4-11. Value Line sheet from Jan. 1983 for Gulf States Utilities. (Reprinted from Value Line Investment Survey, © 1983 Value Line, Inc. Reprinted with permission.)

next three years in terms of price, percentage change from the present, and an annual total return percentage. Little charts in the lower left-hand corner of the price graph show the buy and sell decisions of insiders—company officials, directors, and others close to the "inside" of the company—each month over the past year, as well as institutional buy and sell decisions by quarter for the last five quarters. On the bottom right of this top portion are two small charts. One shows the Value Line proprietary rankings for timeliness (how the stock) is expected to perform over the next year), safety (how the stock is expected to perform over the next three years), and *beta* (how volatile the stock is—a ranking of 1.0 means the stock moves around as the market moves; less than one means the stock shows less relative volatility than the market; more than one means the stock shows more volatility than the market). The second little chart on the bottom right gives price projections for three years out.

Value Line ranked GSU at four for timeliness (below average), but at two for safety. They obviously didn't see the nuclear madness that would sweep the country later in 1983.

The second part of the Value Line page shows statistics for the last 16 years on sales per share, cash flow per share, earnings per share, dividends declared per share, capital spending per share, book value per share, common shares outstanding, average annual price/earnings ratio, average annual earnings yield, and average annual dividend yield. These statistics are projected out for two years. Statistics are given for the past ten years on sales, operating margin, depreciation, net profit, income tax rate, net profit margin, working capital, long-term debt, net worth, percentage earned on total capital, percentage earned on net worth, percentage of earnings retained to equity in common shares, and percentage of all dividends to net profits. These ratios give the investor a method for making quick comparisons of stocks.

The third part shows the company's current structure in terms of long-term debt, short-term debt, how much debt is owed in five years, long-term interest due on the debt, leases, pension liability, how much preferred stock is outstanding (preferred stock usually pays higher dividends and has the right to be reimbursed prior to common stock in the event of liquidation, among other differences), what the preferred stock dividends are, as well as current assets, current liabilities, and annual rates of earnings and dividends for the last few years.

Part four is a description of the company's business in general terms as well as a description of the company's business over the last fiscal quarter (Value Line issues new quarterly reports soon after companies report their quarterly financial figures).

What makes Value Line a well-known and well-used tool is its proprietary ranking system, which ranks stocks on a one-to-five scale for both timeliness (how Value Line thinks the stock will perform in the next year) and safety (how much it will continue to perform three to five years out). Value Line ranks 1,400 stocks, mostly of larger companies, giving 100 a one rank, 300 a two, 600 a three, 300 a four, and 100 a five. They are ranked in comparison to each other, and the rankings are changed each quarter, although they can be changed more often if drastic news is announced before a new report is issued. Value Line does this by a weekly update.

But let's not get carried away with the Value Line proprietary system. What we really want to do is use Value Line as an example of the variables with which fundamental analysis deals.

When first confronted by a Value Line

page (or by a page from another similar service, or, for that matter, a screen on one of the software programs we will be speaking about), one might be tempted to jump out the window. There's so much information; what does it all mean? Let's take a look at some of the information and think about how to put it all in context.

First is the price. By itself, price means little. Of course, many small investors can only afford to buy inexpensive stocks, especially if they intend to buy a *round lot*—100 shares, otherwise known in broker parlance as a "ticket." The reason to buy in round lots is that transaction costs for *odd lots*—transactions of less than 100 shares—are about the same as for a round lot. So if you have about $2,000 to invest and want to buy a round lot, you have to look for a stock with a price of under $20 per share. Other than that, price really does not mean much by itself. What does become important to look at are the earnings per share, the price/earnings ratio, and the earnings yield (the inverse of P/E). These should be compared in the short-term against other short-term periods for the same company and against other companies in the same industry.

For example, XYZ Corp. and ABC Corp. both manufacture chemicals. XYZ sells for $22, while ABC sells for $14. XYZ has a price/earnings ratio (computed by Value Line by taking the last six months' earnings, adding them to the next six months' *estimated* earnings, and dividing that into the price) of 12, while ABC's P/E is 9. Which is the better buy? It isn't possible to tell because there are so many variables to deal with—one company may be coming back from a few bad years or sliding after a few exceptional years. With diversified companies, a company may have just sold off a subsidiary and be cash-rich, or it could have bought a new division and accumulated a lot of new debt.

Many small, innovative companies trade at astronomical P/E ratios. Some companies issue stock when the company is showing negative earnings. Stock with high P/Es are exceptionally vulnerable to large fluctuations in price—especially downward—if earnings don't measure up to expectations. A P/E of 25 or even 50 is not uncommon for a technology stock, while electric utilities usually have P/Es in the 6 or 7 range.

Per Share Figures

Earnings per share is, of course, the first mark of where the company has been in the past quarter or year. But dividends per share, sales per share, cash flow per share, and book value per share are also important indicators. Value Line shows all of these figures.

Margins could be low, causing earnings per share to decline, but as long as sales per share are still high, the situation may not be drastic. It could be a matter of the prices being behind recent rises in labor, energy to run manufacturing, or raw material costs.

Dividends per share differ with the industry as well as with how "mature" a company is. Electric utilities pay high dividends, since there will always be a need for electricity (or so it is thought) and they can always issue more debt (bonds) to cover expansion rather than having to fund it internally through earnings.

Book value per share is what is left for the common stock holders if a liquidation were to occur at the prices the company states for its plant, equipment, and other assets on the books. If more debt is issued, or preferred stock is issued, book value declines. Book value is somewhat subjective, since some investors count such items as the value of brand names, patents, and other "intangible assets" as part of the book value. Book value is lower in some industries than in others, as well as from business to business.

Cash flow per share is the amount of cash a company can generate internally to replace and expand production capacity, pay its dividends and provide working capital. It is the sum of reported earnings plus depreciation on equipment and physical facilities.

Company Figures

A number of important company statistics must be examined. Among those Value Line keeps track of are sales, depreciation, how much the depreciable assets are reduced in value each year, net profit, what was earned for all stockholders (common and preferred), net profit margin and operating margin, and how much of sales is being turned into operating income and how much is being converted into profit.

Other figures include net worth, equity of all stockholders after deducting liabilities from assets, percent earned on net worth (again for all stockholders), percent retained to common equity or "plowback," net income minus dividends, and the percent all dividends paid to net profit or "payout" (the inverse of plowback).

Putting Fundamentals on the Computer

The computer's job in fundamental analysis is to take large data bases and grind them down into manageable listings of companies that deserve further study. Unfortunately, this is an expensive task. The most successful fundamental analysis packages, therefore, are purchased mostly by money managers, banks, and brokers. There are a few programs that do some statistical analysis to attempt to predict stock prices, but they do not do the real "heavy" analysis that most fundamental analysts want.

Value Line is in the process of putting together its Value/Probe, a sophisticated system that will be updated weekly. Currently, the company's Value/Screen program is updated monthly. A similar program to Value/Screen and Value/Probe is called Micro/Scan, developed and manufactured by the Isys Corp. of Cambridge MA. A program called StockPac was devised by Standard and Poor's in conjunction with a software developer a few years ago, and has recently been redesigned with more power and for the larger and more popular Apple and IBM computers.

Value/Probe, Value/Screen, and Micro/Scan are database programs—data is delivered periodically to the user on diskettes—that allow you to set criteria for the types of investments you are looking for. By asking the program to search its database for stocks that meet each criteria, the program continually narrows the database to those stocks that fit all of your criteria. As you become more stringent with your criteria and reach a manageable number of stocks, you begin to analyze and compare the companies more closely, using both the variables available to you on the program and getting additional research as needed.

For instance, you might start by asking for all bank stocks with a P/E of less than 10. The program may cut the database from 1,400 stocks (Micro/Scan) or 1,650 stocks (Value/Screen) to 130. Then, by asking for only stocks with prices under $30 per share, you may go down to 40 stocks. By having the program crunch the database further to only those stocks that also have a six percent or greater dividend, you may get the number down to ten or twelve, a reasonable number to start comparing them statistically to find subtleties.

Gary Sworek, a pension fund manager for Masco Corp., a diversified metalworking company in Taylor MI, was one of the first Micro/Scan users in early 1982. "Microscan sets the groundwork for us," he says. "The staff doesn't have to go through every company to find investment possibilities. The program comes up with maybe 10 or 20 good names, then we go into more detail on them."

While the Value Line's Value/Screen, which was priced at $495 at the beginning of the year, is the only one of the three programs that is in the price range of the individual investor. (Value/Probe will go for about $20,000 per year in "soft dollars," meaning that the user must guarantee to make transactions worth $20,000 in commissions to a certain brokerage house in conjunction with using Value/Probe. Micro/Scan costs from $6,250 to $8,500 for a single database, more for multiple databases, in hard dollars and can be purchased in soft dollars through a number of brokers.)

These database programs have their limitations. Value/Screen is limited in that it has only 32 variables and these 32 variables are bound by Value Line's definitions. Value/Screen has stock timeliness rank, safety rank, industry timeliness rank, price stability index, financial strength rating, and beta factor as the first six of 32 variables. These six variables are the six proprietary rankings Value Line has set up. In essence, then, Value/Screen is an electronic version of the Value Line Survey Book.

This is not, however, necessarily bad. Indeed, the proprietary rankings Value Line has set up over the years are what has drawn many users to the product. The diskette version (which runs on Apple II+ or *II*e with 80 column screen capacity, 64K memory, and two disk drives or IBM PC with 64K memory) is certainly less combersome than the three-ring-notebook version, which can double as a home weightlifting center. And the ability to screen by criteria—isolate all bank stocks with a P/E of less than 8 and a price under 25—can keep you from going buggy turning pages. When you have narrowed your choices down, you can run tests showing how all of your choices stack up on all 32 variables.

Value/Probe (which was not operational when this book was being written) will, the Value Line company says, allow the user to have the 32 Value Line variables and choose 20 others from a list of many more to do 52-variable comparative studies. It will also allow you to go on-line to get the latest pricing figures over the phone lines. Value/Probe will only be compatible with an IBM PC with at least 128K of memory. Users will also be able to download Value/Probe into spreadsheet programs such as VisiCalc and 1,2,3.

Micro/Scan can be purchased with one or more of four databases: Ford Investor Services Data Base (1400 companies, 54 variables per company), Merrill Lynch Equity Research Data Base (1400 companies, 52 variables), Lynch, Jones & Ryan I/B/E/S (1600 to 2400 companies, 52 variables), and Financial Post Data Base (350 Canadian companies, 52 variables). Micro/Scan diskettes are delivered each month, but updated pricing can be done on a daily basis through Isys Corp.'s One/Source pricing update service for $50 to $75 for a complete database, depending on the database size. The program was first developed to run on the Apple II+; the advanced version runs on the II+ with 64K memory, the III with 128K, the IBM PC with 128K, and the DEC Rainbow.

A Test Run

Let's compare two stocks using the Ford Data Base (Fig. 4-12). The two stocks are Dayton Power and Light and Gulf States Utilities, both electric utility stocks. The way these two stocks were chosen is easy: My wife owns a little DPL and I own a little GSU. Fortunately, they provide a good teaching all ford variables

FORD 08/31/83	DPL	GSU
STK PRICE 8/31/83	17.000	13.750
PRICE %CH 1 MONTH	-0.73	-5.17
MARKET CAP.(MIL)	629	1,019
PRICE TO BK. RATIO	0.91	0.88
PRICE TO INTR. VAL	0.99	0.86
P/E RATIO (NORMAL)	6.80	6.17
TOT RETR/P/E NORM	2.17	2.58
TOTAL RETURN %	14.77	15.93
DIVIDEND YIELD (%)	11.77	11.93
GROWTH RATE EPS	3.00	4.00
DIVIDEND PAYOUT %	0.80	0.74
DIVIDENDS PER SHARE	2.00	1.64
RETURN ON EQUITY %	13.31	14.26
REINVEST. RATE (%)	2.66	3.77
CURRENT EPS	2.42	2.23
NORMAL EPS	2.50	2.23
CURRENT/NORM. EPS	0.97	1.00
EARNINGS TREND	50.29	0.00
GROWTH PERSIST.	C	C
EARNINGS VARIAB.	0.11	0.05
HISTORIC BETA	0.49	0.66
DEBT/EQUITY	1.00	1.04
SH. HELD BY FUNDS%	17	24
INDUSTRY CODE	86	86
QUALITY RATING	B+	A-
INTRINSIC VALUE	17.20	16.08
BOOK VAL PER SHARE	18.78	15.64
PRICE %CH 3 MONTHS	-3.55	-3.51
PRICE %CH 6 MONTHS	-0.73	1.85
PRICE %CH 12 MONTHS	2.26	7.84
12 MONTH EPS GAIN	-12.95	8.78
CURRENT P/E RATIO	7.03	6.17
CURRENT ROE (%)	12.89	14.26
5YR EPS GROWTH %	8.85	5.71
5Y DIV/SH GROWTH %	3.53	5.40
RELATIVE CURR P/E	0.44	0.39
RELATIVE EPS 5YR	1.95	1.26
REL PE TO REL EPS5Y	0.23	0.31
RELATIVE P/E NORM	0.59	0.53
REL PROJ GROWTH	0.26	0.35
REL PE TO REL GROW	2.26	1.54
SALES ($ MILL)	887	1,307
RETURN ON SALES	10.10	12.64
SHARES OUTSTAND.	37	74
SALES TO MKT VAL	1.41	1.28
SECTOR CODE	4	4
FISCAL DATE	82/12	82/12
PROJECTED ROI %	14.76	15.88
#EPS INCR OVER 5YRS	4	3
#DPS INCR OVER 5YRS	4	4
12MO ACT RETURN %	14.63	21.02

Fig. 4-12. A printout of the 54 variables of the Ford Investor Survey as they relate to Dayton Power and Light Co. and Gulf States Utilities. (Reprinted with permission of ISYS Corp.)

example of fundamental analysis.

Which stock is a better deal?

First, we have to understand all the definitions used by the database.

Stock Price and Price Change are obvious. Gulf States has taken a bigger price drop in the last month.

Market Capitalization is the current price of the stock times the number of shares outstanding. Gulf States has a much larger number of shares outstanding—its market capitalization is almost $400 million more than Dayton Power and it sells for over three dollars less per share.

Price to Book Ratio is the ratio of the price to the book value. Both stocks sell for about 90 percent of book value. Book value is how much of the company is owned by the investors. This has some relation to the percentage of equity a company has as opposed to debt; if the book value is $15 per share and the debt/equity ratio is 1/1 (50 percent debt, 50 percent equity), we can assume the company's assets per share are somewhere around $30 (plus a few dollars per share for all those adjustments we found on the capitalization statement that didn't fall into debt or equity.

Price to Intrinsic Value is one of Ford's distinctive criteria. The Micro/Scan user's manual tells us that Intrinsic Value Theory says a stock is worth the present worth of all future payments. Future payments are the price the stock can be expected to sell for after a growth period and all dividends it will pay between now and then. This must then be discounted by differing amounts depending on the quality—another subjective value—of the stock. In this case, Dayton Power is selling for its intrinsic value while Gulf States is selling for only nine-tenths of its intrinsic value, hinting that for an investor who is willing to hold the stock for the entire growth period—which, we are told, is typically figured at ten years —Gulf States is current undervalued and may be considered a bargain.

P/E Normal is the ratio of the current price to "normal" earnings per share (EPS). EPS is calculated by Ford at current, twelve months back, projected (either to the end of a quarter or fiscal year), or normal (those that could be expected under normal operating circumstances). Dayton Power sells at a higher price to normal earnings multiple, suggesting that perhaps it is overextended or Gulf States is discounted. To draw that conclusion, this variable should be studied against other electric utility stocks.

Total Return on normal P/E is what could be expected to be returned per $1 of earnings in a dollar figure. This is higher for Gulf States, and is shown as a higher percentage in the next variable—Total Return %. Given the dividend and estimated growth, the stock would return this over the next year.

The Dividend Yield is obvious—yield as a percentage of share price. You can calculate this by going down three items to dividends per share and dividing the $17 selling price of DPL by the $2 dividend and dividing the $13.75 selling price of GSU by the $1.64 dividend it pays.

If you subtract the Dividend Yield from the Total Return you get the next item, the Growth Rate.

Dividend Payout is the ratio of current dividend to normal EPS. In other words, how much of the company's earnings is it paying to its common stockholders and how much is it retaining in earnings for investment in plant and utility. This figure says a lot about the sources of funds for investment statement from the consolidated financial statements section we discussed earlier.

Return on Equity is normal earnings as a percentage of the equity held by common stockholders. Why is Gulf State's higher? The figures won't really tell you. It could be because the company is younger, has more debt, or is trying to grow. It might be demographics—a growing customer base in Louisiana and need for more generating capacity as opposed to DPL's declining customer base in Ohio. It could be diversification—do these companies own other companies that drain equity and increase debt? It could be regulation—difference in regulation in the states where these companies do business. The electric utility industry is fully regulated and different state public utility boards have different state public utility boards have different ideas about reasonable return on investment. These are the kinds of things you have to ask when you read the company's 10K, if you research a company that deeply.

The Reinvestment Rate is plowback.

Current, normal, and current/normal EPSs are obvious.

Earnings Trend is a Ford-determined variable for short-term predictions. A positive value shows an uptrend, a negative value a downtrend, and a zero a flat trend.

Growth Persistence Trend is a Ford-determined variable. Most stocks are assigned C. A and B stocks have shown well-above-average growth.

Earnings Variability is a year-to-year figure of stock earnings as a percentage of normal earnings. This can give you a fast look at how the company has fared one year against the last few, without having to dig back through the Value Line charts.

Beta is the relative sensitivity of a stock to market fluctuations. Stocks with beta of 1.0 react the same way the market reacts. Below 1.0 beta stocks react less forcefully; above 1.0 beta stocks can swing wildly with moderate market fluctuations. Both stocks here trade in a rather narrow range.

Debt/Equity is a ratio of long-term debt to stockholder equity. DPL is 50 percent funded by dept, 50 percent equity. GSU has 52 percent debt.

Shares Held by Funds shows how much stock is held by institutional investors. Utilities have traditionally been "Ma and Pa Kettle stocks," with most small, conservative investors holding at least some utilities in their portfolio.

Industry Code is Ford's system.

Quality Rating is a Ford rating based on company size, financial conditions, and stability. This is similar to the Value Line ratings for timeliness and safety, except Ford uses its own proprietary scheme for figuring this out.

Intrinsic Value and Book Value have already been explained. Price Changes are obvious.

The twelve month EPS change and the current EPS will show you how far from "normal" EPS the company is operating. Current return on equity should be compared with ROE based on normal EPS above.

EPS and Dividend Growth are for the last five years, as are the following relative five year statistics.

Relative Projected Growth projects the company's growth against the growth of all companies in the database.

The only other things that need explanation are Fiscal Date (the end of the preceding fiscal year), EPS increases over the last five years, dividends per share increases over the last five years, and the twelve month actual return. In this case, combining growth and dividends, Gulf States has shown 150 percent the return of Dayton Power.

Users of Micro/Scan who purchase subscriptions to more than one database can compare stocks by variables from more than one database at a time. In Fig. 4-13 we see our model portfolio of DPL and GSU compared by a few variables from the Ford Database as well multi data base portfolio

		P/E RATIO (NORMAL)	DIVIDEND YIELD (%)	GROWTH RATE EPS	DIVIDEND PAYOUT %	DEBT/ EQUITY	BOOK VAL PER SHARE	OPINION CODE	PROJ 5YR DIV/SH %
DPL	DAYTON PWR + LT ...	6.80	11.77	3.00	0.80	1.00	18.78	337	5.50
GSU	GULF STATES UTIL ..	6.17	11.93	4.00	0.74	1.04	15.64	347	4.70
	SUMMARY	6.62	11.81	3.26	0.78	1.01	17.81		5.29
	Market Averages	2,425.29	3.94	5.06	15.19	N.A.	15.11		11.78
	Source	FORD 08/31/83	FORD 08/31/83	FORD 08/31/83	FORD 08/31/83	FORD 08/31/83	FORD 08/31/83	M/L 8/31/83	M/L 8/31/83

ASSUMPTIONS FORD 08/31/83

SUBSET	#FIRMS	SCREEN
1	1400	UNIVERSE
2	2 [P]	INPUT LIST

Fig. 4-13. A printout of a comparison of GSU and DPL for eight variables, six from the Ford Investor Survey and two from Merrill Lynch. (Reprinted with permission of ISYS Corp.)

as some variables from Merrill Lynch. In addition to comparing one stock against the other, this Micro/Scan report compares the holdings in the portfolio against the market averages for the entire database.

Numbers Aren't Enough

To understand the machinations of stock movements, just studying the numbers is not enough. The example of these two stocks, I think, points this out very well.

Both stocks have what became in the public utilities and securities industries in 1983 a dreaded woe—nuclear problems. Both companies are involved in constructing nuclear power plants.

Back in its Jan. 28, 1983, reports on the two stock, the Value Line reported that the dividend yield of GSU (which it estimated at 12.5 percent after the May 1983 dividend hike to $1.64) would be about a point above the industry average and reflected uncertainty about the company's exposure (70 percent of financing) in the River Bend nuclear facility. At that point, the stock traded for $14 per share. River Bend, like all nuclear plants designed in the '70s and begun in the late '70s and early '80s, is running over budget, behind schedule, and into regulatory and public relations problems. But the problems at River Bend had been known for a while, and the GSU stock moved pretty much with the utilities market through the year. It went up as high as $16.50 in the late spring when the utilities were pacing the market, slid to $13.75 at the time we took the above reading at the end of August 1983, and closed on Jan. 10, 1984, at $13.50 after dipping as low as $12.50.

Dayton Power and Light, on the other hand, was creamed in the later part of the year with its nuclear bad news. In the Value Line Jan. 28, 1983, report, DPL was selling for $18.00, yielding 11.1 on dividends of $1.90, raised in the spring to $2.00 per share. Value Line reported that with the finishing of the Killen coal-fired generator, DPL's construction costs were way down, the only construction also being its exposure to nuclear blues, a 31.5 percent ownership in the Zimmer facility being built. The lead company in that project is Cincinnati Gas and Electric. Work on Zimmer had been suspended by the Nuclear Regulatory Commission in November 1982, and Cincinnati Gas and Electric had been coming under pressure since then, with its price and P/E dipping and its yield increasing. DPL climbed as high as $19.00 in the late spring utilities runup, then slid to the level we saw it at ($17.00) by the end of August with the rumors that trouble was brewin' in River City with Zimmer. That was indeed the case, and the stock began to plunge in about October, falling as low as $12.00 and closing on Jan. 10 at $12.75, a loss of about one-third of its market value from the high.

Why was it that the numbers did not tell us this on Aug. 30? Because numbers only tell us what has happened in the past and project what will happen in the future based on statistical information, not on the news of the day and what effect it will have on the market-playing population. Obviously, as news of Zimmer spread, DPL owners bailed out, and as the stock went down, more owners bailed out. Where the spiral will end no one can guess, but such a spiral of downward pressure opens the door for an investor who either chooses stocks *as stocks* and not as companies, or an investor who thinks the company will be around in a few years and will find ways to make up for the Zimmer debacle to pick up a bargain-basement stock.

If that investor is shrewd, he may even be able to acquire one of these stocks at a time just before the dividend payment and pick up a few extra dollars on the dividends—especially if a dividend increase is going to be declared soon.

To do this, an investor—more likely a money manager—might use the Ex Dividend Stock Monitor System by Computer Aided Decisions, Boston MA. Ex Dividend Stock Monitor is another example of how computers can pull very small groups of data out of large databases.

Before we look at the program's report, let's take a look at the practice of "dividend rolling," trying to pick up five quarterly dividends in four quarters plus a few days.

The day a stock pays dividends is not the important day for a potential investor or potential seller of that stock. That is because dividends are paid to "shareholders of record," and to be on record with the company you must have bought the stock a few weeks ahead of the dividend payout date—with most companies the "record" date is four or five weeks before the payout date. But since the stock brokerage business takes five business days to settle a trade, you must have made the trade six business days or more ahead of the record date to actually be a shareholder of record. The fifth day before the date of record is called the "ex" date. A stock "going ex" tomorrow is a stock that you must buy today in order to be a shareholder of record one week from tomorrow (unless there is a holiday in the next five business days) and get your dividend five or six weeks hence. In the same way, if you own a stock that is going ex tomorrow, you can sell it the day after tomorrow and still get your dividend. Given that a long-term hold is one year and one day, you can get the benefits of long-term ownership and five quarterly dividends by holding a stock for only one year and two days if you buy it the day before it goes ex and sell it the day after it goes ex one year later.

The Ex Dividend Stock Monitor, unfortunately, again, costs over $1,000 and is therefore out of the range of most smaller investors. But it is being bought by brokers and money managers.

Below is a report generated by the Ex Dividend Stock Monitor (Fig. 4-3). The program is designed to give you the 70 highest-paying (in terms of total yield) stocks with market capitalizations big enough so you can either purchase or sell 20,000 shares without disturbing the market—in other words, large capitalization stocks.

Because of its target—current income via large yield—the majority of these stocks are electric utilities. By running a report of all

TEST COMPANY
============
EX DIVIDEND STOCK MONITOR
ANNUAL YIELD REPORT
BASE DATE: JAN 6, 1984
SECURITIES GOING EX WITHIN
NEXT 60 DAYS

DATE	TICKER	COMPANY NAME	CURRENT DIV.	CURRENT YIELD	DIV. FORECAST MONTH	DIV. FORECAST AMOUNT	DIV. FORECAST YIELD*	YEAR'S HIGH	CURRENT PRICE	% CHANGE
====	======	======= ====	====	=====	=====	======	=====	=====	=====	======
JAN 7 83	NVP	- NEVADAPOWER	2.72	9.67%	APR	$0.12	12.52%	30.000	28.125	-6.25%
JAN 9 84	CIN	- CINCINNATI GAS & ELECTRIC	2.16	16.00%	SEP	$0.08	20.30%	19.375	13.500	-30.32%
JAN 9 84	PSR	- PUBLIC SERVICES COLORADO	1.84	9.95%	MAR	$0.12	13.08%	19.000	18.500	-2.63%
JAN 9 84	RTC	- ROCHESTER TELEPHONE	2.28	7.35%	FEB	$0.16	9.71%	33.500	31.000	-7.46%
JAN 10 83	RGS	- ROCHESTER G & E	2.04	11.25%	JAN	$0.12	14.90%	18.875	18.125	-3.97%
JAN 14 83	NGE	- NEW YORK STATE E&G	2.32	11.46%	JUL	$0.16	14.91%	22.875	20.250	-11.48%
JAN 17 83	CMS	- CONSUMERS POWER	2.52	16.26%	SEP	$0.04	20.45%	21.875	15.500	-29.14%
JAN 17 83	CVX	- CLEVELAND ELEC ILLUMINATE	2.40	12.63%	SEP	$0.12	16.11%	23.000	19.000	-17.39%
JAN 25 83	NI	- NORTHERN INDIANA	1.50	10.26%	OCT	$0.02	12.89%	15.500	14.625	-5.65%
JAN 25 83	WPL	- WISCONSIN P & L	2.40	8.24%	JUL	$0.08	10.51%	29.125	29.125	0.00%
JAN 26 83	AZP	- ARIZONA PUB. SVC.	2.60	12.68%	JUL	$0.08	16.15%	27.875	20.500	-26.46%
JAN 26 83	PNH	- P.S. NEW HAMPSHIRE	2.12	16.79%	JUN	$0.08	21.46%	20.000	12.625	-36.88%
JAN 31 83	DPL	- DAYTON PWR. & LT.	2.00	14.81%	JAN	$0.08	19.26%	19.125	13.500	-29.41%
JAN 31 83	PNM	- P.S. NEW MEXICO	2.84	10.87%	MAY	$0.12	13.93%	29.625	26.125	-11.81%
JAN 31 83	TE	- TECO ENERGY	2.04	7.63%	APR	$0.16	10.13%	26.875	26.750	-0.47%
FEB 1 83	CSR	- CENTRAL & SOUTH WEST	1.78	8.90%	JAN	$0.10	11.25%	20.750	20.000	-3.61%
FEB 1 83	SO	- SOUTHERN COMPANY	1.80	10.59%	AUG	$0.06	13.50%	17.750	17.000	-4.23%
FEB 2 83	WPC	- WISCONSIN ELECTRIC	2.10	7.53%	APR	$0.16	9.99%	28.500	27.875	-2.19%
FEB 3 83	ED	- CONSOLIDATED EDISON	1.88	7.41%	JAN	$0.16	9.42%	25.875	25.375	-1.93%
FEB 4 83	AEP	- AMERICAN ELECTRIC POWER	2.26	12.64%	APR	$0.04	16.03%	20.125	17.875	-11.18%
FEB 4 83	HE	- HAWAIIAN ELECTRIC	3.12	9.38%	DEC	$0.16	11.85%	33.875	33.250	-1.85%
FEB 4 83	ITT	- INTERNATIONAL TELEPHONE	2.76	6.03%	FEB	$0.10	7.81%	47.750	45.750	-4.19%
FEB 4 83	XON	- EXXON CORPORATION	3.20	8.56%	NOV	$0.15	10.90%	39.750	37.375	-5.97%
FEB 8 83	PIN	- PUBLIC SERVICE INDIANA	2.88	22.15%	APR	$0.12	28.62%	27.375	13.000	-52.51%
FEB 9 83	CTC	- CONTINENTAL TELEPHONE	1.64	7.29%	FEB	$0.08	9.56%	25.875	22.500	-13.04%
FEB 9 83	SPS	- SOUTHWESTERN PUB. SVC.	1.74	8.75%	JUL	$0.10	11.32%	20.125	19.875	-1.24%
FEB 10 83	GSU	- GULF STATES UTILITIES	1.64	12.26%	MAY	$0.08	15.92%	16.250	13.375	-17.69%
FEB 10 83	HOU	- HOUSTON INDUSTRIES	2.32	11.25%	JAN	$0.16	14.25%	24.250	20.625	-14.95%
FEB 14 83	DUK	- DUKE POWER	2.36	9.30%	JUL	$0.12	11.98%	26.375	25.375	-3.79%
FEB 14 83	NMK	- NIAGARA MOHAWK	1.92	12.00%	MAY	$0.12	15.75%	18.500	16.000	-13.51%
FEB 15 83	GTE	- GEN'L TEL. & ELEC.	3.00	6.88%	NOV	$0.08	8.69%	48.375	43.625	-9.82%
FEB 17 83	UT	- UNITED TELECOM	1.84	8.66%	AUG	$0.10	11.18%	25.000	21.250	-15.00%
FEB 18 83	DQU	- DUQUESNE LIGHT	2.00	13.33%			16.67%	19.000	15.000	-21.05%

FEB 18 83	FPL	- FLORIDA POWER & LIGHT	3.60	8.94%	APR	$0.24	11.78%	42.250	40.250	-4.73%
FEB 18 83	KU	- KENTUCKY UTILS.	2.28	9.65%	JAN	$0.08	12.15%	24.125	23.625	-2.07%
FEB 18 83	POM	- POTOMAC ELECTRIC	1.78	8.28%	JAN	$0.12	10.49%	22.250	21.500	-3.37%
FEB 22 83	WPS	- WISCONSIN PUB. SVC.	2.32	8.44%	JUL	$0.16	10.98%	30.500	27.500	-9.84%
FEB 23 83	NU	- NORTHEAST UTILITIES	1.38	10.93%	JAN	$0.10	13.86%	13.875	12.625	-9.01%
FEB 23 83	VEL	- VIRGINIA ELECTRIC & POWER	1.60	10.67%	NOV	$0.10	13.67%	15.875	15.000	-5.51%
FEB 25 83	UTP	- UTAH PWR. & LT.	2.32	9.67%	MAY	$0.08	12.42%	25.000	24.000	-4.00%
FEB 28 83	FPC	- FLORIDA PROGRESS CORP.	2.04	9.71%	NOV	$0.12	12.43%	22.625	21.000	-7.18%
FEB 28 83	PE	- PHILADELPHIA ELEC.	2.12	13.35%	JUL	$0.12	17.26%	18.375	15.875	-13.61%
FEB 28 83	PEG	- PUBLIC SERVICE ELEC & GAS	2.64	11.06%	MAY	$0.08	14.16%	26.500	23.875	-9.91%
FEB 28 83	TXU	- TEXAS UTILITIES CO.	2.20	9.12%	FEB	$0.16	12.23%	27.375	24.125	-11.87%
MAR 1 83	OEC	- OHIO EDISON	1.80	13.46%	DEC	$0.04	16.97%	16.125	13.375	-17.05%
MAR 1 83	UEP	- UNION ELECTRIC	1.72	12.29%	JUL	$0.12	16.00%	16.250	14.000	-13.85%
MAR 4 83	BGE	- BALTIMORE GAS & ELECTRIC	3.00	9.30%	AUG	$0.16	12.00%	34.250	32.250	-5.84%
MAR 4 83	NES	- N. E. ELECTRIC	3.40	8.61%	MAY	$0.08	10.96%	43.375	39.500	-8.93%
MAR 4 83	PPL	- PENNSYLVANIA P & L	2.40	11.43%	FEB	$0.08	14.38%	24.500	21.000	-14.29%
MAR 4 83	SCG	- SOUTH CAROLINA E & G	2.00	10.81%	JAN	$0.08	13.62%	21.250	18.500	-12.94%

AVERAGE PRICE CHANGE FOR GROUP -11.42%

* YIELD ASSUMES 5 QUARTERLY DIVIDEND PAYMENTS

Fig. 4-14. A printout of the top dividend yield companies that will be "going ex" in the next 60 days, from the Ex Dividend Stock Monitor. (© Computer Aided Decisions, Inc.)

those stocks that have gone ex in the last 30 days and all those that are due to go ex in the next 60 days, you can get a picture of the entire group of 70 stocks (since they all pay dividends quarterly).

Let's take a look at an Ex Dividend Stock Monitor report, and see how our old friends Dayton Power and Light and Gulf States Utilities are faring. Both are in the subset of the 70 highest-paying stocks.

The information on the report is pretty straightforward. The forecast can be purchased or can be put in by the purchasing company, depending on the assumptions it wants to use.

The dividend forecast columns are the place to focus our energy, and the percentage change from the year's high is the benchmark to use when deciding relative merits. Remember also that the current yield forecast assumes five quarterly dividends in the "going ex" report and the past four quarterly dividends in the "gone ex" report.

Let's first look at the averages to get an idea of what the overview is like, reminding ourselves that dividend yield is determined to some extent by the risk involved in an investment.

For possible purchases, we want to look in the portion of the report on stocks that will go ex in the next 60 days (Fig. 4-14) that have fallen off their high more than the average, that will have the highest yield after their dividend increase, and that will have a dividend the soonest.

When looking for candidates to sell, we want to look at stocks that have gone ex in the last 30 days, that have the lowest decrease from the year's high relative to the average (which will be calculated only for the "gone ex" subset), which show the lowest increase in yield after a dividend increase, and which will have a dividend increase the furthest down the road.

Let's look at "going ex" and see how DPL and GSU fare (Fig. 4-15). Notice that the stocks are listed by date when they will go ex, rather than in alphabetical order, for easy tracking. Remember the report's date—Jan. 6, 1984.

The average price change for stocks going ex is −11.42 percent. Let's start at the top of the list with Nevadapower, which will go ex tomorrow. If we want it, we have to buy it *today*. It has only dropped 6.25 percent from its high, so we can pretty much dismiss it as selling at its full value—or at least above our target level.

The next stock is our old friend Cincinnatti Gas and Electric, the point company in the Zimmer project that has helped croak Dayton Power and Light. CIN, as you might guess, has lost much of its market value, 30.32 percent off its high for the year. Given CIN's current 16.00 percent yield and a prospective dividend increase of eight cents in September, we get a calculation for 20.30 percent yield over the next year and two days encompassing five dividend payout periods.

Let's go down the list a bit to Jan. 31, when Dayton Power and Light will go ex. DPL currently yields 14.81 percent, quite a bit above its dividend yield in August, when it sold for 17.00. Today it sells for 13.50. Given a dividend increase scheduled for this month of eight cents (which we will collect five times if we purchase the stock before it goes ex and hold it long-term). Ex Dividend Stock Monitor calculates a 19.26 percent yield. It is down 29.41 percent from its high.

Now let's slide down a little further to Gulf States Utilities. GSU will go ex Feb. 10. Currently yielding 12.26 percent, it is expected to increase its dividends by eight cents in May and, over the next five dividend periods, to yield 15.92 percent. It is down 17.96 percent from its high.

Which of these stocks would be the best purchase?

Cincinnati Gas and Electric will have the highest yield over five dividend periods, but it is also in the most immediate danger of future selling if the Zimmer plant becomes an issue again—if it is scrubbed. Dayton Power and Light has been hit just about as hard as CIN over the Zimmer issue, and would provide one percent less yield for pretty much the same risk. GSU has weakened more than the average, but is not as sensitive as DPL and CIN. Still, it would provide a healthy 15.92 percent yield, about 6 percent more than you could get with the bank or about as much as you could get with a solid growth stock with less intrinsic value. For a quick hit, DPL will have a dividend increase the soonest and will have the highest yield over a three or even a four-dividend payout period.

What Else Is Around?

In addition to Micro/Scan, Value/Screen, and Ex Dividend Monitor System, the following is a list of fundamental analysis software: (Prices may have changed recently.)

The Evaluation Form (Investor's Software, Box N, Bradenton Beach FL 33510, 813-778-5515) runs on the IBM PC, Apple II, Radio Shack TRS-80, and computers that use CP/M operating system and M BASIC language. It costs $50.

TEST COMPANY
============
EX DIVIDEND STOCK MONITOR
ANNUAL YIELD REPORT
BASE DATE: JAN 6, 1984
SECURITIES GONE EX ON OR BEFORE
LAST 30 DAYS

DATE	TICKER	COMPANY NAME	CURRENT DIV.	CURRENT YIELD	DIV. FORECAST MONTH	DIV. FORECAST AMOUNT	DIV. FORECAST YIELD*	YEAR'S HIGH	CURRENT PRICE	% CHANGE
*** THIS YEAR, 1984 ***										
JAN 6 84	CES	COMMONWEALTH ENERGY	2.12	10.40%	MAR	$0.12	10.99%	23.750	20.375	-14.21%
JAN 6 84	AC	AMERICAN CAN	2.90	5.98%			5.98%	49.500	48.500	-2.02%
JAN 4 84	OGE	OKLAHOMA GAS & ELECTRIC	1.92	9.37%	DEC	$0.08	9.46%	21.875	20.500	-6.29%
JAN 4 84	IPC	ILLINOIS POWER CO.	2.64	12.72%	DEC	$0.10	12.84%	24.125	20.750	-13.99%
JAN 4 84	BSE	BOSTON EDISON	3.00	11.16%	NOV	$0.12	11.27%	29.500	26.875	-8.90%
JAN 3 84	TED	TOLEDO EDISON	2.52	14.00%	DEC	$0.08	14.11%	22.500	18.000	-20.00%
JAN 3 84	DEW	DELMARVA POWER & LIGHT	1.80	9.60%	DEC	$0.08	9.71%	19.625	18.750	-4.46%
*** PREVIOUS YEARS ***										
DEC 30 83	CPL	CAROLINA POWER & LIGHT	2.52	11.20%	DEC	$0.16	11.91%	25.125	22.500	-10.45%
DEC 29 83	SCE	SOUTHERN CALIF EDISON CO	3.80	9.50%	SEP	$0.28	9.85%	42.750	40.000	-6.43%
DEC 29 83	NSP	NORTHERN STATES POWER CO.	2.96	7.95%	JUN	$0.20	8.35%	40.750	37.250	-8.59%
DEC 23 83	CWE	COMMONWEALTH EDISON	3.00	11.43%	DEC	$0.10	11.81%	29.250	26.250	-10.26%
DEC 20 83	PPW	PACIFIC POWER & LIGHT	2.16	8.64%	MAR	$0.12	9.12%	25.500	25.000	-1.96%
DEC 12 83	MSU	MIDDLE SOUTH UTILITIES	1.74	11.90%	DEC	$0.04	12.17%	16.750	14.625	-12.69%
DEC 9 83	PCG	PACIFIC GAS & ELECTRIC	1.60	10.67%	MAY	$0.12	11.27%	16.750	15.000	-10.45%
DEC 9 83	DTE	DETROIT EDISON	1.68	11.79%	SEP	$0.06	12.00%	16.000	14.250	-10.94%
DEC 9 83	ATE	ATLANTIC CITY ELECTRIC	2.36	10.20%	MAY	$0.12	10.59%	25.875	23.125	-10.63%

* YIELD ASSUMES 4 QUARTERLY DIVIDEND PAYMENTS   AVERAGE PRICE CHANGE FOR GROUP -9.52%

Fig. 4-15. A printout of the top dividend yield companies that have gone ex in the last 30 days, from the Ex Dividend Monitor. (© Computer Aided Decisions, Inc.)

The program uses six years of published data about a stock (keyed in by user) to project a risk/reward ratio, yields, yearly returns, and buy-hold-sell ranges. It can be used with any stock on the market.

Market Maverick (Financial Software, Inc., 11401 Westridge Circle, Chardon OH 44024, 800-392-2669) runs on the IBM PC or Apple II and costs $175, $295 with a year's subscription to the updated data.

This program was discontinued in October 1983 and the author was working on an

Reg check Sept 2, 86

enhanced version—which may have been given another name—he hoped to have on the market in the first quarter of 1984.

The program used in financial model with a projected inflation rate to project from past data the future P/E of companies in a 920-stock database. A target P/E for the market was found and each stock's P/E compared to it. Stocks are then ranked to show potential upside movement and downside risk. Changes in assumptions could be made, and comparative graphs showing differences between stock P/Es given differing assumptions could be made.

Market Microscope is part of the Dow Jones software package. Developed by National Softworks and Dow Jones, this and other Dow Jones programs (Market Analyzer, technical analysis and Market Manager, portfolio management and accounting) are available by calling Dow Jones at 800-257-5114. Market Microscope runs on the Apple II, II+, *II*e and III and costs $699.

By hooking into the Dow Jones News/Retrieval Service you can get up to 20 different financial indicators out of the 68 Media General Financial Services and Corporate Earnings Estimator variables. You can store this information on as many companies as you like and compare them. A special "price alert routine" will print out a report of all stocks you are storing information on that have reached critical buy or sell levels based on your criteria and the program's analysis. You choose how to rank the stocks.

Micro PMS (The Boston Company, One Boston Place, Boston MA 02106, 617-722-7939) runs on the Apple II and costs $595 including monthly data diskette updates.

The program can scan a database of 1500 stocks to make a selection on the basis of a number of criteria. The program has similar portfolio analysis capabilities to Value/Screen and Micro/Scan.

Stockcal (RLJ Software Applications, 306 N. Wolcott St., Hillsdale MI 49242, 517-439-9605) runs on the IBM PC and costs $39.95. The program calculates rates and ratios using the criteria laid out by the National Association of Investment Clubs' Stock Selection Guide. The printout plots past sales and earnings and projections of future sales and earnings, as well as giving numerical information.

Stockfocus (Centennial Software Inc., 410 Seventeenth Street, Suite 1375, Denver CO 80202, 800-525-2003) runs on IBM PC, Apple II, TRS-80 models I, II, and III, CP/M eight-inch disk machines, Osborne, Northstar Horizon and KAYPRO II. It costs $59.95.

The program uses company data for the last five years keyed in to project both graphically and numerically the lowest and highest reasonable prices the stock may attain in a year and the current price in relation to these prices.

Stockpak II (Standard & Poor's Corp., 25 Broadway New York NY 10004) runs on the IBM PC and Apple II and costs from $275 for a composite database of 1,500 NYSE, ASE and OTC stocks to $1,070 for 4,500 stocks from the three exchanges. This is another database program that allows the user to compare stocks by fundamental variables. Stockpak II is graphically oriented rather than numerically, making large use of bar charts.

Stock Price Forecast (J.R. Software, P.O. Box 693, Florissant MO 63032, 314-741-6907) runs on the Apple II and costs $135. It does much the same work as Stockfocus, taking the last ten years of company history from the Value Line Survey and computing the lowest and highest reasonable stock prices in a year.

Stock Pricing Model (Kustom Software,

4652 Cass. St., Suite A-238, San Diego CA 92109, 619-483-7119) runs on the Apple II+, TRS-80 Model III, Osborne, and CP/M eight-inch models and costs $39 ($45 for eight-inch disk models.) This is a template loaded into the VisiCalc spreadsheet used to compute future stock price by calculating past earnings increases and the consensus of future earnings increases by a team of analysts who contribute this information to the Dow Jones News/Retrieval Service. Information is obtained via a modem.

Chapter 5

Technical Analysis

It is more than interesting that people working from the same basic assumption—that prices in the stock market (or any market, for that matter) discount all available information—can come up with such radically different ideas about how to "play" the market.

As we have previously noted, the advocates of the Random Walk theory believe that all information is discounted as reflected in the current price and that no one can grasp, digest, and account for all information fast enough to act on it before more information is available. Therefore, they argue, you may as well throw darts at the stock reports each day to pick your investments—given that you are prepared to hold them long enough to amortize your transaction costs.

Adherents to fundamental analysis believe present price is a reflection of all given information, and they believe the idea is to determine which stocks will do better in the future economic circumstances of the country (considering a company's management, the industry it is in, etc.). That way you can get beyond current price to find the "next generation" of investments.

Technical analysis, the area we will discuss in the next few pages, holds that all information is discounted and that any new developments will reflect themselves in price movements.

Technical analysts believe the market moves in patterns, and that stock (and other) markets have trends that are determined by changes in investor attitudes.

The technical analyst, we could argue, is closest to Asimov's psychohistorian, trying to judge human nature by studying how "the people" have reacted to similar situations in the past. To do this, the technical analyst uses a panoply of indicators, which he usually tries to graph for a more clear, concise picture.

Three basic types of indicators are used.

Sentiment indicators try to keep track of how various market participants react to the changes in market patterns and trends. Among the participants who are tracked are insiders (those close enough to companies to have advanced warnings of company actions), so-called "odd-lotters" (people who buy less than 100 shares in a trade), specialists (the stock exchange members charged with trading specific stocks in order to maintain an orderly market), mutual funds (otherwise called investment companies, the funds that pool the money of small investors in order to diversify or target a portfolio), and other groups.

Different groups behave in different ways, according to technical analysts. For example, odd-lot traders are theoretically late to get the news. As one major institutional broker said to me a number of years ago, "When the little investor comes to me and says, 'Get me 25 shares of XYZ,' I know the run is over." Insiders, conversely, are theoretically early to get the news.

Flow of funds indicators show who is buying and who is selling by showing how much purchasing power certain groups of market players have. For every sale there must be a purchase, and if there are more sellers than buyers, the price must fluctuate until the supply/demand situation comes into balance. Flow of funds analysis keeps close track of the cash position of the banking industry as well as mutual funds and other larger investors. It also tracks how "short interest" moves. Short interest is the number of shares sold short—borrowed from brokerages and sold in the hopes that the stock will drop so the shares can be repurchased at a lower price and paid back to the brokerage house with interest while still leaving a profit for the short seller.

Market structure indicators take a closer look at the actual price and volume trends. These are the indicators technical analysts put most of their faith in. These indexes measure certain market averages—the Dow Jones 30 Industrials (DJIA), the New York Stock Exchange Index, the Standard and Poor's 500, etc.—cycles, market breadth, market volume, and other structural indexes.

The market structure indexes are the technical analyst's bread and butter. As Timothy Slater, President of Compu Trac, a company that produces a number of technical analysis programs, puts it:

"A true technical trader feels that everything other than price movement and volume—and in the case of commodities, open interest—is irrelevant. The technician feels that all fundamental factors, of whatever nature occurring wherever on the globe, manifest themselves in price . . . The technical trader takes the attitude that he as an individual couldn't possibly know all of the factors bearing on a particular stock or commodity that will cause it to go up or down. But, by close observation of the price movement, of the volume and open interest, he can detect changes in public sentiment towards that particular issue. A pure technical trader analyzing a market in its lowest common denominator would say to the observer, 'Don't bother me with facts. I'm not interested in facts. Show me prices, because prices in themselves will reflect everything that is known.'"

The Techniques of Technical Analysis

Between 1900 and 1902 Charles Dow wrote a series of editorials in the *Wall Street Journal* in which he looked at stock market movement as a barometer of business activity. Over the next 25-30 years, Dow's ideas were reinterpreted and massaged until his work emerged as what we now call the Dow Theory—the theory that the stock market moves in cycles, and that by studying the closing price and the day's volume, a trader can learn much about the behavior of the market and can give himself an edge in trading.

The Dow Theory's first tenet is, of course, that everything that has or can occur in regards to supply and demand in the market has been discounted in the current price.

Next is the idea that the market has three cycles: *primary, secondary* (or intermediate, and *minor*. The primary trend is the long-term trend, which manifests itself in what is commonly called a "bull" market (rising) or "bear" market (falling).

Let's take our example of Fig. 5-1. This is a five-year chart, with a general bull market. But within that five-year time frame, there were periods when the market moved down. We will see them when we look more closely at smaller time frames in greater detail.

Intermediate trends run against the grain of the primary trend—drops in a bull market or rises in a bear market. For an intermediate trend to be official—not just a short bout with profit-taking or a quick runup on bargain-basement shopping—it must last a few weeks and can last the better part of a year. The countertrend (the rise or the drop) must be precipitous—as much as half or two thirds of the price rise since the last intermediate trend. But as long as the bottom of one intermediate trend (in a bull market) is higher than the last bottom time after time, the bull market has not been broken. The converse applies to a bear market (Fig. 5-2).

Minor trends can last a few hours (interday or intraday) to a few weeks, and within each intermediate trend there can be a number of minor trends in both directions (Fig. 5-3).

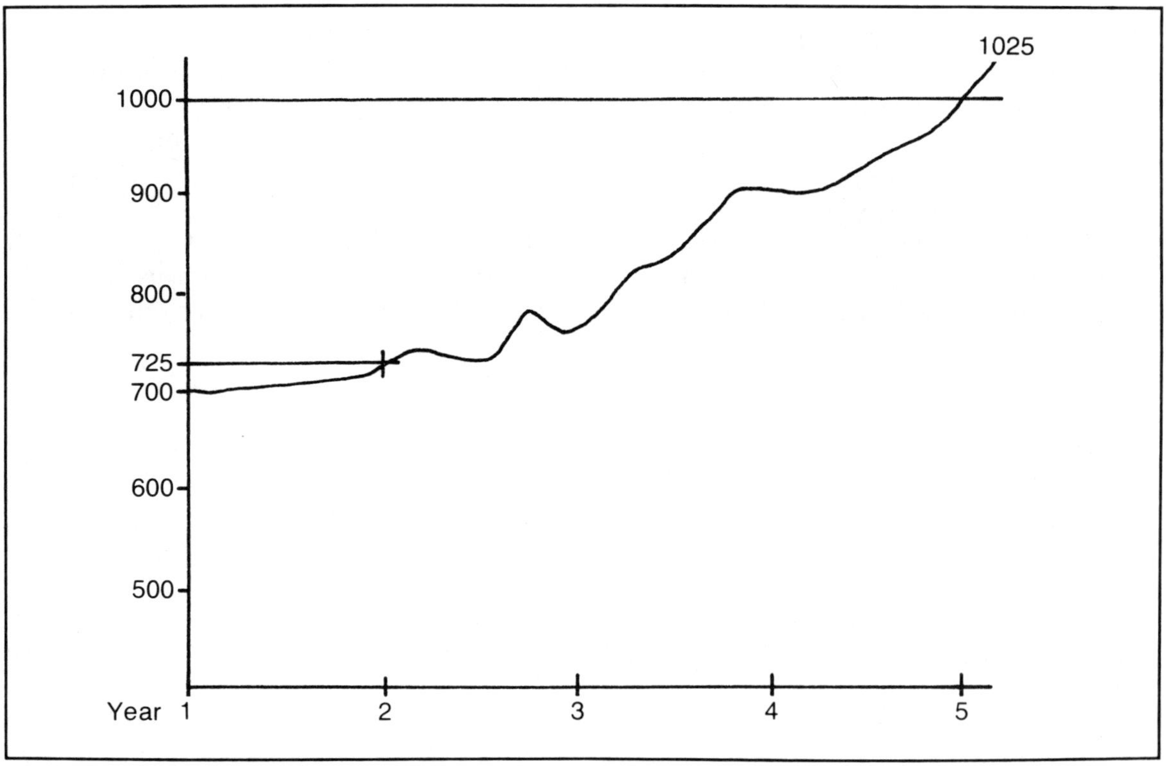

Fig. 5-1. A five-year primary trend bull market.

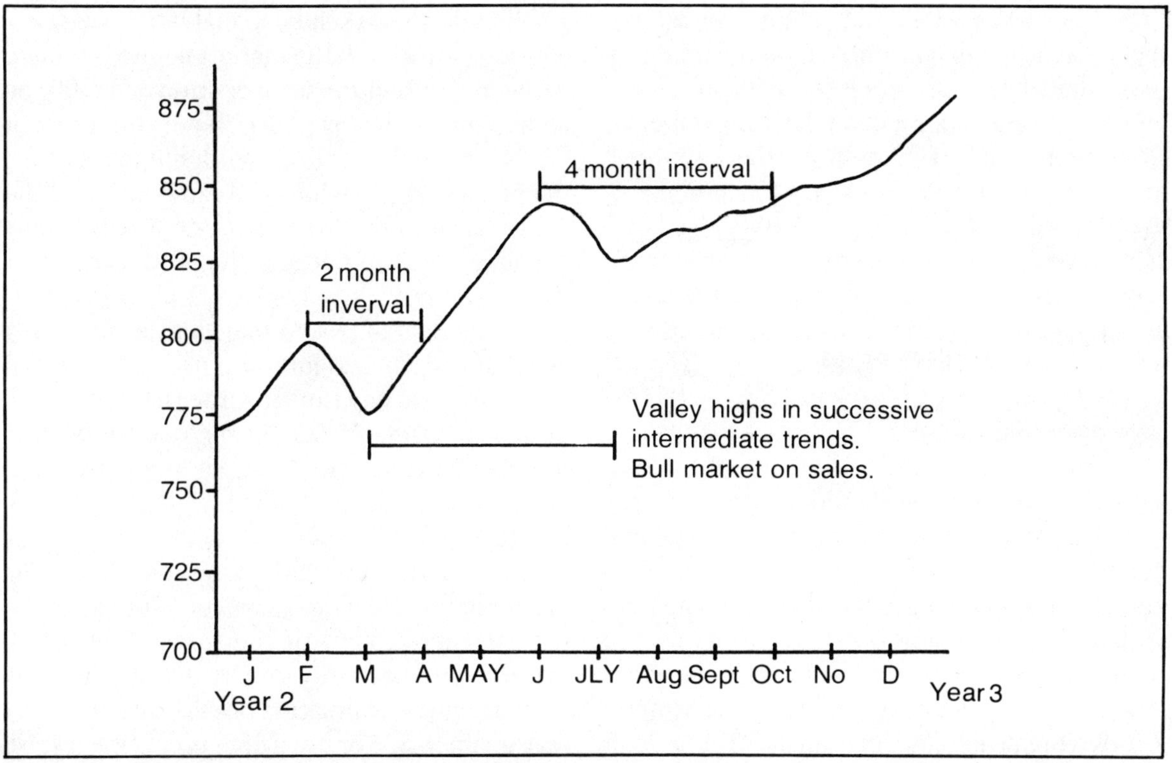

Fig. 5-2. One close-up of one year in the bull market, with two troughs, but successively higher bottoms to the valleys, signifying an unbroken bull market.

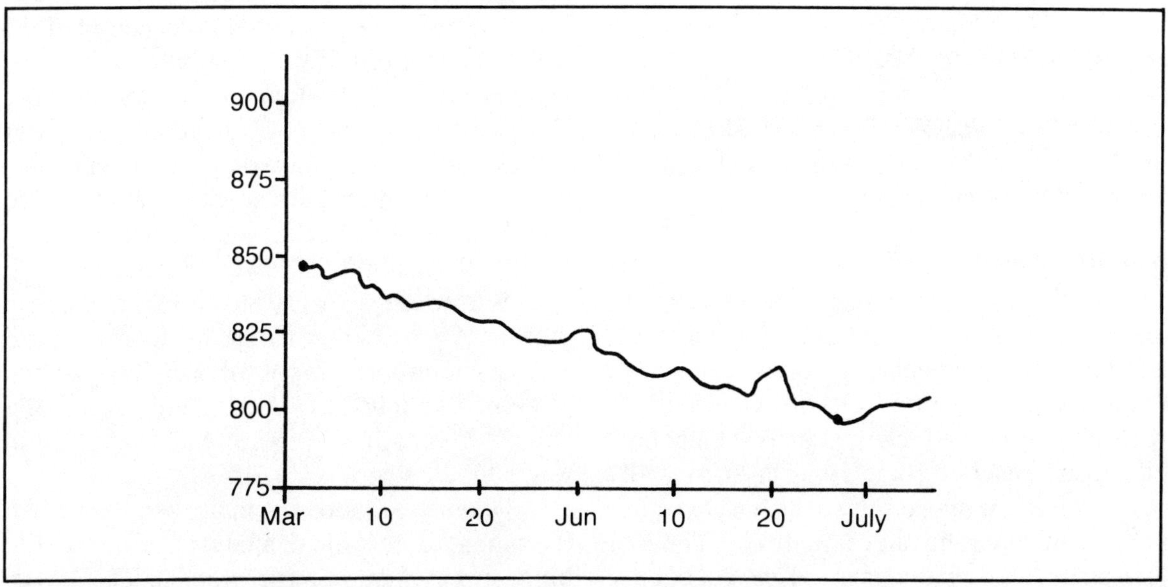

Fig. 5-3. A close-up of two months, showing a minor downturn in the bull market.

While it is often the minor trends that technical analysts concentrate on most keenly (especially heavy traders who can make a lot of money on half a percent or less movement), these trends are of no help for the long-term investor, in contrast to intermediate and primary trends, which can be used by the long-term investor to gain perspective on where he might expect the market to go in the near-and-longer term. (Indeed, many investors who primarily use fundamental analysis use technical trend analysis to try to gain a timing advantage in conducting their transactions.)

Price and volume work hand-in-hand. Theoretically, volume should expand on a rally and contract on a drop. Increasing volume and declining prices signal a prolonged bear market, the technical analysts tell us, but when the volume begins to slow down, a change for the better may be in the offing. In a similar way, while rising prices on rising or continued strong volume means a continuation of the bull market, a slowdown in volume while the market is still rising could mean all the buyers are in and a turnaround is in the offing.

The Dow Theory looks at both the averages of the industrial stocks and the transportation stocks. For a Dow Theory analyst to be convinced the market is doing what it is supposed to do, both averages must run in tandem, or "confirm" each other.

One Step Ahead

To the market technician, the idea is to be one step ahead of the market—buying in the last few days or weeks of a decline and selling in the last few days or weeks of an advance. As with all people, the technical analyst must fight off greed, the feeling that if only he stays with a stock for a few more days, the last possible penny can be wrung out of the trade. The idea is to protect the change in trend and get out just before the peak (or trough, in short selling).

To do this, technical analysts keep track of price patterns. If the market bounces around between 700 and 750 for weeks on end, 700 can be said to be the "support" level (the price at which demand equalizes with supply because the price is right) while 750 can be termed the "resistance" level (the point at which supply equalizes demand because the profit is good for those who currently hold stock).

This kind of closed-end "battle" of supply and demand can last for any length of time, and can show up at any time in either a primary bull or bear market. At some time one can expect this deadlock to "break out" into a more open pattern that signals a "new leg" in the primary market.

In a more open-field situation, the levels of support and resistance will continually move with the movement of the market. In a bull market, we may see support at 750 for a few months until the situation breaks, then support may go up to 825 or even 850, etc. Conversely, in a bear market the resistance level may constantly go lower.

The levels right around support and resistance are often called the "accumulation" and "distribution" areas. In a bull market, investors accumulate stock around the support level waiting for the next leg of the bull market to push prices up. Conversely, in a bear market, investors distribute stock around the support level in the expectation that the primary trend will push prices lower in general.

Within these general rules, there are dozens of more subtle variations that technical analysts look for. This is all done by charting price and volume movements over time. And this is where the computer has come to the forefront in investing.

Of course, there are many skeptics when it comes to technical analysis. One of the biggest was Adam Smith, who, in *The Money Game*, wrote, "If one could depend on these charts, it would be a very neat world indeed. But if things were really this cut-and-dried, all the 22 million active investors would simply load up with charts and the Game would be over. Stocks have a way of blitzing right through the Resistance or the Support, pausing only long enough for the chart followers to sell (at resistance) or buy (at support). And while the chartists can then look back and point this out as a Trap, that doesn't make the poor people caught in the trap feel much better."

While computers have made fundamental analysis easier by taking large databases and grinding them down into manageable groups of stocks that meet certain criteria, they have given the technical analysts—otherwise known as "chartists"—the opportunity to conceptualize to a greater degree than ever before because they no longer have to worry about the grunt work of penning in all those lines connecting yesterday's price to today's. In addition, technical analysis programs, when hooked into databases, open up vast storehouses of historical data to chartists that otherwise would fill notebooks.

While our first few illustrations in this chapter were crude charts, many of the charts created by technical analysis software are truly magnificent.

Technical analysts use computers to not only keep track of the high, low, close, and volume of markets and stocks, but to do sophisticated time studies that show market behavior overlayed on "scientifically"-determined business, social, and historical cycles, studies that include moving averages, oscillators, on-balance volume, and other technical tools that try to make sense of price and volume.

But before we look at some of the studies from one of the popular (and, I think, best-researched) technical analysis programs, let's discuss for a moment market sentiment and flow of funds.

The Bulls and the Bears

A lot has been written about market psychology, and it has often been called "herd" psychology. To be sure, the "feeling" of the market continually wavers from fear of economic doom to mild pessimism up through optimism to overconfidence and outright greed.

As in any other field, there is a communications gap in market watching. Some market participants are well-informed, others not so well-informed. While a number of people tend to think of market sentiment as monolithic, it is not. Where you are on the sentimental pendulum depends on where and when you get your information.

There have been interesting studies done showing that the *Wall Street Week* Index, a composite of stocks that are touted on the *Wall Street Week in Review* television show each Friday night, have risen precipitously in the few weeks prior to getting touted, go up slightly after the show as all those people who were touted to the stock by the *WSW* expert put in their orders, then dive as all the people who ran the stock up before it was touted sell out and take their profits. The same has been shown of "advisory" letters. When the market advisor letters get bullish, the "insiders" have already taken their positions and are ready to sell them out to those who read the letters. The theory goes: Strong information sells to weak information.

There is good reason for this. Part of it has to do with the amount of time spent keeping up with possible investments and the amount of information available to the potential investor—an information gap that can be closed to some extent using a personal computer.

But another part of the reason has to do

with just how far inside you are in the investment community. Brokers, who are really salesmen, have to be careful about what they tell and to whom it is told. Getting back to the Securities Exchange Act of 1933 and the Securities Exchange of 1934, we see that there is a precedent in the enforcement of the anti-fraud provisions to hold brokers accountable for making recommendations of "unsuitable" investments. In other words, if a broker convinced a widow who had slated investment goals of investment and capital preservation to put $10,000 into the stock of a genetic engineering company and the company went bust, there would be a good chance for that investor to get a court judgement against the broker for violating the securities laws by getting her involved in a unsuitable investment.

For that reason, the "research" distributed to small investors by brokerage houses is highly distilled from the more complete data and opinions sent to the institutional clients. As Milton Weiler, a former institutional broker and now chairman of Computer Aided Decisions, puts it, "If a management company gets put onto a stock and it turns bad, they sweep it under the rug. They're big kids. If the brokerage house gives the same information to a little investor, that's an accident waiting to happen."

There is some question as to whether sentiment indicators will continue to be as valid as before in the computer age. More small investors will have access to raw data and to earlier information than they did before, when they had to wait for a story in the *New York Times* business section or for a call from their broker, who was confident the stock had enough movement that he could safely suggest it without going out on a limb if it fell off four or five months later while the investor was still waiting to take a long-term capital gain.

Suffice it to say that technical analysts feel odd-lot trading—trading by those who buy and sell less than 100 shares at a time—runs contrary to the trend. When odd-lot trading turns bullish, you can pretty well count on the fact that everyone and his aunt—and it's often everyone's aunt who is an odd-lotter—knows about the stock. Conversely, the indicator of the end to a bear market, they say, is odd-lot short selling—when the odd-lotters go out on a limb and borrow from the broken to sell short in the hopes of falling prices. Odd-lotters don't get too many original ideas.

On the other hand, watching what members and insiders are doing can often give advance warning of the primary trend, technical analysts argue. Each week a ratio is computed of member short sales/total short sales. Between 70 and 80 percent of short sales by members is about average, according to Martin J. Pring, author of *Technical Analysis Explained* (McGraw-Hill, 1980). When the level of shorts being sold by members gets higher, it's a bearish sign—short selling is bearish in nature—and when it dips below 70 percent into the 60-65 percent range, that means the public is catching on and the market trend is bullish.

How come all these members are shorting (60 percent minimum of all shorts by members) even in a bullish market, you might ask. Selectivity would be the answer. The ratio doesn't tell you what companies are being shorted. Even in the best of markets there are some stocks that go down.

There is the chance that these figures have become skewed in the past few years by the advent of listed option trading. Options will be explained more deeply later, but basically an option gives the purchaser the right to buy or sell 100 shares of stock at a set price on a set date, and selling a "call" option (the right to sell the stock at a later date) has taken the place of selling short for a lot of investors as a hedge against the stock you own dropping in price.

Some analysts of market sentiment also look at how mutual funds are putting their money to work. They look at the cash/asset ratio and the cash/redemption ratio.

Cash-to-assets shows both how much cash the mutual fund manager is holding on the side, waiting for a market upswing to get "fully invested," as well as how much pressure the manager feels will be brought to bear by shareholders wishing to sell out their position in the fund.

Cash-to-redemptions shows how much pressure has come on the mutual fund in the past few months. If cash on hand/redemptions for the last three months is high, then there is still a lot of buying power in the fund (mostly institutional money) and not much selling pressure by the general public. If cash/redemptions is low, selling pressure has eaten into the fund's buying power.

An indicator that presents a good transition from sentiment to flow of funds is margin debt. Buying on margin means using securities you own as collateral for a loan made by your broker to purchase more securities. In effect, you can double your holding by allowing your broker to keep your holding and loan you an equal amount. If you purchase 100 shares of XYZ at $10 ($1,000) and allow the broker to hold it, he will loan you $1,000 to buy another 100 shares.

If the stock goes up, you double your profit without tying up more capital. If the stock goes down, your loss is doubled. However, win or lose you pay interest on the loan—usually a few points above prime interest rates—and this adds to the transaction costs in determining whether or not your overall trade is profitable. In addition, if you have borrowed to your margin limit and the stock goes down, the broker can call your debt—known as a *margin call*—and liquidate part of your holding to pay the portion of the loan no longer covered by collateral.

For example, if you have used your $1,000 and the broker's $1,000 to purchase 200 shares of XYZ at $10 and the stock drops to $8, your 200 shares are now worth $1,600. But "your" 100 shares are only worth $800 and your debt is $1,000 plus interest. The broker can issue a margin call and if you can't come up with $200 plus interest, he can sell enough stock to cover the difference.

In any event, margin debt is a sentiment indicator since it shows how many people are willing to go out on a limb. As the market climbs, so does margin as investors are willing to take on the debt burden to share in the rising market. Margin buying adds fuel to the fire of the market, and when margin buying begins to fall off, many of the speculators are cashing in their chips. In a market drop, margin debt sinks—sometimes precipitously—as the market contracts and the value of people's equities shrink.

The reason that margin debt provides a good transition into flow of funds considerations is that interest rate changes affect margin debt.

Interest rate changes affect equity markets in other ways. First of all, if interest rates go higher, bonds become a more attractive investment with their steady interest payments. In addition, as interest rates go higher and companies have to pay more to borrow, they have less cash to generate corporate growth and to pay dividends to equity shareholders.

Short-term interest rates usually move prior to long-term rates, so when the Federal Funds rate goes up—the Federal Fund rate is the rate one bank has to pay another to borrow money that must be held in reserve in order to meet Federal Reserve Bank regulations—other short-term interest rates are likely to follow, such as the rate of 30-180-day commercial paper. Six-month Treasury bills are likely to follow before we see a rise in Treasury bond rates, municipal bond rates, and corporate bond rates.

Compu Trac

Perhaps the most sophisticated technical analysis program is Compu Trac, a series of over 35 programs developed by the Technical Analysis Group, (P.O. Box 15951, New Orleans LA 70157, 800-535-7990 or 504-895-1474).

The technical analysis group works somewhat like a cooperative, in that "members"—who pay an initial fee of $1,800 to receive all the programs to date and $200 per year to receive updates and all new programs—often contribute ways to enhance programs or new ideas for programs, which are then programmed by professional computer people.

The group began in 1979 when Timothy Slater (who is still group coordinator and was

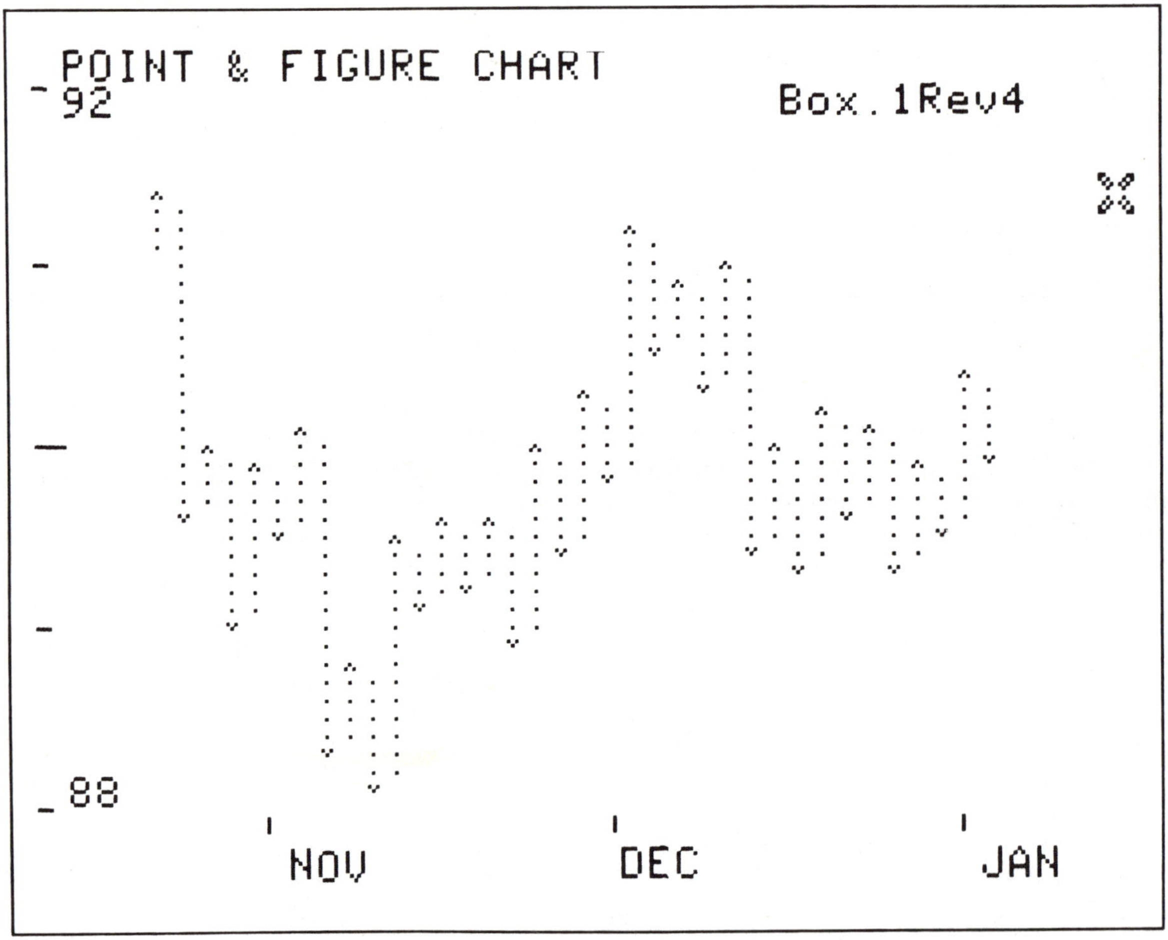

Fig. 5-4. A point and figure chart for two months, showing each day's movement. (Reprinted with permission of the Technical Analysis Group.)

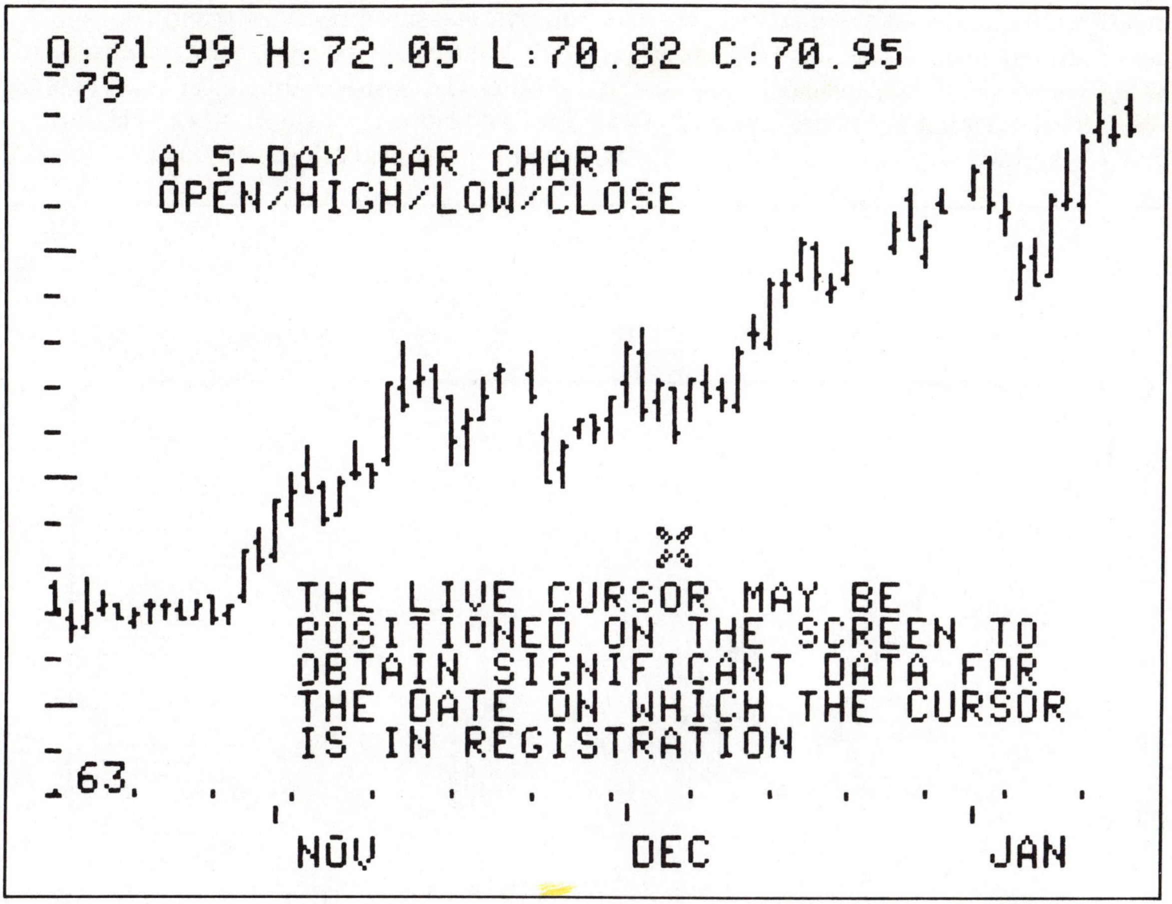

Fig. 5-5. A five-day bar chart open/high/low/close. (Reprinted with permission of the Technical Analysis Group.)

then a private investor) got together with two professional writers of technical analysis news letters and a professional broker. The four men were all advocates of using market structure technical indicators to signal investment opportunities. Over the years, word of mouth spread the news about the success of the programs the four men developed and the group grew.

The idea was to "let the computer do the day-to-day drudgery" and the "boring math and logging" necessary to maintain a large portfolio, look for opportunities, and make sure the current holdings are not slipping.

Compu Trac uses two forms of charts—point and figure charts (Fig. 5-4) and bar charts (Fig. 5-5)—to record data. The bar chart extends from the high to the low with the little nub somewhere on the bar representing the closing price. It can be used either for a single stock or commodity, or for the market. Users can define the price and time parameters for any chart. The precision chart (Fig. 5-6) has a much smaller price scale for close-up inspection.

Figure 5-7 shows a bar chart of the Dow Jones Industrial Average ending on Nov. 11, 1980, with a relative strength index overlayed at the bottom of the chart. Relative strength was originally developed by Welles Wilder to measure the commodities markets, but has been adapted to measure the DJIA. It measures the strength of "up close" or "down close" in the market each day. The RSI chart mimics the Dow chart to some extent. RSI is always measured between 0 and 100.

Figure 5-8 consists of two charts together. The first is a simple bar chart of high, low, and close for a single stock. The bottom chart represents both the closing prices (solid

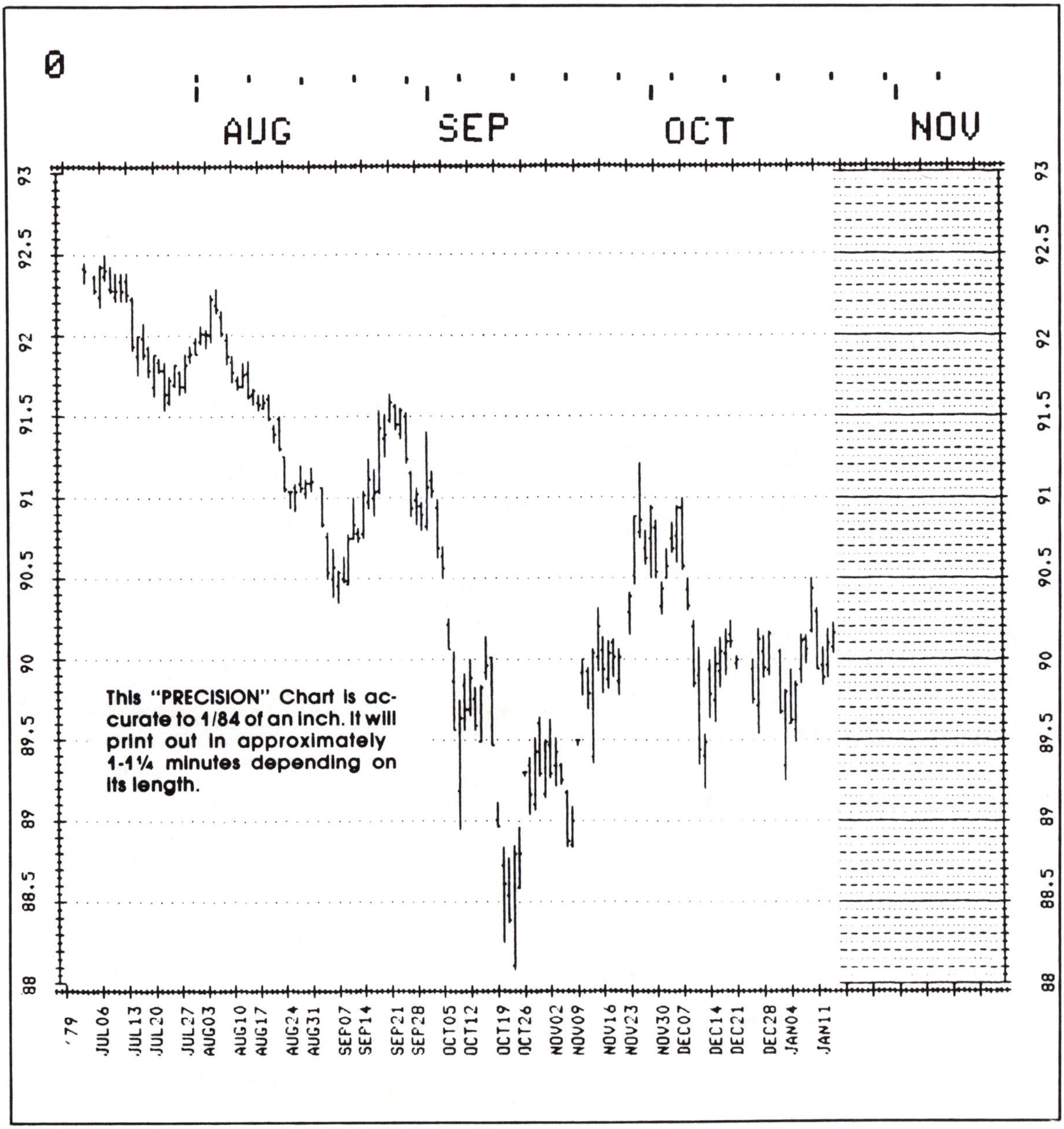

Fig. 5-6. Compu Trac precision chart. (Reprinted with permission of the Technical Analysis Group.)

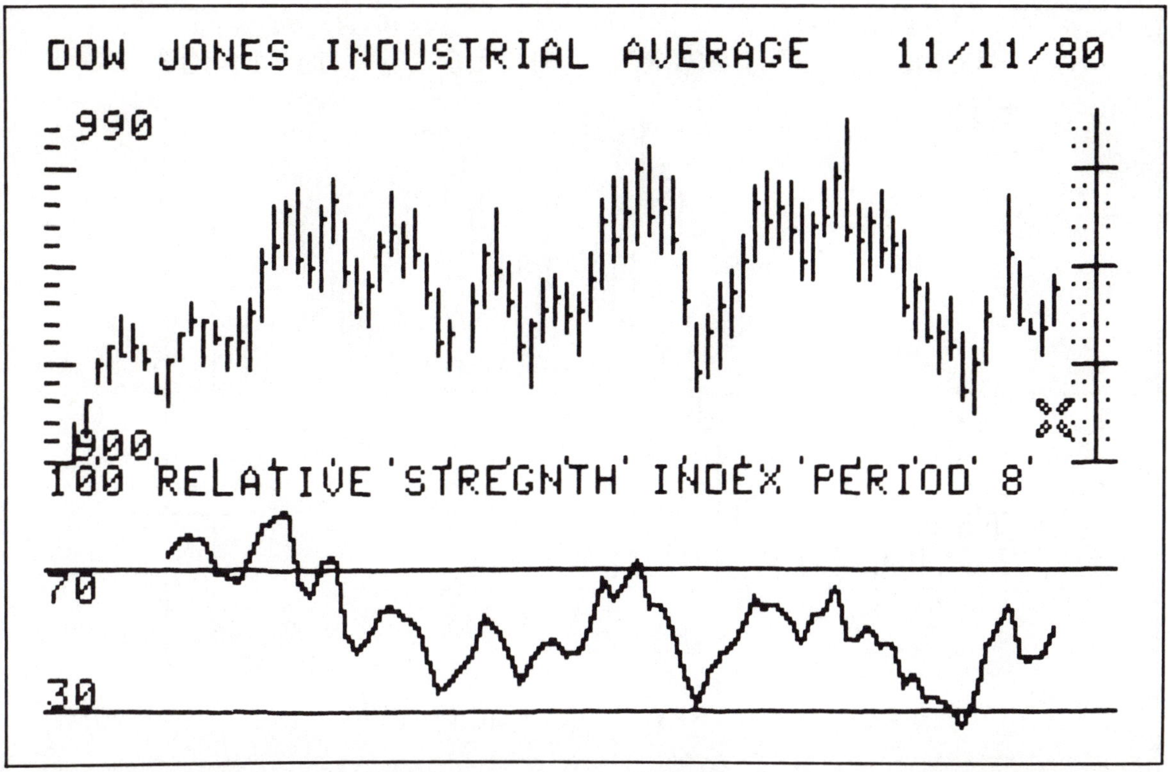

Fig. 5-7. A double chart showing a bar chart of the Dow Jones Industrials along with a relative strength chart. (Reprinted with permission of the Technical Analysis Group).

line) and the moving average (dotted line). Moving averages smooth the movement of a security or commodity and give an indication of trend over time as opposed to the jittery movements of day-to-day closing prices.

A trend line (Fig. 5-9) is drawn from the high points (peaks) over a period of time. A channel is drawn from the highs and the lows. In this case, the trend line is down.

On-balance-volume (Fig. 5-10) measures volume over a period of time, subtracting a smaller volume than the day before from the total volume and adding a larger volume to the total. Figure 5-10 is a busy chart that shows three graphs at once—a five day high, low, close bar chart; the on-balance-volume line; and the daily volume.

Jim Sibbet, publisher of *Let's Talk Silver and Gold,* has developed the Demand Index (Fig. 5-11), a combination of price and volume data configured to become a leading indicator.

The overbought/oversold index is developed by subtracting the number of declining issues each day from the number of advancing issues each day. A high positive number—500 or so—signifies an oversold condition while a high negative number— −500 or so—constitutes an overbought. The Compu Trac variation (Fig. 5-12) was developed by Walt Bressert, and works hand-in-hand with a momentum index.

Compu Trac makes use of oscillators in a number of its composite charts. Oscillators are relatively new to technical analysis, since they are very difficult to construct by hand. An oscillator is the difference between two moving

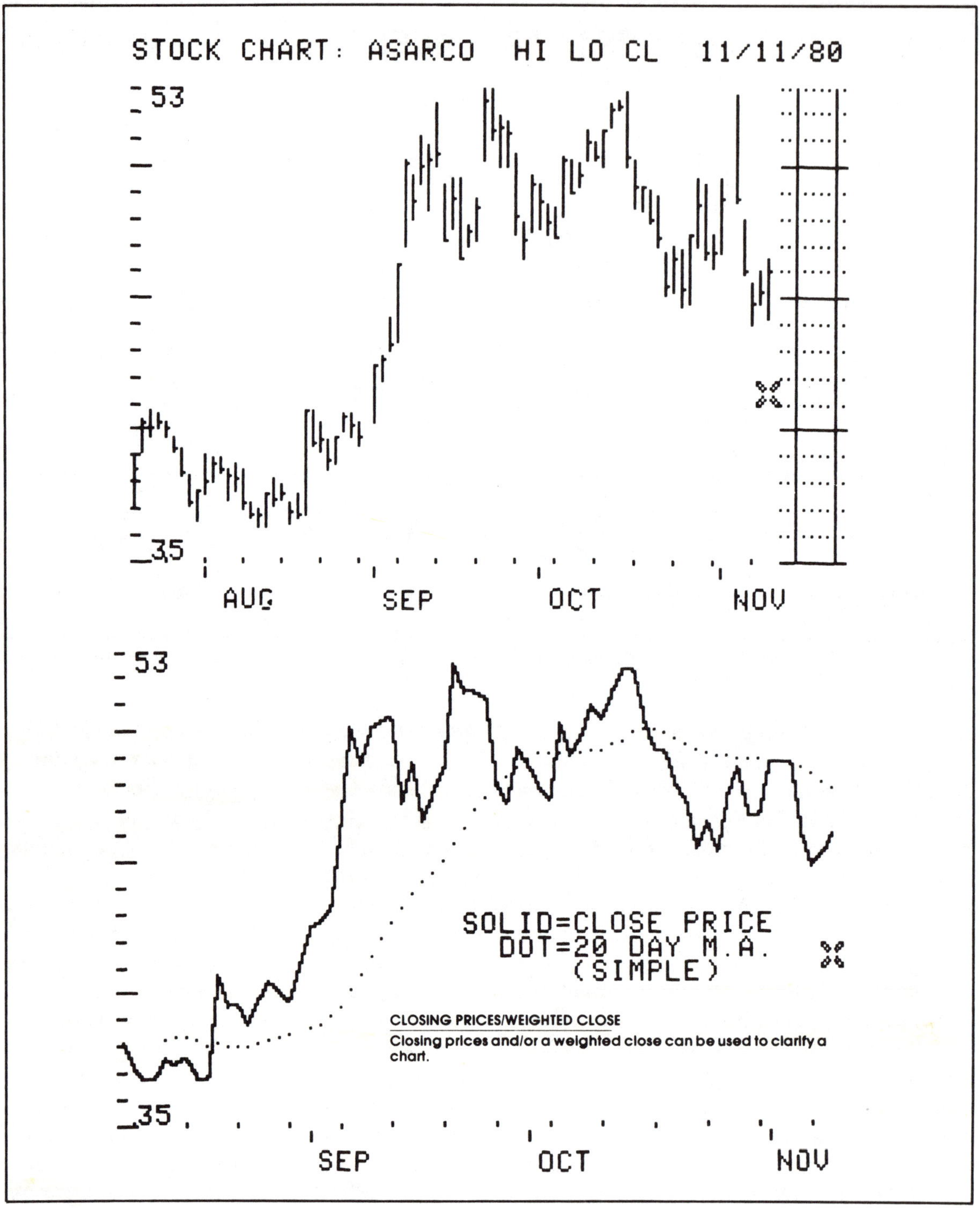

Fig. 5-8. Closing prices/weighted close. (Reprinted with permission of the Technical Analysis Group.)

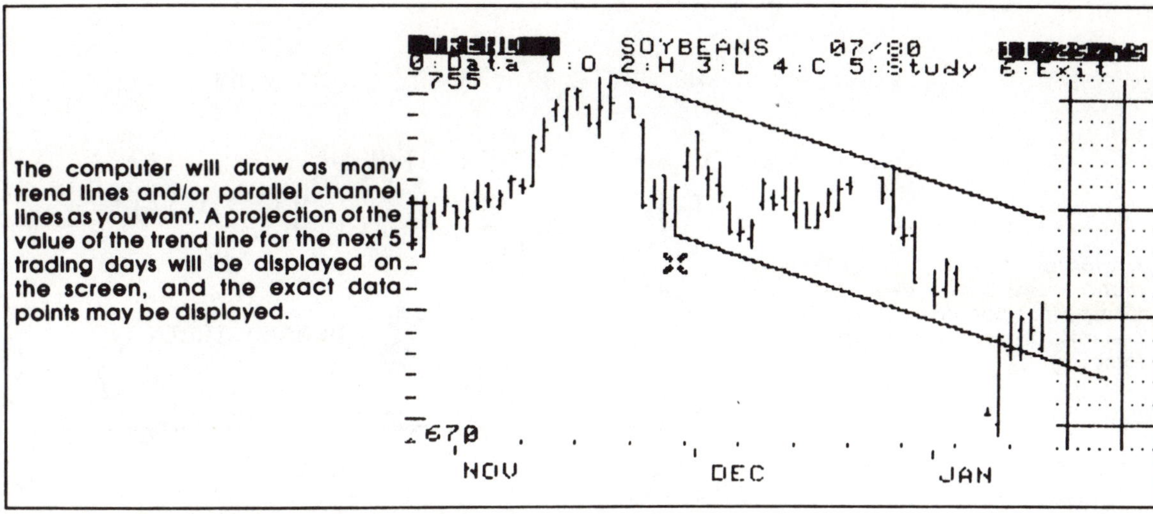

Fig. 5-9. Trend line. (Reprinted with permission of the Technical Analysis Group.)

averages and can be used to show subtle strengths and weaknesses.

As you can see (Fig. 5-13) in the top chart of the Dow Industrial Average and the rate of change, the oscillator more closely parallels the average, while in the bottom chart it more closely parallels the momentum index used to offset the price chart for Federal Express.

The variations available for technical studies are almost infinite, given that changing one variable will often present a whole new graph. Compu Trac is continually coming up with new studies.

As Timothy Slater says in the cassette

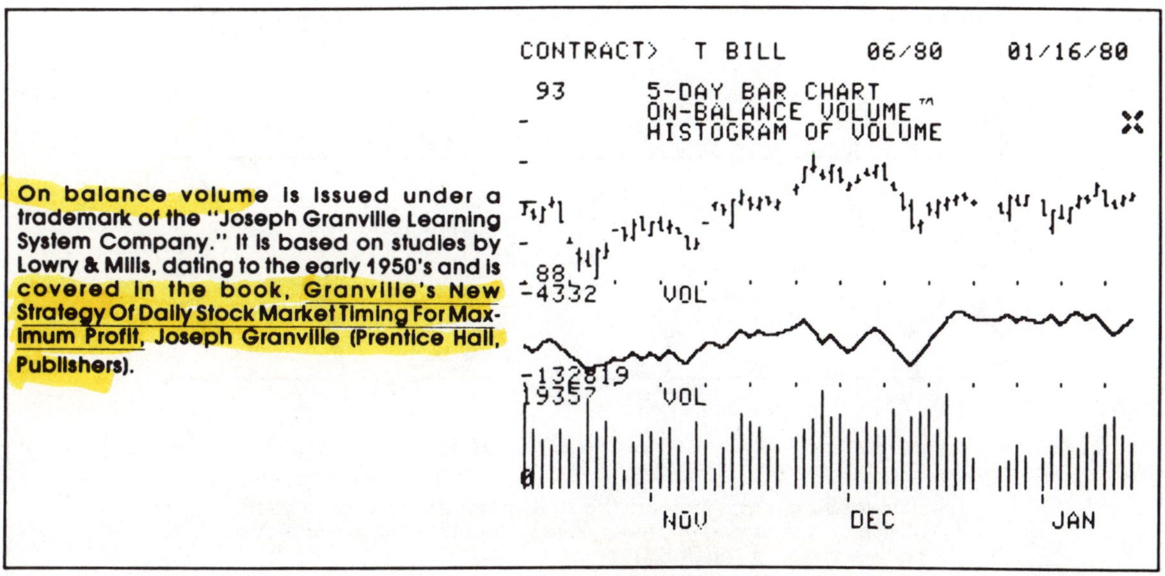

Fig. 5-10. On-balance-volume. (Reprinted with permission of the Technical Analysis Group.)

A program feature, Jim Sibbet's Demand Index, is fully explained in the Compu Trac documentation--it is an excellent tool to spot broad tops and bottoms.

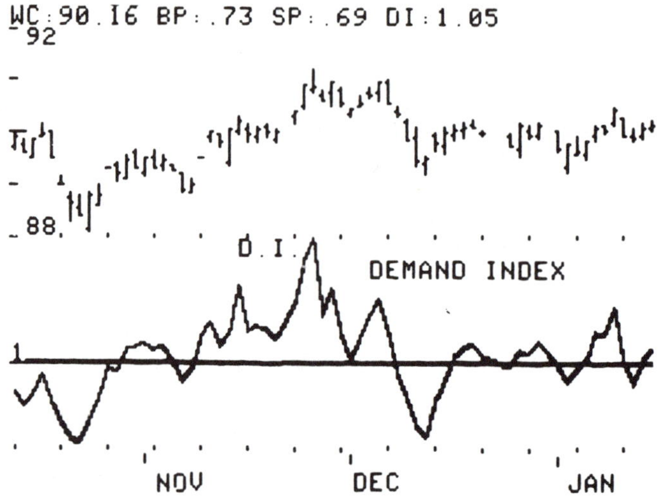

Fig. 5-11. Demand index. (Reprinted with permission of the Technical Analysis Group.)

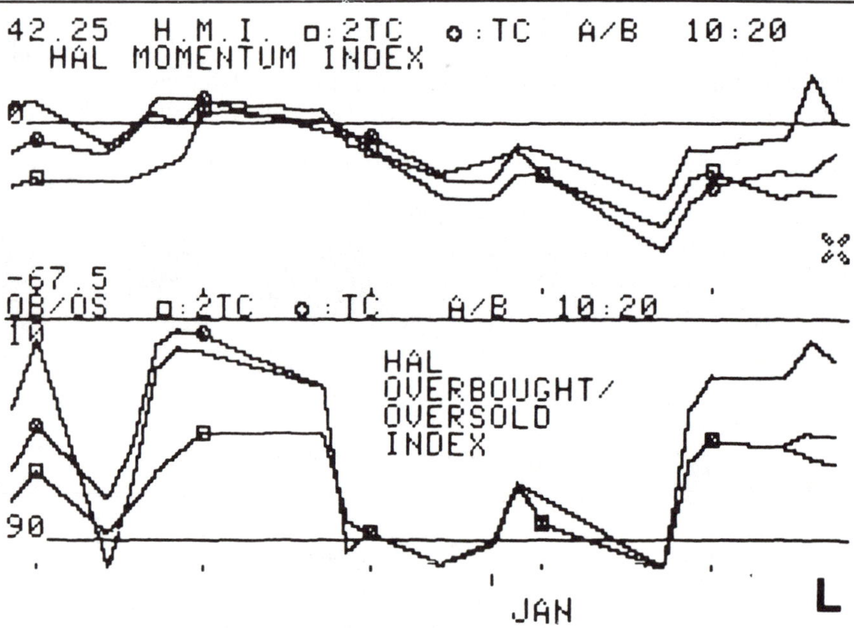

Developed by Walt Bressert, this program uses the natural cycle length of a commodity or security to calculate momentum and an overbought/oversold indicator.

Fig. 5-12. Momentum and overbought/oversold index. (Reprinted with permission of the Technical Analysis Group.)

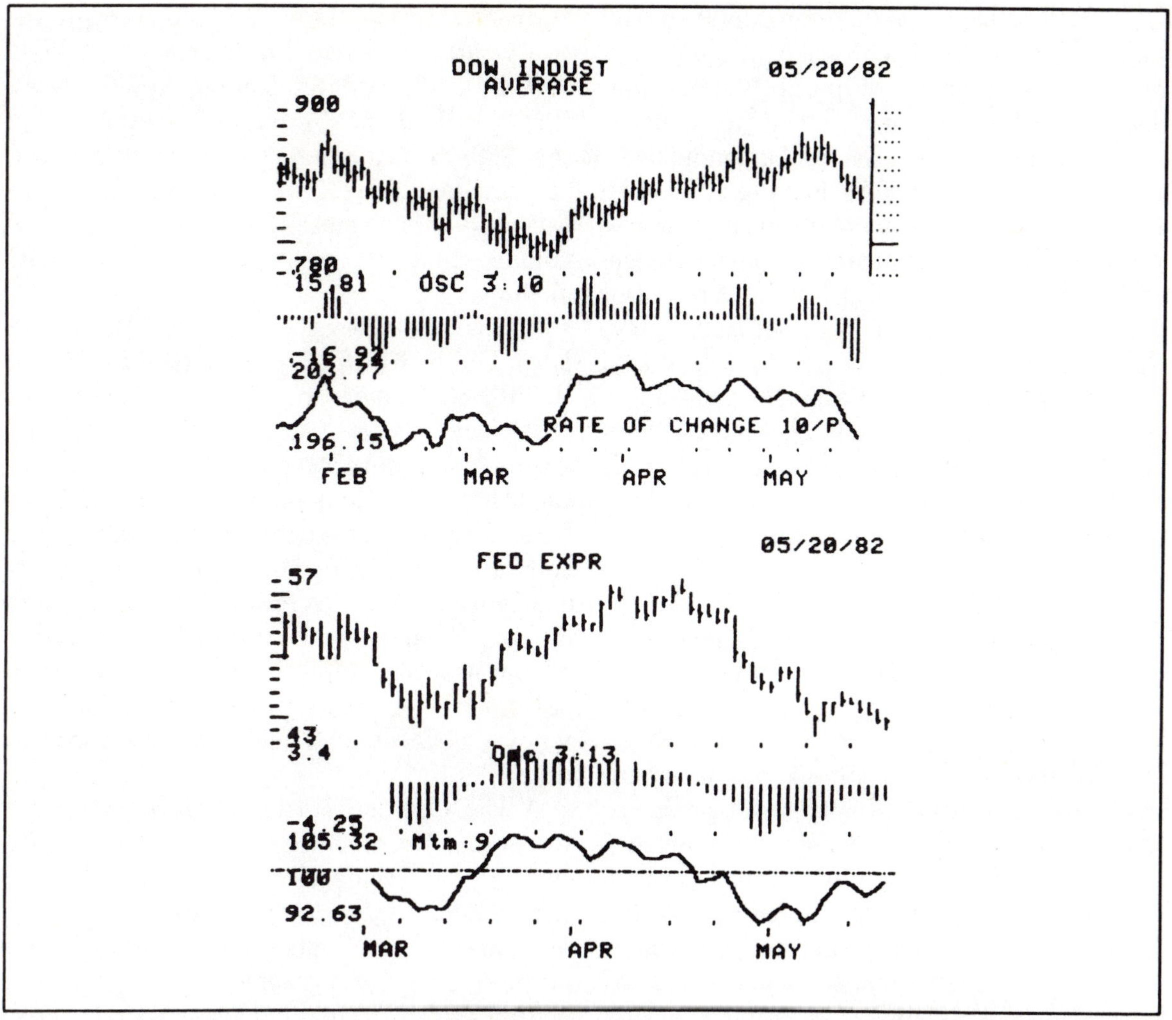

Fig. 5-13. A triple chart using a standard bar chart, the rate of change, and an oscillator, comparing the Dow Jones Industrial Average to the Federal Express Corp. (Reprinted with permission of the Technical Analysis Group.)

tape introduction to the Intra Day Analyst, the Technical Analysis Group's other product, "There is no single system, no single study, that will give you consistent answers. It needs some human interpretation. It takes *you* to use the studies you best understand. I can't write a system that other people can trade with. But you can configure a system that you can trade with successfully."

Intra Day Analyst provides a number of studies that run on a very short time span and record movements made in one trading day. The software includes communications with the stock and commodity markets so that users can follow the markets in real time.

Some will find the Compu Trac series of programs far too complex and too numerous. Some will want to look at more sentimental indicators, while others will only want to use a couple of indicators to make their decisions.

Another argument Slater makes should be taken to heart. There is probably no such thing as a purely technical or purely fundamental analyst of investments. Technical analysts must take into account the fundamental conditions of a company before looking at it as an investment. If a company dives in price, it may go below what would ordinarily be a technical marker that would signal an imminent rise. But if the company is on the verge of bankruptcy, the technical indicators would do no good.

In the same way, if a stock looks like a good investment, a quick study of some technical indicators could show that the market is likely to slide a way in the near term, and the stock may be able to be purchased at a better price.

Although the technical indicators and the math involved often look daunting, one can get beyond that and find some important information to help in the timing and choice of investments.

Most other technical analysis programs take a portion of the studies involved in the Compu Trac group, while some have original studies or different computational methodologies. It is important when deciding whether to purchase a technical analysis program to read the documentation and understand the underlying mathematics of the studies, or else the studies can become nothing more than black magic.

Other Programs

Analyst (K-Wave Financial Services, P.O. Box 1675, Sausalito CA 94965, 415-332-9434) runs on the IBM PC and PC-XT, Compaq, DEC Rainbow and North Star and costs $1,500.

The program can be customized to do more than the standard technical analysis charts and graphs, including bar charts, logarithmic price plots, and volume displays.

Chart Eas-alyser (Wall Street Graphics, P.O. Box 562, Wall St. Station, New York NY 10268, 212-498-6225) runs on the Apple II and cost $395. It is a graphics program to produce bar or line charts, moving averages, on-balance volume, and other charts. Price and volume data can be keyed or obtained by modem.

Chartist (Nexus Research, P.O. Box 1024, Dillon SC 29536) runs on IBM PC, Apple II, TRS-80, Vector Graphic, Altos, Televideo, DEC, and other standard CP/M operating system computers and costs $495. Purchasers can also get the Houston Instruments DMP-29 flatbed plotter for $1,995 when ordering the software. This is a comprehensive set of programs that does five-day, seven-day, and monthly charts of such studies as relative strength index, directional movement indicator, spreads, moving averages, on-balance-volume, overbought/oversold, and momentum.

The Chartist (Pardo Corp., 515 Sheridan Rd. #105, Evanston IL 60202, 312-866-9342) runs on the Apple II and costs $75. It can accommodate Compu Trac formatted information. Time intervals are user-defined. The program provides a graphics tool kit for doing speed lines, price channels, trend lines, geometric shapes, and a number of other charts and graphs.

Chartmaster (Decision Resources, Inc., 21 Bridge St., Westpoint CT 06880, 203-222-1974) runs on the IBM PC, Apple II, and Apple III and costs $375. The program produces graphs, charts, and signs using up to eight different colors, up to 600 bars for bar charts, four pies with up to 20 slices per pie chart, and signs with up to 100 lines of text.

Disk Trendex (Radio Shack, 1500 One Tandy Center, Fort Worth TX 76102, 817-

390-3155) runs on the TRS-80 Models I and III (32K) and costs $59.95. The program provides statistical procedures for analyzing market trends—primary, intermediate, and minor—and plots trend changes.

Radio Shack also puts out Trendex Stock Trend Analysis, the same program as Disk Trendex only for TRS-80 model I or III computers with cassette drives. Its cost is $49.95.

A company called Dogwood Software (3905 Dogwood Dr., Greensboro NC 27410) sells an enhancement to Trendex called, logically enough, Trendex Enhancement, which runs on the TRS-80 models I, III, and IV, as well as the Lobo Max 80; cost is $20.

Dynamic Volume Analysis (RTR Software, Inc., 444 Executive Center Blvd., Suite 225, El Paso TX 79902, 915-544-4397) runs on the Apple II and costs $200. The program charts on-balance-volume for individual stocks, graphing net cumulative volume against price. In addition, a number of other indices are graphed and summarized. An autorun allows charting of a number of stocks on a data diskette. Historical data input and updating are done manually.

RTR has two other technical analysis programs. Market Charter II works on the Apple II and costs $250. A stock charting program, it displays volume and price data in linear and semi-log bar charts. It charts trendlines, speed-resistance lines, exponential and weighted averages, and more. Stocks and stock averages can be compared. Historical data input and updating are manual.

RTR Point and Figure Charting runs on the Apple II and costs $125. Using standard X and 0 point-and-figure technique, this program shows current price level and well as trendlines. An auto-run feature allows you to chart a number of stocks on a data diskette. Historical data input and updating are manual.

EASI/ARIMA (The Winchendon Group, 3907 Lakota Rd., Alexandria VA 22310, 703-960-2587) runs on the IBM PC (cost: $500) and the Apple II ($300). The program forecasts stock prices using an advanced time-series analysis formula. Reads Compu Trac formatted files.

Fundgraf (Parsons Software, 118 Woodshire Dr., Parkersburg WV 26101) runs on the TRS-80 Color Computer (16K, extended basic needed for full presentation) and costs $69.95 for diskette and $49.95 for tape. The program does graphic and numerical comparisons of any stock of mutual fund for up to 200 weeks. It will plot price changes, calculate percentage price changes, and generate buy/sell signals based on moving averages.

LeInvestor 2.0 (LeSoftware, 3224 Magnolia Ct., Bettendorf IA 52772, 319-335-0134) runs on the Apple II, II+ and *II*e and costs $150. The program is nine modules based primarily on moving average relationships. The user has flexibility to fine-tune databases without destroying data. Reports and graphs are generated.

Market Analyst (Anidata, Inc., 318 South Black Horse Pike, Blackwood NJ 08012, 609-228-3034) runs on the IBM PC, Apple II, II+, and *II*e, and costs $495. The program does all the standard technical charts, including daily, weekly, and monthly volume, moving averages, oscillators, trendlines, and price/volume. Multiple graphs can be produced on one screen for comparison.

Market Analyzer (Dow Jones & Co., P.O. Box 300, Princeton NJ 08540, 609-452-2000) runs on the IBM PC (color graphics card), Apple II+, and Apple III and costs $350.

Market Analyzer is the technical analysis member of the Dow Jones family of software. The system automatically collects data from the Dow Jones News/Retrieval Service and creates a number of graphs and charts on market trends and movements.

Market Analyzer (N-Squared Computing, 5318 Forest Ridge Rd., Silverton OR 97381) runs on the Apple II+ and costs $295. This product is one of three technical analysis programs by N-Squared; the other two are Market Illustrator and Stock Analyzer.

Market Analyzer does exponential smoothing, arithmetic averaging, detrending, time-lag analysis, and more using indicators such as the Trading Index (TRIN) and the Advance Decline Line.

Market Illustrator does price, volume, and on-balance volume charting for stocks and futures/commodities. It also uses a split screen for comparing data with program-generated indicators. The package works on the Apple II+ and costs $195.

Stock Analyzer charts such indicators as high-low-close-volume with linear or semi-log auto scaling, relative strength, price/volume indicators, momentum, and more. Also for the Apple II+, this program costs $295.

Market Counselor (Capital Management Systems, Inc., P.O. Box 11595, Denver CO 80211, 303-595-9998) runs on the IBM PC and the Apple II+ and costs $149. A historical database updated to within one week of delivery plus your manual updating of information provide tools to analyze indicators such as overbought/oversold markets, odd-lot trading, advance-decline ratios, and other indicators.

Market Maestro (AJH Systems, 3032 S. Saulsbury St., Denver CO 80227, 303-985-9062) runs on the IBM PC, KAYPRO, and Osborne and costs $125. The program uses historical data either loaded manually or downloaded from the Dow Jones News/Retrieval Service or CompuServe to generate buy and sell signals for any stock.

Market Mood Monitor (Computer Asset Management, P.O. Box 26743, Salt Lake City UT 84126, 801-964-0391) runs on the Apple II+ and *IIe* and costs $185. The program allows you to create your own "sentiment indicators" by combining any of the indicators the program can plot, including advance/decline, new highs/lows, NYSE Index futures premium/discount, public/total shorts, and others. Includes database with all data from 1975 on; update manual.

Market Time (Hourglass Systems, P.O. Box 312, Glen Ellyn IL 60137, 312-690-1855) runs on the IBM PC, Apple II, Osborne, Televideo, and most other CP/M machines. The program assists in spotting trends using weekly price, volume informaton on the NYSE, advance/decline information since 1971, and total issues traded issues since 1975. It graphs moving averages to even trends.

Market Tracker and Stock Tracker (H and H Trading Co., P.O. Box 549, Clayton CA 94517, 415-672-3233) run on the Apple II and TRS-80 models I and III. Both cost $295. Stock Tracker will store data on up to 30 securities per diskette and generate buy/sell/hold recommendations using volume-based analysis. Market Tracker uses six market indicators to generate buy/sell signals on stock futures of the DJIA.

Market Trend Analysis System (Personal Equity Computing, Inc., P.O. Box 2105, Ocean NJ 07712) runs on the IBM PC and PC XT; it costs $300. The program has three modules that build, maintain, and interpret a database of daily and weekly indicators. Percentage change and divergence analysis can be performed on major indicators.

Market Information and Plotting System (Data Express, 4009 Pacific Coast Highway, Torrance CA 90505, 213-326-8440) runs on the Apple II and costs $300. You define your portfolio, then get MIPS to automatically dial Dow Jones News/Retrieval Service to get daily prices and news about your portfolio. Annotated charts showing price, volume and smoothing for 60 or 120 days are coupled on the screen with news stories.

Market Technician (Datamost, 8943 Fulbright Ave., Chatsworth CA 91311) runs on Apple II or II+. The program uses a 120-day database and updates (manually or via Dow Jones News/Retrieval Service) to create user-defined graphs based on moving averages, momentum, or statistical projections.

Market Trend Analysis System and Buy/Sell Trend Analysis System (Personal Equity Computing, P.O. Box 2105, Ocean NJ 07712, 800-431-6082) both run on the IBM PC and PC-XT, Columbia, Compaq, Hyperion, and Seequaa. Market Trend costs $350 and Buy/Sell Trend costs $295.

Market Trend Analysis System graphs moving averages, as well as comparative studies using technical indicators for three exchanges, currency and interest rates, market psychology and more. Buy/Sell Trend Analysis System looks for trends as well as changes in market strength both before and after market tops and bottoms.

MTS Market Charter (Market Timing Software, Inc., 6912 N. Sheridan Rd., Chicago IL 60626, 312-743-8184) runs on the IBM PC ($195) and the Apple II+, TRS-80 models II, III, and Color Computer ($95 for all models). This program graphs up to 120 days of volume, high, low and close per stock and can store up to 100 stocks per diskette. It calculates moving averages, rate of change, oscillators, and more.

On-Balance Volume Charting (Stock Market Software, Inc., 44 Front St., Ashland MA 01721, 617-881-5190) runs on the Apple II, II+, and *IIe* and costs $1,200. The program allows you to set parameters and look at more than one stock at a time to get OBV information showing price and variable moving averages. It can overlay stocks on the same chart.

Pear Technical Analyzer (Remote Computing Corp., 1044 Northern Blvd., Roslyn NY 11576, 800-645-3120) runs on the Apple II and costs $995. The program can be set up to assist meeting personal trading goals and decision rules for portfolios involving stocks, commodities, and futures. The program retrieves and stores price, volume, and other data and generates a variety of technical studies.

SMAS (Spiral Enterprises, 308 Crown Rd., Willow Park TX 76086, 817-441-8901) runs on the TRS-80 models I and III and costs $172.95. The program uses a moving-average system and its own database to provide buy/sell signals on 196 common stocks and five market indexes.

StockAid (Dynacomp, Inc., 1427 Monroe Ave., Rochester NY 14618, 800-828-6772) runs on the Atari (32K) computers with disk drives and costs $29.95. The program handles up to 239 days of data on individual stocks (manually entered) and creates graphs of trend lines, short-term oscillator and long-term moving average, along with high, low, close, and volume.

Dynacomp produces three other technical analysis programs, NYIndex, Microcomputer Stock Program, and Buy/Sell.

NYIndex also works on ATARI (32K) computers with disk drives. It graphs up to 700 days of the NYSE Index high, low, close, volume, and graphs oscillators and moving averages; cost is $29.95.

Microcomputer Stock Program runs on all computers and generates buy/sell signals for the past eight weeks using autoregressive price trend analysis. Cost is $59.95 for diskette and $55.95 for tape.

Buy/Sell runs on IBM PC and CP/M operating system computers and costs $149.95. It generates buy/sell signals using four distinct systems based on moving averages, price channels, the "buy low, sell high" system, and dollar-cost averaging.

Stock Charting (Diamond Head Software, 2937 Kalakaua Ave., Ste. 28, Honolulu HI 96815) runs on the IBM PC (color graphics) and costs $69.95. It stores 30 days of high, low, close, and volume for 20 stocks, and superimposes actual daily price and volume movement on a stock's moving average over a month.

Stockcraft (Decision Economics, Inc., 14 Old Farm Rd., Cedar Knolls NJ 07927, 201-539-6889) runs on the Apple II+, *II*e, and III (in emulation mode) and costs $188. The program has a technical analysis module (also a portfolio management module) that generates buy/sell signals using moving averages and does trading optimization strategy.

Stock Helper (Magreeable Software, Inc., 5925 Magnolia Lane, Plymouth MN 55442, 612-559-1108) runs on the VIC 20 and ATARI 400, 800, and 1200. It costs $30. The program calculates 52-week moving averages and maintains history of stocks or markets.

Stock Market Advance/Decline Timing Program (Dr. R. Altman, P.O. Box 1197, Hightstown NJ 08520) runs on the Apple II and costs $149. The program makes short-term (3-7 day) and intermediate-term (4-7 week) projections for markets using daily and weekly advance/decline values. Up to two years of trading information can be stored and used.

Stock Momentum Studies (Troy-Folan Productions Inc., 29 Miller Rd., Wayne NJ 07470, 201-694-0424) runs on the Apple II, II+, and *II*e and costs $325. The program generates buy/sell indicators using four technical signals. It can store past prices and other data, update manually or through Dow Jones News/Retrieval Service or Bridge Data, and uses momentum, moving averages, percentage change, and other indicators to prepare multiple-stock or test overlays.

Stock-TAS (Financial Applications, Inc., P.O. Box 34094, Houston TX 77234-4094, 713-484-5026) runs on the VIC-20 and costs $24.95. It charts up to 147 days of high, low, close, and volume for individual stocks, adjusts for splits, and will plot moving averages for user-defined time period.

Stock Watch (Micro Program Designs, 5440 Crestline Rd., Wilmington DE 19808, 302-738-3798) runs on the Apple II, II+, *II*e, and III (in emulation mode) and costs $59.50. It features manual data entry on up to 45 stocks that are monitored for high, low, close, and volume, displays moving averages, and also does simple portfolio maintenance.

Stox (Sydney Development Corp., 600-1385 West 8th Ave., Vancouver B.C. Canada V6H 3V9, 604-734-8822) runs on the IBM PC (color graphics) and costs $200 Canadian. The program produces price charts, relative strength indexes, moving averages, on-balance-volume, momentum, and more.

Strohl Stock System (Strohl Systems Group, Inc., 661 West Germantown Pike, Plymouth Meeting PA 19462, 215-825-6220) runs on the IBM PC and costs $495. The program makes daily buy/sell/short and buy/sell/stop recommendations. Up to 45 stocks can be maintained per diskette and the program comes with an automatic log-on to Dow Jones.

The Technical Investor (Savant Corp. P.O. Box 440278, Houston TX 77244, 800-231-9900) runs on the IBM PC (color graphics) and the Compaq and costs $395. Updates come via modem from Dow Jones or any other commercial database. After update, a summary report is generated showing price, volumes, and changes since the previous update. Up to four independently controlled miniscreens can be charted at the same time. Multiple stocks can be charted on the same screen, or miniscreens can be used to compare various securities for the same criteria.

Techni-Stock Software System (Toco Technology, P.O. Box 98, Santa Claus, IN 47579, 812-937-4611) runs on the Timex/Sinclair and costs $24.95. The program charts price/volume charts on a logarithmic grid, technical evaluations based on risk/return, moving averages, momentum, and regression formulas.

Telescan (Telescan, Inc., 802 The Interfin Building, 1400 Post Oak Blvd., Houston TX 77056, 713-877-1206) runs on the IBM PC and costs $300 per year. This program includes access to the Telescan database, which the company says is cheaper to use than any commercial database. The program does composite graphing of two or more variables at a time. A key at the side of the screen tells you the variables being graphed at any time. It does relative strength, moving averages, inflation adjustments, insider trading, and more.

Trend Analysis Program (Harley D. Wilbur, 9709 Elrod Rd., Kensington MD 20895, 301-949-8131) runs on the TRS-80 models I, III, and IV and costs $45. The program allows the user to create and maintain data files and do moving average studies. It features linear or logarithmic graphs.

The Unfair Advantage (SSB Programming, P.O. Box 30285, Indianapolis IN 46230, 317-758-4401) runs on the Apple II and *II*e and costs $895. The program has six modules to retrieve both text and prices from Dow Jones, generate buy/sell and close signals, weigh volume and price fluctuations, and compute trends. Graphs include moving averages, volume balance, and others.

Visi Trend/Plot (VisiCorp, 2895 Zanker Rd., San Jose CA 95134, 408-946-9000) runs on the IBM PC and the Apple II and III and costs $300. The program works with the VisiCalc spreadsheet to allow the investor to perform statistical tests and do graphics including line charts, pie charts, high/low/close charts, and bar charts. Statistical functions include multiple regressions, cumulative total, lead, lag, percent change, and moving averages.

Wall Street Plotter (Dickens Data Systems, Inc., 3050 Holcolm Bridge Rd. Suite A, Norcross GA 30071, 800-241-6753) runs on the Apple II and costs $125. The program plots high/low/close/volume, moving averages, and trend analysis plot of trading cycles for stocks, commodities, and market averages.

Wall Street Plotter (Spring Dale Software, 1507 Evesham Rd., Voorhees NJ 08043, 609-795-1457) runs on the IBM PC and costs $169. It will keep up to 300 days and 210 weeks of data for nine stocks per diskette and plot price/volume 30-day moving average, on-balance volume, and other graphs. It also charts earnings, dividends, market averages, interest rates, commodities, and option prices.

Wall Street Micro Systems, Ltd. (500 Fifth Ave. #520, New York NY 10110, 212-371-5940) produces two pricing services. Both run on the IBM PC, Apple II+ and *II*e. Pricing Service provides daily open, high, low, close, number of trades, and number of shares traded for all NYSE-listed stocks. Delivery of database is weekly. Daily prices cost $3,000, weekly $999. Historical Prices has the monthly closing price for the past 18 months for all NYSE stocks; cost is $199.

Chapter 6

Macroeconomics

Macroeconomic research is another type of analysis that goes into a full-scale investment research program. This brief discussion follows those of fundamental and technical analysis because few, if any, individual investors, will do much of this analysis themselves. However, money managers and brokerage houses do this kind of research and individuals should know that the personal computer has made it much more economical.

Macroeconomic research, often using econometric models, is a highly technical form of analysis that tries to take all the variables of the total national (or multinational) economy, and determine from their changes the possibilities for economic growth or decline in the future and where that growth or decline will manifest itself.

To get the raw numbers for any macroeconomic model, the modelmaker must look at the aggregate corporate output (like taking every page covering every stock in such sources as Value Line, Ford Investors, and Merrill Lynch and adding all the columns—all the net sales, all the depreciation, etc.) as well as all the flow of funds data on interest rates, savings, bank reserves, etc., as well as welfare statistics, employment, householdspending, and reams of other data.

A little bit of this is done crudely in both fundamental and technical analysis, but only in a rudimentary way.

This analysis is watched very closely by corporations that will have to borrow, banks that both borrow and lend, politicians who want to know which way the wind is blowing (and whether to rail against unemployment, inflation, deficits or what), as well as a number of other individuals.

In terms of investing, projecting the future economic circumstances can give one an idea of how the market will fare—using comparisons of how the market has done in prior similar circumstances.

What Is "The Economy?"

We have all heard the expression "The economy took a turn for the better/worse" on the evening news. Indeed, we hear it almost every day. But what exactly is "the economy?"

As Woody Allen said in a recent movie, "without being didactic or facetious," the economy is the state of the world. The economy is all of the reality and all of the perception of how the world is working: Are businesses making money, are people being paid, are people spending, saving or hoarding the money they have, how is the government raising and spending money? And there's a whole raft of other questions.

Economists study the current state of the economy both to cull information with which they can modify and refine their mathematical models, and to help both the public and the private sector set policy. A number of different policies can be designed for any economic circumstance, depending on what a company or country would like to do in the future.

First, let's briefly look at the government's role in the economy, and then how private industry—and investors—might react.

Henry Hazlitt, in his classic book *Economics in One Lesson,* states the lesson this way: "The art of economics consists in looking not merely at the immediate but at the longer effects of any act or policy; it consists in tracing the consequences of that policy not merely for one group but for all groups."

Hazlitt starts with the example of the broken window. A store window is broken. To replace it will cost $500. One person standing in the crowd watching the storekeeper sweep the shards of glass says, "Well, at least the glazer has work." The fallacy, Hazlitt says, is that the storekeeper was that very day going to buy himself a new suit and put some money into his money market account. So while the glazer has more work, the suit manufacturer has sold one less suit and the money market fund has less money with which to invest in securities. While there is a winner, there are also losers.

Lester Thurow, the Massachusetts Institute of Technology economist, describes the economic dilemma posed by Hazlitt's broken window metaphor of winners and losers as a "zero sum game."

When taken from the microeconomic (individual) to the macroeconomic (city, state, country, or world) context, the broken window/zero sum game becomes the "push/pull" economy. For every economic push given, there is a reactive pullback in some other area of the economy—a social science version of the classic physics theorem that for every action there is an equal and opposite reaction.

Since the time of Franklin Roosevelt and the New Deal, Americans have come to see the push/pull dilemma in terms of inflation and unemployment. When inflation rose, unemployment usually fell, signaling that much of the country's productive capacity was being utilized. When unemployment began to rise, signaling a slowing in the manufacturing economy, inflation usually abated. Why? This has been the classic debate among economists, as well as politicians, at least since the Great Depression.

For a while—from the end of World War II until the mid-1960s—government spending tended to alleviate recessions and unemployment but usually at the cost of higher inflation. But in the last 15-20 years, everything has become skewed.

In a pure market economy, government

would have no role in the economy. Unfortunately, once you create a government, you create government involvement, or, as some put it, government "intervention" in the economy. If you have a village of 100 people and assign one person the task of being the village administrator, those who produce food and shelter must produce enough for the administrator also. A way of taking enough from the population to keep the administrator fed, housed, and clothed must be determined. But how?

Everyone could contribute an equal amount, but not everyone will have an equal amount. One person might farm an acre of fertile land while another farms a less fertile acre. One person might have an aged grandmother in the household who makes clothing while all the other women her age in the village have died. One family might have four children, another two, and thus be able to produce more.

So those who have more can be asked to pay more for the administration of the village. The village administrator has to make some decisions—after all, that is what he gets paid for. He must decide how much the rest of the villagers should give to the man whose once-fertile field was flooded during the sudden summer rains so that the man's family doesn't starve between now and the time the fields dry out for planting again. He must decide whether or not the village has grown enough corn to trade it with another village in exchange for more goats, how much each farmer will contribute to the trade, and how many goats each will get in return.

Of course, if the village has over 250 million people and the village administration has millions of workers doing everything from making laws (Congress) to delivering mail (Postal Service) to keeping economic records (Department of Commerce) to managing land (Department of the Interior) to planning for the defense and possibly the next war (Department of Defense), the government must take in a lot more money—and distribute a lot more money.

How it distributes that money has more to do with politics than it does with economics. Regardless of whether the country is democratic, autocratic, oligarchic, party-committee-state, or any other aberation, decisions about what the country should produce and how it should distribute what has been produced are necessary.

Of course, in a cash society, the decisions become even more difficult. In addition to questions about how to distribute the cash that the government takes in and what goods and services to purchase with the cash, there is the need to set policy on how much money is actually in the economy to be used. A very delicate monetary balance is kept in this country. It is a well-known fact (that few people like to even think about) that if suddenly one morning everyone got up and decided to go to the banks and withdraw their cash, call their brokers, and sell their positions in all the markets, there wouldn't be enough cash to pay but a few pennies on the dollar—if that. If we all called in the government debt (about $1.4 trillion as of early 1984), the country's economy would go down the tubes in about 35 seconds.

Economic Policy, Political Policy

Over the last 40 years this country has charted a wavy course in economic management. It has vacillated between tax increases and tax cuts, while at the same time trying to increase the amount of money it spends producing arms *and* increasing the amount it spends on programs to assist the poor.

The tax code is constantly amended so that it is now over 2,000 pages and so convoluted that increasingly, it takes high-powered, high-priced tax assistance to pay only the taxes you must pay and take advantage of all the "loopholes" in the tax laws that you legitimately can. At the same time, there is a continuous philosophical debate over whether government should try to do more or do less in terms of both managing the economy and redistributing the nation's wealth—as well as a debate over whether you should *increase* taxes to generate more money for the government or *decrease* taxes in order to stimulate production and wealth (in order to generate more tax money).

The idea of a constantly larger role for the government—larger in terms of the military, larger in terms of social welfare, larger in terms of the size of government and the amount of regulation it imposes over the daily activities of the individual and corporate population—worked fine during a time when America's economy was predominant and the "economic pie" was growing. But much of this had to do with inexpensive raw materials—materials we had in this country, or purchased from major European countries or newly post-colonial countries that had always been depended upon by the colonial powers to supply these materials. When these materials became more expensive, the cost of production increased dramatically. Increased regulation of our own natural resources in an attempt to overcome depletion, pollution, erosion and a number of other outcomes of resource utilization, as well as dramatic price increases by post-colonial "third-world" nations in an effort to generate more cash for modernization and industrialization, drove raw material prices through the roof.

The most dramatic of these price increases, of course, was in the cost of petroleum produced by the Organization of Petroleum Exporting Countries (OPEC) in the early 1970s, virtually tripling the price of a barrel (42 gallons) of crude oil overnight. Our energy-inefficient economy was jolted. Countries that were more energy-efficient in their manufacture—and that had far lower labor costs—drove huge amounts of imports into this country.

Most economists believe there are solutions to our economic problems. There are two major schools of thought about where those solutions lay. They parallel the thought about increasing or decreasing taxes. One school, characterized by Thurow and his zero-sum game scenario, says that for us to get back on an even keel, a number of people are going to have to endure relative economic hardship (he nominates many of the upper class individuals and corporations). We must close the gap between the top of the economic scale and the bottom.

The other school, characterized by a number of the "supply-siders" in the Reagan administration, believe that the wealthy have to be allowed to invest in more production and get the economic engines of the country moving again, pulling the less wealthy up the economic ladder with them. During the Reagan administration the latter approach was tried, and, as we saw, it nominated the lower classes to bear the brunt of the economic dislocation and rearrangement and caused severe hardship for many of them.

The New Industrial Revolution

The rise of the computer has had a part to play in changing the face of the American economy. The computer has skewed the economic picture in two ways. First of all, production of the computer and use of the computer for a myriad of tasks has created what many people like to call "the new industrial revolution." Along with this industrial revolution will have to come a major change in the composition of the workforce as well as the goods and services the country produces. How this transition occurs will have lasting effects on the economy.

Already we are seeing changes in emphasis in higher education—away from broad liberal arts studies and toward more narrow engineering and computer science majors. In addition, the computer is helping managers work more productively while at the same time generating a need for more clerical work to amass the raw data these managers transform, often using personal computers and "decision support software," into information. This threatens to cause a two-tier economy, with people only at the top and at the bottom, cutting into the ranks of middle management—and therefore, the middle class.

The rise of the computer has also caused the beginnings of change in this country from a manufacturing economy to an "information" economy. In this new economy, many skilled workers, it is argued, will be displaced by computers and computer-aided manufacturing processes. They will be forced to take less-skilled, lower-wage jobs, often in the clerical or service sector, while our needs for manufactured goods are met by other countries. This again will tend to displace a large segment of the skilled middle class.

Second—and more importantly for our current discussion—the computer has made the continuous collection and analysis of economic data a manageable task, and has served to disseminate this data much more widely than ever before. The advent of an econometric modeling tool for the personal computer (discussed later in the chapter) can only add to this dissemination. And with this huge body of information in the hands of many more people than two decades ago (or even one decade ago) there are more people reacting to it in their investment decisions. This only enhances the desire of investors to become preemptive in their investment decisions, so that an investment in a company now might not be made on the basis of what the company's fundamentals—or even the technical indicators—are, but what the economy shows happening there, six, nine, or more months out.

As an example, in February of 1984, the prime interest rate (the rate at which a bank will lend to its best customers) was 11 percent. President Reagan submitted a fiscal 1985 budget showing a deficit of almost $200 billion. Immediately, "the experts" on Wall Street began predicting that the second phase of the bull market (the one that began in August 1982 and went into a "correction" in June 1983) might not begin in the spring as they had earlier thought. It might not begin until after the election, they reasoned, or it might not begin at all. Why?

The reasoning went something like this: With the federal budget $200 billion in the red for fiscal 1985, on top of about $1.4 trillion in accumulated debt over the last 50 years since the first deficit spending of the Roosevelt administration, there might be such a demand by the government for credit (issuing treasury bonds and bills) that there might not be much room for private companies to get credit.

This would do two things. First, it would force companies to put off expansion of modernization, thereby slowing production in all the industries that supply goods and services to other industries. Companies wouldn't buy new trucks, nor lathes, nor even computers. Second, for the business that really needed credit, it would be forced to pay more for that borrowing to, in effect, outbid the government. Interest rates would no doubt rise. The government would then raise the rates it paid on its bonds in order to outbid others who sought credit.

This, in turn, would have investment fallout.

First, if investors could get high enough guaranteed interest on bonds, why take a chance on stocks? Second, since "tighter money" in the form of higher credit costs would slow production, companies would not have as good fundamentals; their stock prices would not go up, so why buy the stock? Third, higher credit costs can force the smaller investor out of the market because he must pay more for goods he buys on credit.

If you can get beyond this reasoning, there are opportunities to make money on stocks in an inflationary market. There are stocks known as "defensive stocks"—stocks in companies that manufacture necessities such as prescription drugs, food, and basic clothing. Then there are stocks that might be somewhat interest rate-proof, such as stock in a movie theater company or a middle-priced chain restaurant. These are the kinds of treats people might buy themselves even if a new car or stereo has been priced out of their range by high credit costs or inflation.

So now we are all sitting here watching the economy and trying to second-guess the statistics to figure out what will happen six months or a year out. In a year like 1984, this becomes especially difficult since the shape of the economy will be vastly different depending on who is elected president in November.

It is hardly coincidental that, while the economy is in such a rapid state of flux (or maybe transition from one based on manufacturing to one based on information) tools are being developed to keep up with that change in a way that was never before possible.

The question, however, becomes one of the chicken-or-egg variety: Which came first, the computer or the need for it? Have we created the apparent need for all of this information as something to do with the microelectronic hardware, or has the development of the hardware fulfilled a need we had for more, better, and faster information? Is the "information society" a step toward a higher form of economic society or merely a self-fulfilling prophecy, a delusion of the corporate management in this country, and a hoax perpetrated on the rest of the society in order to consolidate economic power that has been seen slipping into the hands of the mass middle class since the end of World War II?

The Mechanics of Computing the Economy

Because of the pure volume of data, this has been a computer timesharing chore—with such information providers as Chase Econometrics/Interactive Data, Data Resources, and Wharton Econometrics selling this information. Each provider of the information uses a slightly different model and each makes certain assumptions when analyzing the results.

In the past few months, however, a macroeconomic model product has emerged for the IBM PC. Called the FairModel (after Ray Fair, the Yale economics professor who designed it), was programmed and is being sold by Urban Systems Research & Engineering, Inc. (2067 Massachusetts, Ave., Cambridge MA 02140, 617-661-1550).

The program comes in a stand-alone model or a model that runs in cooperation with Lotus 1,2,3 an integrated software package that has spreadsheet, word processing, and database management. FairModel also runs on a number of IBM-compatible machines.

Whereas much fundamental and technical analysis software is time-saving, FairModel is billed as primarily a *money* saver. With timesharing systems costing $50 per hour and up, if an analyst wants to change a variable on the model and do another run to compare how the economy would react to, say, a difference in interest rates of 10 percent or 12 percent, that can be an expensive change. With the PC, the analyst can change this or any of 110 "exogenous" or user-defined variables and make another run in only a few minutes. The other 128 variables in the 238-variable model are "endogenous" (defined by the model itself).

With a price tag of approximately $2,500 for a yearly subscription (which includes quarterly updates with all the new national economic data), analysts can make numerous passes at the model changing one or many variables each time so as not to be locked into the model designer's assumptions. In addition, the analysis is not weighted by the model designer before being given to the user, as is the case with some timesharing systems.

The model projects the state of the American economy out by 12 quarters—three years—using data from three years prior to the date of the analysis and estimates of data projected out 12 months. Each quarterly update provides figures for all the exogenous and endogenous variables. The exogenous variables are assigned by Fair using his knowledge and previous experience with the model. Each of these 110 variables can be changed by the user if he feels it is not accurate or if the real economic picture has changed suddenly.

For example, in February of 1984 major banks in the country raised their prime interest rate by one-half point from 11 to 11½ percent. This rise would not be reflected in the FairModel until the end of the January-March quarter, when a new set of numbers and projections were issued. But to a user wanting to find the state of affairs in early March, it is important that he be able to change that prime rate number immediately to see the effect on the rest of the economy and the investing picture.

In addition, the program projects voter behavior in the presidential election of 1984 (and it can be assumed that this will be recomputed for the 1988 elections) given the state of the economy and how an incumbent president could be expected to change economic policy if he decided to become a lame duck.

In December of 1983, using data through the third quarter of 1983, FairModel was predicting a more expansionary economy than many other models, with real Gross National Product (GNP) growing at a rate of 5.6 percent over the five quarters from the fourth quarter of 1983 to the fourth quarter of 1984. "The expansions driven in large part by the expenditures of the household sector," the summary of results shows.

Fair's five variables of household income show that interest rates are lower than in the recent past; decreases in income taxes have led to a rise in after-tax income; recent increases in the stock market and the relatively high savings rate during the recession when people were putting more away for a rainy day; after tax non-labor income is up because of lower tax rates and labor constraint is eased as unemployment has fallen.

"Another way of looking at this forecast is that there is currently an expansionary fiscal policy and a fairly accommodating monetary policy, which leads to a strong expansion," the summary suggests.

What would this information mean to an investor?

It would probably cause him to expect continued strong earnings, especially in consumer items, which are cyclical stocks. He might feel tempted to invest in "big ticket" consumer good companies—autos, building materials (home additions and new home building), appliance companies, etc. The stock market probably looks better than the bond market at this time. In addition, because it is a presidential election year with an incumbent running, inflation should stay low.

But given the increase in the prime rate and the sluggish stock market through the first three months of 1984, the investor who went along with this enthusiastic prediction for economic expansion might have been stung.

Indeed, the FairModel in late 1983 was predicting a Republican victory in the 1984 presidential election based on low inflation in 1983 and projected low inflation for 1984 (it began creeping up around February), and a continued high growth rate through 1984. If Ronald Reagan sought a second term, the Dec. 1983 prediction was that he would receive 57.14 percent of the popular vote. If Reagan did not run, the projection was that the Republican candidate would receive 52.65 percent of the vote.

We'll just have to wait and see.

Fair's book, *Specification, Estimation, and Analysis of Macroeconomic Models,* published by Harvard University Press, comes along with a subscription to FairModel. The book explains his theoretical background and methodology for the model and suggests that people keep testing econometric models in order to refine them.

The more traditional providers of econometric and macroeconomic work—the timesharing companies—are also beginning to come up with their own personal computer programs that help users link with the company mainframes and allow fast downloading and messaging of the data of the personal computer. This will, no doubt, cut costs for those users and may help stave off disk-based macro programs, although there will also probably be a proliferation of macro programs for personal computers as time goes on.

How FairModel fares will, for the time being, be a benchmark for other purveyors of macroeconomic material.

Chapter 7

On-Line Trading

We all have pictures in our mind of John D. Rockefeller, J.P. Morgan, and the rest of the "Robber Barons" of the late 19th and early 20th centuries sitting in their cigar-smoke-filled clubs thinking about investments. The picture we draw is often of one of these men getting up from his chair and walking over to a little bubble-like machine—almost like a light bulb with a paper dispenser in it instead of a filament—taking a thin little stream of paper in his hands, reading a few unintelligible combinations of letters and numbers, and resuming his seat with a satisfied grin.

From the time Edward Callahan designed the first stock ticker—which was modified and upgraded three years later by Thomas Edison—until the 1930s, when a company called Teleregister introduced the first electronic tote board, these glass-domed "tickertapes" dominated Wall Street and other financial centers throughout the nation. These machines that transmitted stock exchange information were the public's link with the exchange. This was wonderful for men who watched how much more or less they were worth as the price of their steel, utility, and maybe—for the daring—automobile stocks fluctuated.

But in today's world of high-speed trading, where a second's hesitation could mean a change of a quarter-point in the price of a stock, the 15-minute delay of the tickertape could be the difference between profit and loss.

Staying on Top

Today's investor now has a few products that can keep him on top of the market—Tickertec, The Monitor, and Track Man. All give a continuous, no-time-delay readout on your personal computer of one market throughout the trading day.

Bill Fredriksson, an options trader in San

Francisco, was the first person to use Tickertec for the Apple. Since options don't trade as frequently as the underlying stocks, watching the stock market like a hawk can get an options trader a few moments advantage and maybe a bargain.

Before using Tickertec, Fredriksson was "calling my broker every ten minutes to find out what a certain stock was doing. Now I have a much broader scope of information instantaneously. I have better information than they have on the floor. I can call up the last 50 or 100 transactions on a stock and get a video display." Fredriksson can also make a hard copy to help determine trends and make decisions.

Fredriksson sets buy and sell limits on specific stocks and keys the information into the computer, which lets him know if a limit has been reached by buzzing and flashing.

You can either set the system up to monitor many trades in one security, a few trades in a few securities, or only the last trade in a larger number of securities. While you are watching your target stocks, the ticker is moving constantly along the bottom of your screen.

Tickertec also allows the user to monitor daily highs and lows, receive uptick and downtick information, track big block trades, and receive all four Dow Jones averages.

The program is available from Max Ule and Co. Inc. (6 East 43rd St., New York NY 10017, 800-223-6642 and 212-687-0705). Tickertec comes in an *a la carte* fashion. The price runs from about $2,000 to about $7,000. In addition, the exchanges charge monthly fees for telephone hookups. The program runs on a variety of different machines, including Apple, IBM, TRS-80, and some CP/M machines.

The Monitor (First Flight Data Systems, P.O. Box 555, Kitty Hawk NC 27949, 919-441-6480) has many of the same features as a moderately-souped up version of Tickertec. For $1,800 plus $110 installation, you get the tickertape, a portfolio monitor, advance/decline indicator, tick index, and data files on about 2,000 stocks. Stocks' closing prices are automatically updated at the end of the day and you can do analysis after the close of the market. There is also a program that allows the user to write his own utility programs on the diskette in BASIC. The system runs on an Apple II with 32 or 48K of memory and only needs one disk drive.

Track Man (Track Man Systems Inc., 11 Broadway—3rd Floor, New York NY 10004, 212-269-5460) is a slightly different product from the previous two. With Track Man, you play "what if" games by determining a possible strategy, then Track Man computes the percentage change of successfully carrying out that strategy.

If you want to sell one stock and buy another, Track Man will compute for you your profit or loss on the trade by trading now, or by waiting for future circumstances to arise. Once you have decided which set of circumstances you would like to place your trade at, you set Track Man to monitor the situation until those circumstances come up. When they do, it signals you to conduct your trade. This system can be very helpful if dealing with tax swap strategies and options strategies.

Track Man runs on the Apple II+ and *II*e, with some peripheral equipment (including a modem) necessary. Its cost is $325 for the software, about $500 per month for the Monchik-Weber database to receive quotes and exchange fees.

Just Like the Big Kids

Some of the traditional brokerage house quote vendors are getting into the act, attempting to sell systems to the individual investor who uses a computer.

Bunker-Ramo will lease you one of their little three-inch Telquote III monitors for $425 a month.

Quotron offers the VuSet, installed by the local phone company for $300 and costing $266 a month after that, plus extra for the specialized Quotron databases. Quotedial will also be offered from Quotron for personal computer owners. The databases will be available from the close of the market each afternoon until 7:30 A.M. For $160 per month plus exchange fees, the user can get round-the-clock service.

Tymeshare Inc. sells the Scanset XL terminal for $895 through mail order businesses.

Teleware Inc. has designed Teleminder and Telebroker for the IBM PC and Apple II. Telebroker is an on-line portfolio maintenance program that costs $1,495; Teleminder is an automatic dial-up and download program that can be programmed to call a database and retrieve information without the user being around. Its cost is $295.

ADP Comtrend hopes to be out soon with its Trendsetter system, a hardware and software product that will allow users to pick up via microwave dish antenna or hooking into an antenna all the latest quotes as well as information from the Dow Jones News/Retrieval Service and other sources. This will, it is hoped, do away with paying on-line time charges. The system will be compatible with IBM PCs and CP/M operating system computers, or will come with its own hardware from Convergent Technologies.

For $600 per month plus exchange fees a single user will receive the complete hardware/software package, including a 10-megabyte hard disk. The system can handle up to five more terminals at $150 per month per terminal, so the neighborhood investment club can all plug into one system if they want.

For those who are still into smoking their cigars and drinking their port while the ticker clackety-clacks in the corner of the office, Trans-Lux, which has served the denizens of Wall Street since 1925, offers a leased paper ticker for $85 per month. Their top-of-the-line ticker goes for $1,350 per month. (By the way, Trans-Lux invented the mirrored prism projection system that enlarged the ticker and made it convenient for large numbers of people to press their noses against the broker's windows to catch a glimpse of their fortunes as the last trade passes by.)

New Technologies

In addition to the computer hardware and software for staying on top of the market, there are devices based on some of the newest technology that some style-conscious investors will *just have to have.*

The most notable system currently is Pocket Quote, an 11-ounce radio receiver from Telemet America Inc. that picks up over the FM radio band quotes on stocks and options, as well as automatic alerts to breaking news and preselected stocks. This is so you don't miss anything while you're driving from your home computer to your office computer. The unit costs $349 and the service costs $249 per year. So far, the service only, extends 50 miles out from each one of its receivers, which are located in Boston, Chicago, Los Angeles, Miami, New York, and Washington D.C. And you thought all those joggers running through Central Park during their lunch breaks were listening to music on those headsets. The day will surely come—and not too far in the future—when you will be able to listen to your quote radio while sitting on your tractor, walking to lunch, or camping in the Grand Tetons.

Chapter 8

Bonds

Some investors wish to diversify their portfolios further than is possible by investing in a number of different stocks—or equities. These investors, especially the more conservative ones, tend to look at investment in bonds as one of the primary answers to the diversification issue.

Bonds are debt instruments, an obligation on the part of the company to pay the holder of the bond the face value of the bond at the date of maturity. Bonds provide little capital gain potential in comparison to stocks. Because of this, a reasonably high rate of interest is offered to bondholders by the company for the right to hold and use the investor's money.

If an investor purchases a new bond issued by a corporation, he pays face value (par), usually $1,000. Each year from then on until the bond matures or expires, the corporation pays a fixed rate of interest to the bondholder. Bonds can also be purchased in the open market, or aftermarket. If interest rates should go up, old bonds, with their lower interest, will be less desirable and command lower prices on the open market. By buying these bonds and holding them until they either command more on the open market or until they mature, an investor can make a capital gain (either long- or short-term, depending on how long the bond has been held).

In addition to corporate bonds, government entities issue bonds. The federal government issues Treasury bonds, which have maturities of five years to 30 years; Treasury bills, which run from six months to five years; and Treasury notes, which run from seven to 90 days. State governments issue bonds for all sorts of capital projects from roads and sewers to new jails and universities. Local governments issue bonds to cover capital projects and also to borrow money for regular expenses during times of the year when they have no income (property taxes are usually paid twice a year and between the property tax dates many communities live off "general revenue" or "tax anticipation" bonds). Bonds issued by cities and towns are known as municipal bonds. Many of these state and local bonds are exempt from all state and federal taxes, making them a way that many investors shelter money from taxes.

Bonds have traditionally been thought of as a safe haven for capital, since in the event of a company's liquidation, holders of corporate bonds are the first investors to be paid after banks and other lending institutions, holders of short-term notes, and holders of mortgage-type bonds "secured" by the company's real assets. After bondholders are paid, holders of "subordinated debentures" (a *debenture* is another term for an unsecured corporate bond) are paid, then equity investors. In addition, bondholders are guaranteed first that they will be paid their yearly interest rates. If you remember the Gulf States Utilities financial statements from Chapter 4, interest expenses were listed above the "bottom line" net revenue figure that was used to compute earnings per share. A company can declare a lower dividend or no dividend at all for a quarter or longer, but it can't declare that it will not pay its interest payments without going into default.

But even a bond portfolio must be diversified in order to ensure safety, as we have seen in the recent past with the failure of the Washington Power Pool in Washington State and the default on that system's interest payments to its bondholders. Since bonds come in minimum denominations of $1,000 ($500 for some municipal bonds) and commissions don't really become reasonable unless you buy $5,000 or $10,000, diversification in the bond market is a rich folk's game.

Recently the municipal bond unit trust has become popular with smaller investors, providing a diversified portfolio of tax-exempt bonds. Taxable bond funds have been around longer. Most of these funds allow $1,000 minimum investment in the funds, diversify each fund over dozens of bond issues, and provide reasonably high rates of return. Funds also narrow the range of bonds they invest in so participants can tailor their investments. Some funds invest in only the highest grade bonds, those rated AAA by Standard and Poor's or Aaa by Moody's Investor Services. Other funds buy "junk bonds," which are more speculative and often graded BB or B by S&P or Ba or B by Moody's. These two rating services rate bonds from "investment grade" of Aaa for Moody's and AAA for S&P all the way down to C, which is a highly speculative bond. The better the bond rating, the less money the corporation or government entity has to offer as interest to attract investors. Many investors invest in only the safest, least speculative, and lowest-interest paying bonds.

Bonds pay a fixed rate of return each year with payment made semiannually. Some bonds are *coupon* bonds, while others are *registered*.

A coupon bond is delivered to a holder as a certificate with a number of coupons attached. One coupon must be clipped each half year and taken to a participant bank for redemption (hence the derisive term "coupon clipper's elbow," reputed to be one of the health scourges of rich people). Registered bonds are registered on the books of the issuing company and semiannual checks are sent to the bondholders. Registered bonds are theoretically safer, since the bonds cannot be stolen or lost and interest redeemed or sold. The coupon bond is payable to the bearer and the company has no record of the purchaser (hence the term "bearer bond," a favorite way of hiding ill-gotten cash from the IRS). All bond funds are registered. The bonds are held by the brokerage house underwriting the fund and payment is made to the fundholders monthly, quarterly, semiannually, or annually in the form of checks, shares in the brokerage house's money market mutual fund, or further investments in the bond fund.

How Does the Bond Market Work?

Although bonds pay a set rate of interest, they still have the intrinsic ability to move up or down in price from their face value or *par*. This is because of the change in interest rates. The interest rate in the general economy determines the interest rates of bonds. If a bond issued last year has an interest rate of 11.0 percent and interest rates have dropped since then so that a new (comparably rated) bond issued today only pays 10.2 percent, then the 11 percent bond will sell at a "premium" over par. Conversely, bonds that are 10 and 15 years old might only pay 6 percent and will sell at a "discount" from par in the secondary bond market.

The bond market moves to some extent in relation with the stock market, although this has been true in the past to a much greater extent than at the present. There are many reasons for this.

First, you must understand that there are really *two* bond markets. There is the new bond market and the secondary bond market. While new bonds often attract investors during bad stock market periods, the market for old bonds tends to move in tandem with the stock market. However, this has been skewed to some extent by the money market mutual funds.

Before we try to sort out this complex relationship, let's take just a moment to explore the money market funds. To a great degree, these are like stock market mutual funds, or bond funds—a group of investors pooling their money to get the best possible rate of return with the least possible risk. But instead of investing in stocks or bonds, they invest in "money market instruments," short-term lending often called "commercial paper."

As a comedian once said, "there is $149.95 in cash in the whole world; the rest is on ledger books."

Companies often need money and they often can't go to the "public" to float bonds or sell more stock. Other businesses are privately owned and can only borrow on the private money market.

We were all involved in the money market well before we knew it. As I have said before, we are all investors of one sort or another. We pay premiums to insurance companies and put money in pension funds. We also put money in checking and savings accounts—only when we got 5¼ percent we were called savers; now that we get 9¼ percent we're called investors. Well, there is a *quantitative* difference in what we invest in through those different accounts, although not a *qualitative* difference.

When you put money in a traditional savings account at a savings bank, your money is pooled with other people's to invest in mortgages, car loans, home-improvement loans, college loans, and all sorts of other person-to-person type loans. Deposits made in commercial banks often went to make loans to the small businessperson—long-term at fixed rates, or rates that floated with the prime interest rate.

What many of us didn't know was that, in addition to these loans, banks also make very short-term loans at very high interest rates to other banks and to companies, often for as little time as overnight or over the weekend. By using a certain amount of our savings (or invested money) for these lucrative loans, the banks could afford to loan long-term at rates that had little built-in margin for them (keeping borrowers happy), and to give us some services (tellers, record-keeping, cashiers' checks, etc.) that cost them money.

Then along came brokerage houses that decided to take small investors' money away from banks with money market mutual funds. These funds were designed specifically to pool investors' money into accounts to invest in these short-term loans and pay the investor a much larger percentage of the return. With bank deregulation, many banks set up their own funds to do the same thing, thereby luring customers back to the bank with slightly lower rates but the same Federal Deposit Insurance Corporation (FDIC) insurance that investors had on traditional savings accounts.

Now, what effect has all this had on the bond market?

Let's look first at the way the stock market and bond market traditionally related to each other.

In the good old days, individual investors—even big investors—kept some money in the banks and invested the rest in stocks and bonds. If interest rates went up, many investors would leave the stock market and buy new bonds that paid a high interest rate: the stock market usually sinks in times of higher interest rates because the cost of borrowing money for a company is rising, thereby lowering the amount of after-interest-payment income that is reflected in earnings per share. At the same time, the market for old bonds would usually drop—not in lockstep with the stock market, but usually close. Old bonds with lower interest rates weren't worth as much to prospective buyers. There were, of course, some people looking to buy discounted bonds for their capital gains potential but not that many.

Of course, the stock market and the bond market reacted to different kinds of news in different ways. Higher interest rates might move the new bond market higher, the old bond market lower, and the stock market lower. (Of course, the stock market is not uniform, as our understanding of beta tells us.) Good news of lower interest rates might raise the stock market and old bond market by relatively equal amounts, while other forms of good economic news—higher family income, for instance—might not lower interest rates but might get some stock market play from investors who think that consumers with more disposable income will spend rather than save, specifically because they only get 5¼ percent no matter what.

The cause of higher or lower interest rates can have an effect on how the bond market/stock market relationship works. Higher inflation might not hurt the stock market as long as corporate profits remain high (prices rising faster than wages), but might hurt the bond market because interest rates drift up in an effort to reflect higher inflation and even moderate inflation by getting people to borrow less and spin each $149.95 into the economy fewer times. This is called *lowering the money supply*. Higher federal deficits without high inflation might cause interest rates on bonds to go up as the government competes against private business for borrowing funds while stocks remain fairly high because with low to moderate inflation, corporate profits are still relatively high. (This was the situation, to some extent, in the first half of 1984.)

Money market mutual funds throw a wrench into all this by giving investors a place to park their money when stocks are going bad without having to commit it to bonds, and by giving bondholders an alternative place to earn fairly high interest rates.

The presence of money market funds seems to have set new floors on the level of interest Americans will accept for their savings. This floor seems to be about 8½ percent, well above the previous level for savings accounts. How will this affect the future of the bond market, and how will it affect the future of the way the bond market relates to the stock market? For the first few years these funds were in effect they were still paying interest that was less than the rate of inflation. But in 1982 that all turned around, and in 1984 the funds were paying *double* the rate of inflation and going up in tandem with the prime interest rate and other lending interest rates rather than in relation to the inflation rate.

Who Does What Investing in the Bond Market?

Why would one buy a bond at premium or discount rather than a new bond at par? A big part is taxes. (We'll discuss taxes a lot more in our chapter on portfolio management.) Another reason is the need for current and continuous income.

Let's look at two brief examples.

One is a widow who just collected $100,000 in life insurance. She would like to get as much income from that money as possible. By buying bonds at a premium, she will get bonds with higher interest rates. If the general trend of interest rates is down, she will do better to buy the bonds earlier, before the premium gets even higher. She doesn't much care if the market for bonds goes down or stays even, but if it goes up she may lose her advantage.

The other example is of a youngish couple (in their 40s) who earn $75,000 per year and want to transfer some income to capital gains. By buying discount bonds, they receive little income now (but they don't need it) and sell the bond for a capital gain (the difference between the face value of the bond and the price paid). They don't care if the market goes up or stays even, but if it goes down they could lose their capital gain advantage.

Of course, it's not that simple, as can be seen from the complexities of bond pricing and computing yield.

In order to determine if a bond should sell at a discount or a premium, you must calculate the holding-period yield, current yield, and the yield to maturity. The discount or premium is determined in an effort to even all bonds in terms of current yield and yield to maturity. Of course, not all bonds will have the same yields; this will depend on the longevity of the bond and the rating, as well as the supply/demand for bonds of that general type.

The holding-period yield can be shown in the following formula:

$$HPY = \frac{(P_1 - P_0) + I}{P_0}$$

where the following representations are made:

HPY	is the holding-period yield.
I	is the interest payments.
P_0	is the beginning price.
P_1	is the ending price.

As you can see, the price is the important variable here. If you are anticipating holding the bond until maturity, P_1 is the par, while P_0 is the price you paid.

The yield to maturity is equal to the annual interest minus the amortization of the premium you pay over the life of the bond (or plus a yearly percentage of the discount) as the numerator over a denominator made up of the cost price plus the maturity price divided by 2. The maturity date of the bond is important, since to get the same yield to maturity for a bond with a shorter lifespan you will have to pay more than for one with a longer life. Conversely, the farther out the maturity period, the deeper the discount.

The yield to maturity can be understood from the following formula:

$$Y + \frac{I + \dfrac{1{,}000 - M}{N}}{\dfrac{P + M}{2}}$$

where the following holds:

- Y is the approximate yield.
- I is the annual coupon interest.
- P is the par value of the bond ($1,000).
- M is the market price of the bond.
- N is the number of years during which the bond will remain outstanding.

In effect, the approximate yield to maturity equals the average annual return divided by the average annual investing in the bond.

Bond prices are quoted in terms of *bid* and *ask*. Sometimes they are quoted in terms of a price such as 102, meaning a $1,000 bond would sell for $102 for each $100 of face value, or $1,020 total. Other times it is quoted in terms of the yield one would like to either get after buying the bond, or sell the bond for. A $1,000 face bond bid at 7.0 means the buyer would like to get a 7 percent yield *to maturity* on the bond. If the interest rate is also 7.0 percent, the bidder is bidding 100.

If the ask price is 6.75, it means the seller wants to sell the bond so the yield is only 6.75, not 7.0. In order to get a 6.75 yield to maturity on a 7.0 percent bond, you must pay 102.72, or $1,027.20. (In this case, the prevailing rate for current bonds is 6.75 and the buyer is buying a bond wth a higher coupon—hence the premium on the bond price.)

In addition to the basic price of the bond, the purchaser must pay the *accrued interest* from the date of the last interest payment to the date of the purchase.

This is only the beginning of the complexities of investing in bonds. There are *floating rate* bonds, *zero coupon* bonds (similar to U.S. Savings Bonds in that they pay no regular interest but sell at a deep discount from face value and pay full face value at maturity), and *government reinvestment mortgage* bonds such as Ginnie Maes (Government National Mortgage Association) and Freddy Macs (Federal Home Loan Mortgage Corporation) bonds.

As you can see, the widow and the young couple have a lot to take into consideration. When it all boils down, our instincts—income for her, capital gain for them—are probably right.

Things to Consider in Buying Bonds

Bond analysis goes beyond the simple interest rate risks and inflationary or purchasing power risks, and beyond weighing bonds against the alternatives of money market funds. It must take into account a number of the other factors the macroeconomic model maker dealt with: employment, credit demands, and consumer spending, as well as the government's monetary and fiscal policy.

In addition, there are a number of unsystematic risks that must be examined.

What are the earnings and charges associated with the purchase? A company must be looked at in terms of its earnings before interest and taxes to see if it has proper coverage for making timely interest payments on all its bonds, including subordinated debentures. After all, if the company goes bankrupt, even the mortgage-bond holders can lose their money.

A look at the capitalization figures of a company would do a potential bond investor well. How much debt is there as opposed to equity, and in what form is that debt? How long are the maturity dates, and are they spread out? What are the interest rates? How much preferred and preference stock is there?

The liquidity of the company must also be examined. Companies can be cash-poor yet asset-rich.

Another thing to look for is how the company foresees buying the bonds back—all at once or at various times—and how well it has funded the mechanism to do that. Sometimes companies put money in an escrow account that collects interest and will buy back all the bonds at once. Other times the company puts the money in a sinking fund to buy back portions of the bonds at various times, either through the marketplace or through calling them in from purchasers. If a bond is "called," par value is paid. Sometimes companies promise bondholders not to pay too much in common stock dividends so as not to weaken the cash position of the company and jeopardize future payments of interest and principal.

Municipal bonds must also be studied for how they can be expected to cover their debt and how much they are borrowing in relation to their taxable base (real estate property tax for a city).

A Word about Taxes

As I mentioned earlier in the chapter, part of the reason for deciding which bond to invest in is determined by taxes.

Think of two investors buying bonds that yield 10 percent to maturity. One bond pays interest of 10 percent, the other pays interest of 7 percent and was bought on a discount. Their total after-tax yield is different.

Assuming they are both in the 50 percent bracket, the purchaser of the 10 percent bond will have after-tax yield of five percent (half of 10 percent). In figures it looks like this: $50\% \times 10\% = 5\%$ taxed $= 5\%$ after-tax income.

The other bondholder will have after-tax yield of 5.9 percent (half of 7 percent plus 20 percent of 3 percent). This equation looks like this: $(50\% \times 7\% = 3.5\%) + (20\% \left[\text{capital gain rate} \right] \times 3\% = .6\%) = 4.1\%$ taxed $= 5.9\%$ after-tax income.

Interest from state and municipal bonds is exempt from federal income taxes, although capital gains are not. In addition, many states exempt interest from their own bonds from state income taxes.

What's on the Computer?

Choosing the particular bond to invest in can involve a lot of calculations. Bond computations are real sliderule-and-scratch pad work and ideal for computerization. A number of programs have been designed for personal computers.

Bonds and Interest Rate Software (Programmed Press, 2301 Balis Ave., Elmont NY 11003, 516-775-0933) runs on the Apple II, II+ and *II*e, IBM PC, and all models of TRS-80. Its cost is $100 and $19.95 for the handbook of programs. There are 16 programs that calculate bond and interest rate data to help evaluate price, risk, and return. This is one of several packages of Programmed Press software. A total package, Investment Software Package, contains 50 programs. For those who don't mind copying programs out of books onto diskettes, Programmed Press sells their 220-page guidebook, including all 50 programs, for $19.95.

The Bond Manager (Analytical Service Associates, 21 Hollis Rd., Lynn MA 01904,

617-593-2404)costs $150 and runs on the IBM PC and the Apple II+. Information is keyed in by the user. Bond Manager has nine programs that handle price projections, charting, portfolio management and maintenance, yield computations, return computations, and more. You can keep track of your own portfolio on a data diskette and do "what if" projections to determine how your portfolio would be affected by changes in the bond market. Charts can be made that show changes in yields, interest rates, percentage down from high, percentage up from low, and more. The program also does analysis of convertible bonds but the company has a program, The Convertible Bond Analyst, that does this in more depth.

Convertible bonds are somewhat like Minotaurs—they have the head of a bond and the body of a stock. They allow the investor to take part in the best and worst of both worlds—the stability of a "base" interest rate and base price for the bond below which it will not fall, and the possibility of getting capital gains in the form of stock.

"A convertible is for an investor who would like to participate in a company's growth but doesn't want to take the pure gamble," says Michael McNamara, formerly with Prudential-Bache in Chestnut Hill MA. George Manna of Analytical Services, an investment advisor who designed The Convertible Bond Analyst and The Bond Manager, calls convertidles "a poor man's hedge."

Here's how they work: The convertible is issued with a face value of $1,000 as subordinated debentures. It is convertible at any time before the maturity date by the purchaser for a set amount of shares in the company's common stock. The bond can also be called by the issuing company, which then either pays face value or issues stock—forcing the investor to convert or liquidate.

Because the bond has a coupon and yield to maturity like a straight bond, it can never fall below open market value for a straight bond with the same yield. If interest rates go down, this base price moves up. Since stock prices are also interest-sensitive to some extent, a double gain can be attained this way if the stock price rises. The convertible provides some income for the investor who believes a company's stock has future potential while he waits for the "inevitable" price rise. There is a point at which the value of the instrument as a bond and as stock crosses, and the decision on whether to convert has to be made on thoughts of appreciation as a stock as opposed to the income value of the bond.

Strategies for playing convertibles can be as conservative or aggressive as an investor wants, and depend on how the trading in the convertible is tracking—closer to the bond value or the stock value. If the convertible is selling near the open market bond value, a drop in the stock price can't force the price of the convertible down much. But a rise in the stock value can make the convertible worth that much more—a conservative buy. On the other hand, if the convertible is selling near the value of the stock, a slight drop in stock price can send the value of the convertible plummetting—a sell.

Convertibles have become more popular in the past few years from the points of view of both investors and the companies that issue them. Investments in convertibles have gone from $1 billion to $18 billion between 1980 and 1983, according to McNamara.

In terms of companies, convertibles offer flexibility. They don't have to dilute stock value by issuing more equity, yet they don't have to get tied down with more burdensome long-term debt. In addition, convertible bonds pay lower interest rates than straight bonds, and at a future time the company can retire the debt by calling the bonds and issuing stock to those who want it. It is also a convenient way to issue more debt in a bull market, since investors will want the possibility of stock appreciation.

Since convertibles don't trade heavily, there is opportunity to pick up undervalued issues. The Convertible Bond Analyst is designed to calculate such things as premium over investment value (in both points and percentages), conversion parity, premium over conversion in percent, current yield, payback in years, break-even time, and yield to maturity. The program provides graphic as well as numerical readout. Its cost is $225 for IBM and $175 for Apple II+.

Bond Master (Outwater and Wells, 15 Exchange Place, Jersey City NJ 07302, 201-434-8900) runs on the Apple II+ (64K) and IBM PC and costs $1,100. In a question-and-answer format, Bond Master allows you to set up portfolios with up to 110 bonds in memory and an infinite number stored on diskettes. It calculates prices and yields, bond swaps, compares two complete packages of bonds including rating, par value, price, average coupon, annual income, and block size.

Bondscholar (Investechnic, P.O. Box 1006, Jackson MS 39205, 601-355-1335) runs on the IBM PC and PC-XT, the Hewlett Packard 80 series, and the Apple II and *II*e. Basic price is $1,995; four $500 modules are available.

Bondscholar is geared toward the professional bond trader. On a single screen or page printout it gives all the standard data for corporate bonds and calculates internal rate or return, after-tax IRR, taxable yield in annual and semi-annual equivalent, and semi-annual IRR. Compound after-tax rate of return (for variable tax rate) and future value (on a per-dollar basis) are computed for variable reinvestment rates, whereas many programs compute the reinvestment rate as the original interest rate.

One module handles bond swaps, while a second handles mortgage-backed securities. A third module does leverage analysis—tax arbitrage to determine your total after-tax rate if you borrow (interest payments on borrowing are tax-deductible to invest in high yielding securities). The fourth module, the "reinvestment scan module," helps determine how three securities compare against each other at all different reinvestment rates from 11 to 18 percent.

The Bond Swap Analyzer (Technical Data, Financial Software Division, One Post Office Square, Boston MA 02109, 617-482-3341) runs on an IBM PC (128K double density diskettes) or Apple II+ (80 column board) and costs $675.

This is one of a series of four bond programs by Technical Data. The other three are The Fixed Income Portfolio Manager, The Rate of Return Analyzer, and The Yield Calculator.

The Bond Swap Analyzer analyzes bond swaps under various market conditions. It computes yield, price, duration, and other data and evaluates swaps to a user-specified end period, designation of reinvestment rates and displays cash flows, realized rates of return, and profitability. You can also get a break-even reinvestment rate for each swap. Each side of the swap can involve up to 10 bonds.

The Fixed Income Portfolio Manager is a portfolio management and analysis program that can handle all sorts of fixed income instruments including corporate, municipal, federal bonds, mortgage reinvestment bonds (Ginnie Maes, Freddie Macs and Fannie Maes), Euro Bonds, and Certificates of Deposit. Over 30 indicators are kept up-to-date, including annual income, accrued interest, and book value. Pricing is done manually at the keyboard. The program will do "matrix pricing" if you don't want to update all prices. In matrix pricing, a few benchmark bonds are priced and the rest are automatically adjusted to retain the previous spread in the yield to maturity. The program runs on the IBM PC or PC-XT (128K and double density) and costs $925.

The Rate of Return Analyzer allows you to compute total rate of return for up to 14 securities at a time based on your own assumptions, then perform "what ifs" to see how the total rate would be affected by changes in the composition of the portfolio. The current yield curve, hypothetical yield curve, and rate of return can be graphed on one screen. The program runs on the IBM PC and PC-XT (128K) and costs $700.

The Yield Calculator calculates yields for all kinds of bonds and notes, including yield to maturity, yield to call, and current yield. This is a subset of abilities in the other programs. The program runs on the Apple II+ (80 columns) and the IBM PC (128K); it costs $275 for the Apple version and $375 for the IBM.

Converticalc (RPH Associates, P.O. Box 1155, Weston CT 06883) runs on the Apple II (64K and VisiCalc) and costs $95 for individuals, $195 for corporate clients with duplication privileges. The program is a template that fits over the VisiCalc program to provide computations for the 100 most actively traded convertible bonds on the New York and American stock exchanges. It calculates premium over common stock, yield to maturity, and time it will take for the yield of the convertible to recoup the premium. A monthly and quarterly update service is available.

The Financial Package (Computer Asset Management, P.O. Box 26743, Salt Lake City UT 84126, 801-964-0391) runs on the Apple II+ and *II*e and costs $49.95. While not specifically a bond program, it does compute bond yields, internal rate of return, IRA projections, and more.

Investor (Embassy Computer Products, Inc., P.O. Box 88, Little Neck NY 11363, 212-961-9806) runs on the Commodore VIC 20 and the Commodore 64; it costs $24.95 for diskette and $19.95 for tape. Again, this is not a bond program but it does do bond calculations as well as analysis of IRAs, savings accounts, and other things in terms of cash flow and future value.

Master Brain (Decision Programming Corporation, 10401 Grosvenor Place, Suite G17, Rockville MD 20852, 301-493-6444) runs on the Apple II or IBM PC and costs $225. The program performs all calculations on municipal, federal, corporate, and zero-coupon bonds, notes, and bills. The "what if" method is used to determine total after-tax yield for different holding periods, interest rates, and owner tax brackets. It also computes IRAs and annuities.

Microcomputer Bond Program (Dynacomp Inc., 1427 Monroe Ave., Rochester NY 14618, 800-828-6772) runs on all personal computers and costs $59.95 for diskette and $55.95 for cassette. The program has storage for portfolios and does standard computations such as bond yields before maturity and bond prices estimated over time, at various market interests either to maturity or early call, and bond valuations.

Personal Financial Analysis (Wiley Professional Software, John Wiley & Sons, Inc., 605 Third Ave. New York NY, 10158) runs on the IBM PC and costs $60. The program is not specifically a bond program but a modular program that helps analyze a number of fixed-rate based investment and personal financial obligations. The program has modules on tax-free securities, convertible bonds, retirement funds, home mortgages, and interest rates. Information is keyed in and standard calculations are made.

SOFIE (System of Fixed Income Evaluation) (PM Software, 4101 W. St. N.W., Washington D.C. 20007) runs on the Apple II (80 columns) and the IBM PC and costs $350 to $495 depending on the portfolio capacity. This is mostly a portfolio management system for bondholders, although some standard bond calculations are done. Up to 60 portfolios, each with an unlimited number of securities, can be maintained by the system. The rating, quantity, description, coupon, maturity date, price, yield, and acquisition date are all recorded. Monthly cash flow and total principal invested are displayed, and it can handle bonds, notes, T-bills, DCs, and other fixed-rate securities.

Chapter 9

Options

An *option* is a contract that gives the holder the right to either buy or sell a block of 100 shares of stock at a given price by a certain date. Options can be either a highly speculative or a very conservative investment, depending on whether they are used for hedging or speculation.

The idea behind simply buying or selling—otherwise known as "writing" an option is not complex. However, there are a number of option strategies that call for enough computations that the advent of personal computer programs for analyzing options has made things easier for individual investors.

A *put* option allows the purchaser to sell 100 shares of a certain stock by a given date for a predetermined price. When one sells a put, he is "putting" shares of stock to another person, the buyer of the option.

A *call* option allows one to buy stock by a given date for a predetermined price. When one writes a call option, he is "calling" shares for purchase from another person, the owner of the shares who has written the option.

Options are transacted through brokers. The purchase price of an option is called the *premium* and the price at which the underlying block of stock the option is written against is valued is called the *strike price*. Option contracts expire quarterly—on a January/April/July/October schedule, a February/May/August/November schedule, or a March/June/September/December schedule.

For instance, if a June call is written on ABC company at 25, it means the purchaser of the call has the option of buying the 100 shares of stock represented by the option by June 15 for 25 per share. The premium price of the call will be determined by the price at which the stock traded when the call was purchased.

The premium price for an option is dependent on two variables—the difference between the strike price and the current stock price, and length of time between the present and the exercise date. An option for a strike price closer to the current stock price costs more than a strike price further from the current price. An exercise date further off costs less than a closer one. When analyzing options one also must take into account such factors as the volatility of the underlying stock in order to judge the probability that price prediction will be reflective of true price.

Options were first traded over-the-counter in the 1930s and regulated by the SEC and the National Association of Security Dealers (NASD), the industry's trade association. Since 1973, when the Chicago Board of Options Exchange opened, trading only call options on about 25 stocks, the market has flourished. Today hundreds of options are traded on four exchanges.

Not only are options traded on individual stocks, but options are now traded on stock exchange indexes. And if gambling on the stock exchange isn't speculative enough for you, you can bet on whether interest rates will go up or down, the future price of treasury bills, and foreign currency. The SEC is constantly considering new options. It is almost getting to be like a British bookmaking operation. Options trading is governed by the Options Clearing Corporation. As we will see from further examination of options, this has thrown a wrench in the technical analyst's sentiment indicator of short selling, since speculators can now purchase puts or sell calls as well as sell short if they think a certain stock price will go down.

In terms of carrying out the analysis on an underlying stock issue before purchasing an option, a combination of fundamental analysis and technical analysis should probably be used. Medium-range and long-range technical indicators can help, while many of the highly sophisticated short-term price/volume indicators are probably more difficult to weave into an options analysis.

Who Writes Options and Why

An individual's relationship to the options market depends basically on whether or not he owns stock in a company. For this example, let's look at two people—Bruce and Mara—and follow them through the options game.

Bruce owns 100 shares of XYZ company which sells for $30 per share. Mara has other investments, but no XYZ.

Bruce and Mara each decide to buy a call for XYZ. Bruce is said to be buying a "covered" call, since he owns shares of the underlying stock. Mara is said to be buying an "uncovered" or "naked" call, since she does not own shares.

Why would each one of these people be purchasing a call?

Basically, a call option is bought because a purchaser believes the market will go up. If Bruce and Mara think the stock will go to 40 by September, they may want to lock in a purchase price of 35 in February by purchasing a September 35 call on XYZ. If the price of the stock goes to 40, they have each made $5 per share, minus the premium paid to the writer and the broker's commission. If the price doesn't make it to 35, all Bruce has lost is the commission. If the stock doesn't make it to 35, they don't exercise the option and only lose the premium and commission—usually about 15 percent of the value of the underlying shares.

What if they had been the call writers?

If Bruce had thought the stock would go to 40 per share he certainly would not have written a call for 35, because he could have made more by selling the stock at 40 than by selling a call at 35. The call writer's motives are often some quick income—the premium—and the gamble that the stock won't go up to the exercise price plus the premium. Bruce is essentially hedging.

The naked call writer is in another boat. If the stock goes above the strike price, the naked call writer must go into the open market to purchase a block of stock in order to meet his or her obligation to the call purchaser. Mara is essentially speculating.

In our example, if Bruce and Mara each wrote September 35 calls on XYZ and the stock went to 40, Bruce wouldn't make as much—35 plus the premium—as he would have made had he held the stock and sold it at 40, but Mara would have lost money. Her out-of-pocket expenses for speculating and losing are the same as the added gain Bruce lost by hedging. Put another way, the naked call writer's losses are the call purchaser's gains.

What About Puts?

Puts are written when either a speculator or the owner of an underlying stock thinks the price will fall. In the case of a put, the owner of the stock is the purchaser of the option, not the writer. If the price of the stock at the expiration date is still above the strike price, the put purchaser exercises the option to sell the 100 shares. If he or she does not own the underlying shares, he goes into the market and purchases them at less than the strike price, thereby profiting the difference between the open market price and the put strike price. Writing a put is very much like selling a call or selling stock short.

The writer of the put, who will accept the shares if the owner exercises his option, receives the premium. If the value of the underlying stock does not go down to the strike price, he or she pockets the premium and leaves. (An option writer's potential profit is always no more than the premium.)

For speculators, buying a put is often more desirable than selling short. The premium is usually less than the margin and the downside risk is limited to the premium if the stock price goes up, where the risk of selling short is unlimited.

Getting Fancy

You can set up any combination of option purchases in the hopes of beating the percentages. But remember, stated in the lengthy discourse on fixed costs in Chapter 3, premiums and brokerage costs can eat you alive.

In addition to all the individual investors in the options market, there are market makers, specialists, and registered options traders who are all charged to some degree by the SEC and the NASD with keeping the options trading markets orderly. These traders incur only minimal commissions in their trading and trade in large amounts, so they can take advantage of a lot of situations in which individual investors cannot participate.

While an individual may think a *spread*—buying one call at one strike price and selling another call at another strike price—is fancy and allows for play between the two prices, a sophisticated market player may take the concept a step further and *scalp*—buy an option at the big price and sell it at the offer price immediately—in a game that is played to fractions of percentages. The individual may want to try a *vertical spread,* buying two calls that expire on the same date, or a *time spread,* where the options expire at different dates.

Many of these market players have been using sophisticated computer models for a number of years. While the options programs available to individuals are usually not derivatives of these, they do provide the investor with the ability to play "what if" to determine the different profit potentials involved in multi-option writing or purchasing.

There are a number of other strategies for multi-option games. In the *straddle,* a put and a call are purchased at the same price. The purchaser hopes the price deviates one way or another from the strike price. The writer will get a double premium.

A buyer of a *strip*—two puts and one call—thinks the price of the stock will go down but is hedging and guessing that it will change one way or another from the exercise price. He pays a triple commission. A *strap*—two calls and one put—is the opposite of the hedge-on-speculation game.

Options and the Computer

Many of the options programs available use the Black-Scholes options pricing model, a mathematical model developed in 1973 by professors Fischer Black and Myron Scholes to calculate option prices as changes in stock prices change and the expiration date approaches. The model uses the price of the underlying stock, dividends paid, volatility (expected rate of change of the underlying stock as a percentage over one year), current interest rates, and the time remaining on the option to determine the fair value of an option at any time in the future.

Like all other categories of investment programs, programs for analyzing options range in price from less than $100 to over $2,000, representing varying levels of sophistication and different approaches to user interaction. Updating stock prices to recompute the option valuation is usually done via modem and the Dow Jones News/Retrieval Service, although some programs allow access to other databases and some have manual updating.

Some programs ask you to update a file of the volatility of certain stocks. Volatility is usually determined from historical data. Volatility is the probable percent price change of the underlying stock in a year.

While some programs compare your potential income from an options trade to the interest rate you could earn on your funds if they were invested in short-term instruments, others do not have this capability. And even those that use the Black-Scholes model may have variations in both the modeling and the programming.

Among the programs available are:

Advanced OpValu (Star Value Software, 12218 Scribe Dr., Austin TX 78759) runs on the IBM PC and TRS-80 models I and III and costs $129. Other options software produced by the same company are Optionvue-A ($189), Optionvue-B ($189) and Professional Optionvue ($425). All run on the IBM PC and TRS-80 models I and III. Professional Optionvue also runs on Apple II.

The package of Optionvue-A, Optionvue-B, and Advanced OpValu provides full analysis of options. "A" analyzes basic option writing and buying. "B" analyzes option combinations such as spreads and straddles. "Advanced" will analyze the fair market value for any number of listed options on a single stock, including hedge ratio. The Professional model includes analysis of a trader's position over time, changes in volatility, and more.

ASOC (Automated Summarized Option Comparator) (Mehrtens Financial Data Systems, P.O. Box 45, Ardsley NY 10502, 914-693-8546) runs on the Apple II, II+, *II*e, and III (in emulation mode) and costs $80. The program allows up to 20 options at a time to be calculated for fair price, percentage under- or over-priced, break-even point, and probability of breaking even at expiration. A volatility update diskette allows storage of 100 stocks' closing prices for 52 weeks.

Call/Put Options 2.0 (Harloff Inc., 725

Market St., Wilmington DE 19801) runs on the Apple II+ and costs $499. A non-Black-Scholes model is used to determine theoretical values, option price changes for stock price changes, leverage, and break-even stock prices for hedge positions.

O.A. SYS (Software Resources, Inc., 186 Alewife Brook Pkwy, Cambridge MA 02138, 617-497-5900) runs on the Apple II and III and costs $395. A data base of all optionable stocks (updated each month for $175 per year) is the heart of this program, which analyzes options and strategies. Current option prices are entered manually.

The Options Accountant and Options Analyst Plus (DataLab Inc., 760 College Ave., Haverford PA 19041, 215-667-1640) run on the IBM PC and Apple II+. The Options Accountant also runs on CP/M operating system machines. It costs $125. Options Analyst Plus is a five-module program (Options Analyst Plus stock version, $450; non-stock version, $350; access communications/storage disk for Apple II+, $95; monthly volatility datadisk, $125; and twice-monthly volatility datadisk updates, $250). The programs have information on 358 optionable stocks, stock index futures, interest rate options, foreign currency options, treasury bills and bonds, and more. Manual or automatic updating are available via modem from Chase Econometrics/Interactive Data Corp.

The Options Analysis System (New York Institute of Finance, 70 Pine St., New York NY 10270, 212-344-2900) runs on the Apple II and costs $2,400 plus $600 for an annual subscription to the weekly data service. The program is geared to follow the book *Options as Strategic Investment* by Lawrence G. McMillan (a copy of the book is included), and the current prices are updated via the Bridge Data Company of St. Louis. The program includes analysis routines for a number of strategies, with volatilities and dividends automatically updated.

OPTIONS-80 (Options-80, P.O. Box 471, Concord MA 01742) runs on the IBM PC, Apple II+ and III and TRS-80 models I and II; it costs $125. The program shows graphic and tabular information on analysis of calls, puts, spreads and shares. It takes into account commissions, cost of borrowing money, dividends and risk exposure, as well as showing annualized percent return on investment.

Options Strategy Model (Kustom Software, 4652 Cass. St., Suite A-238, San Diego CA 92190, 619-482-7119) runs on the Apple II+, TRS-80 Model III, Osborne Model I, and CP/M 8″ diskette machines and costs $39 (45 for CP/M 8″). The program is an overlay template for VisiCalc or Supercalc spreadsheet programs. It computes annualized return for six option strategies, and has manual input.

Options Value Software (Programmed Press, 2301 Baylis Ave., Elmont NY 11003, 516-775-0933) runs on the IBM PC, Apple II II+, *IIe* and TRS-80 (all models) and costs $100. This is a series of eight programs using different valuation models that evaluate risk, return, price, and other variables. The programs can be purchased in written form in the Programmed Press Handbook (which comes with the software or costs $19.95 separately) and can be copied onto diskettes using BASIC language and user's time. The handbook contains about 50 investment programs.

Option X (Crawford Data Systems, P.O. Box 705, Somis CA 93066, 805-484-4159) runs on the Apple II and costs $145. This program has three different option price models to choose from, and also allows the user to set specific brokerage commissions. The program especially seeks to find overpriced and underpriced options by using theoretical value models.

Op Val (Calc Shop, Inc., Box 1231, W.

Caldwell NJ 07007, 201-228-9139) runs on the Apple II, *II*e, or III with Apple II emulator and costs $250. The program uses a dividends-adjusted Black-Scholes model to provide forecasts of fair prices for options and positions taken. It can analyze extensive positions and simple strategies. The information is displayed like pages in a book.

PECOS (Programmed Evaluation of Contract Option Strategies (Pecos Systems Inc., P.O. Box 490, Mamaroneck NY 10543, 212-678-7469) runs on the IBM PC and costs $2,000. There are 24 strategies, including four user-defined, in the PECOS system. A new transaction or "leg" can be added at any time and the analysis will be recomputed. Commission and collateral tables are easily modified. PECOS calculates profit and loss, maximum/minimum profit, break-even points, annualized return rate indices, commissions, collateral, and probabilities. An inventory equivalent position report is provided.

Risk/Reward Analyzer (Golden Enterprises, P.O. Box 445, San Famon CA 94583) runs on the Apple II and costs $125. The program can be set for bull, bear, or neutral trends in the market and then will analyze risk/reward factors for various strategies. The printout includes potential gains and losses versus the stock price.

Stock and Option Analysis (Compuware, 15 Center Rd., Randolph NJ 07869, 201-366-8540) runs on the Apple II, II+ *II*e, and TRS-80 Model III and costs $99.95. The program is mostly a portfolio management tool for the options portfolio, including information in graphic or table form of value per share, current value and capital gain or loss, effects of commissions, margin interest and dividends. It also predicts future premiums of an option at a desired time and stock strike price.

Stock Option Analysis Program (SOAP) and Stock Option Scanner (H & H Scientific, 13507 Pendleton St., Ft. Washington MD 20744, 301-292-2958) both run on the Apple II+ and cost $250 each.

SOAP uses the Black-Scholes model to calculate the fair price of any number and class of options. The user maintains a volatility file for up to 75 stocks and changes in volatility are flagged by the program. SOAP provides three commission schedules and analyzes all positions as either current positions or future holdings.

Stock Option Scanner is a companion program that can take up to 1,000 stock options downloaded from the Dow Jones News/Retrieval Service and rank-order the top 100 and bottom 100 by any of five selection criteria based on the annual rate of return.

Chapter 10

Commodities

Commodities are often confused with options. Indeed, both are often lumped under the term *futures.*

Commodities are distinct from options in that they are contracts that represent the purchase and sale of hard tangible goods, rather than just gambling chits that represent an investor's idea of what the price of another financial instrument will be at the end of a certain period of time. Although people who buy and sell commodity contracts rarely take possession of the goods they buy, they sometimes do and they could do so more often if they desired.

In terms of the personal computer, commodities traders use programs and techniques from both the options and technical stock analysis camps to do their analysis of the commodities market. There are also fundamental and economic considerations to take into account when trading commodities contracts.

The Commodity Contract

A commodity contract is an agreement to buy or sell a set amount of a specific item for a defined price at a predetermined date. Commodities contracts, like options, expire quarterly (March, June, September, and December). The price of a commodity contract is set in dollars or cents per unit of measure. For instance, wheat might be $3 per bushel, while gold is $400 per ounce.

Each contract represents a set amount of the goods in question. A grain contract may include 5,000 bushels while a mineral contract may be 100 ounces. The price per unit times the amount of units equals the price of the contract.

Rather than paying a premium, as with an option contract, the purchaser of a commodity contract pays a *margin* payment—a percentage of the total contract—as a down payment. The rest of the money is borrowed from the commodity broker. Therefore, if the value of the contract goes down, the broker may call for more margin payment in cash or may have to liquidate the contract to recoup the money he has lent. This margin payment, however, can mean that a small percentage rise in the market price of a good can increase the value of your investment by a large percentage.

For instance, you have purchased five March contracts for wheat, 5,000 bushels each at $3 per bushel. Each contract is worth $15,000. The total is $75,000. Your margin payment is 10 percent, or $7,500.

The market moves up so that wheat is now $3.25 per bushel. Each contract is now worth $16,250. Your five contracts are worth $81,250, an increase of $6,250—or about an 85 percent increase in your cash investment.

On the other hand, if the price goes to $2.75 per bushel, each contract's value would dips to $13,750—total $68,750—and your cash investment decreases in value about 85 percent. At this point you would probably receive a margin call so the value of the contracts would not dip below the amount you did not put up for the original $75,000 investment.

Who Invests?

The people who invest in commodities fall into the same two basic categories that options investors fall into—speculators and hedgers—although they are not the same people.

Speculators trade pieces of paper that mean little more than money to them. Many wouldn't know the difference between a pork belly and a coffee bean if they fell over them. It is all a matter of price at any given moment. Many trade dozens of contracts in a single day—usually in one commodity—and try to even their positions in terms of long (buy) and short (sell) for each contract expiration date by the end of each day. These people often work for minuscule percentages as they spend day after day in one "pit" or another at the Chicago Board of Trade or one of the other commodity trading floors in the country or outside the country. N.R. Kleinfield's article "The Fast Track of Futures Trading" (*New York Times Magazine,* Dec. 4, 1983) painted a gripping and sometimes grim picture of these people. His book *The Traders* is expected out in mid-1984.

There are two kinds of hedgers, buying hedgers and selling hedgers. A buying hedger might be the jeweler who fears the price of gold may be going through the roof in the next year. Feeling that the price of a gold future commodity contract does not reflect what the price will really be, he may want to lock in a supply at today's future price for a time six, nine, or 12 months down the road. If the price does not go up as much as he expected he can sell out the contract at a lower price—closing his position with one long and one short contract—and take a loss while spending less than anticipated on gold on the open market.

In the opposite way, the grain farmer or elevator operator may think the price of grain will fall between this fall's harvest and next summer due to a big winter harvest. He may not think this price fall is fully reflected in the costs of grain futures, so he sells a contract for a set price now in order to lock in that price. If the price does not drop as much as he thought it would, he can buy a contract at a higher price—closing out his position—and take the loss while selling his grain for more.

Hedging can get more complex by buying and selling in both the cash and futures market. Prices change in commodities, as in options, due to both the underlying market conditions of the goods contracted for and the amount of time before the contract must be honored. The difference between the cash price and the futures price is known as the *basis.* It can either be a *positive value* when the futures price is greater than the cash price, or a *negative value* when the futures price is less than the cash price. It also must be considered that the futures price is reflective of four contract expiration dates.

For instance, a grain elevator operator—who may buy 50 million bushels of wheat at harvest—is a constant hedger. If the elevator pays $2.60 cash per bushel for 5,000 bushels in September and sells a May contract for 5,000 bushels at $3.00, then sells 5,000 bushels for $2.50 cash in January but buys a May contract for $2.75, he has lost 10 cents per bushel on his cash transactions but gained 25 cents per bushel on his paper transactions for a net gain of 15 cents per bushel or $750.

Each hedger will have a different set of circumstances since the basis has a geographical component to it as cash prices fluctuate. The local basis is partially determined by the difference in cash price between the local area and Chicago. This can fluctuate because of transportation costs. For instance, in the late fall of 1983 the Mississippi River froze early and a number of grain barges headed for market to beat the winter were stuck in the ice for the winter. The price of grain in Chicago went up, while in some other locations this was not true, or it didn't go up as much. It can also fluctuate because of crop circumstances in one part of the country, such as the '83-'84 winter freezes of citrus fruit in Florida. While futures prices for frozen orange juice went up, the cash prices in the West, where there is other supply, probably did not go up, or at least not as much.

As the contract expiration date comes closer, basis usually narrows between cash price and that future price. Basis is a hedger's tool much more than it is a speculator's tool, but knowing something about the mechanism and patterns of basis changes can be important to a speculator. However, the speculators will probably not spend too much time worrying over basis since they are not dealing in the marketplace of the actual commodity but only in the paper marketplace.

A Combination of Tools

The typical commodities speculator will use a combination of the investing techniques and computer software previously discussed. Commodities speculators, like equity investors, argue about whether fundamental or technical analysis tells more about the state of the market.

Technical analysts state that when they talk about a perfect market and complete information, they are talking about the commodities markets more than anything else. There are no insiders and no market makers, just open auctions where the price is constantly changing on the basis of supply and demand for contracts in the pit.

Fundamental analysts, on the other hand, will argue that yes, it is a perfect market, but it is natural causes that make it so. There is no human interference, nobody to skew the price. Therefore, it is hard to find undervaluation, but it is not hard to find world economic and natural conditions that will change the prices in the future.

It is probably a worthless argument, since no fundamental analyst could help but look at the grain barges stuck in December 1983 and worry what would happen to prices when they became unstuck. Technical analysts would not worry. When the first water started to flow and the worriers started to sell, so would they until the "support" level was reached and they could buy again.

In addition to our old warring armies, there are those who use options analysis techniques to value the prices of futures. The Black-Scholes model is one frequently used, and the Black commodity modifier of that model was designed by Professor Black to fine-tune the technique to the vagaries of the commodities market.

The Technical Analysis Group's Compu Trac and Intra Day Analyst programs are among the most well-known and well-respected among commodity traders. The Intra Day Analyst is tied into a real-time quote system. One of the Compu Trac's strong points is the ability to vary parameters for profitability tests and optimize any one of the more than 40 trading systems for any particular market.

There are a few specific programs for analyzing the commodities markets. Among them are:

Auto Trader (Avinco Corporation, P.O. Box 189, Sharpsburg, MD 21782, 301-432-7118) runs on the IBM PC and costs $295. The program uses the moving average trading signal technique to generate buy, sell, and hold signals for up to 32 commodities with 260 days of prices per file.

COTS/Fair Value Commodity Options System (Software Options, Inc., 19 Rector St., New York NY 10006, 212-785-8285) runs on the IBM PC with color graphics and the Apple II. Cost is $2,540 plus data update charges for the IBM system and $895 for the Apple II version. The program starts with the "Valuation Kernal" that calculates theoretical values, time and intrinsic values, fair value, and hedge ratios. The Black-Scholes model is used as is the Black enhancement for commodity futures. COTS has also adapted the Black model to provide a valuation for types of options not covered by the models. This allows the user to set up estimates of future volatility and interest rates. The options strategies portion of the program allows strategies with up to five trades. There is a professional module that allows the user to set up matrices for different option maturities and strike prices, as well as a portfolio maintenance module.

The Quicktrieve system, consisting of Quicktrieve, Quickmanager, Quickstudy, Quickplot and Quickmoney (Commodity Systems, Inc. 200 W. Palmetto Park Road, 2nd Floor, Boca Raton FL 33432, 800-327-0175 or 305-392-8663) runs on the IBM PC, PC-XT, Columbia (IBM compatible), Apple II+, *II*e, and III, Franklin (Apple-compatible), TRS-80 models III or IV, and Commodore 64.

All of the programs are contained on one diskette, and the pricing is by how much on-line service you purchase. One, three, and six-month special rates including toll-free daily phone service are sold, and after that it is a subscription service. The company will send a brochure with rate list. Each purchaser acquires a data bank on diskette containing the particular commodities (or other options) he would like to follow.

Each day the Quicktrieve program signs on the CSI computer and retrieves the price and other information for the particular commodities and distributes the information into the diskette data base using Quickmanager. Quickmanager also performs a number of other data manipulation and system maintenance functions.

The Quickstudy module uses an N-day breakout system to generate buy, sell, and hold decisions. Although the user can use the basic program, it is helpful to know the BASIC programming language in order to modify the system for customized use. The N-day breakout system lets the user pick a value for N, then generates buy or long signals when the last N days' high is reached and generates sell or short positions when the last N days' low is reached.

Quickplot is the graphics module that displays up to 100 days per second. It displays moving averages superimposed over high, low, close bar charts, and other displays.

Quickmoney, a new module in the design phase, will generate buy, sell, and hold signals by finding historically repetitive trading patterns.

✓ Technical Trader (Memory Systems Inc., 5312 Hoffman, Skokie IL 60077, 312-674-4833) runs on the Apple II and costs $350, plus $75 for communications software. The program combines techniques from Welles Wilder's *New Concepts in Technical Trading Systems* with moving average and on-balance-volume studies to generate buy, sell, and hold signals for commodities trading. It updates prices via telephone retrieval.

Chapter 11

Portfolio Management and Analysis

Even if you do not use your computer for investment analysis—even if you do no investment analysis to speak of—the computer can be an indispensable tool for keeping records of your portfolio.

Although tax time is not until April 15, by the end of January the paperwork is beginning to flood in—year-end brokerage statements of your purchases and sales, as well as dividend statements from the corporations you own stock in or interest statements from bond holdings. For the investor who has made many trades involving different investment vehicles using numerous brokers, this can set off pre-tax panic. That panic can be multiplied for the investor who has custodial accounts for his or her children, or IRA, Keogh Plan, or Personal Corporation Pension Fund accounts, and the investor who is managing a personal trust account as part of an estate plan or managing an account for a parent or a parent's trust.

The computer may not do away with all the incoming paper and the need to keep files and records for each individual account, but it can help organize the scutwork of simple arithmetic and ledgerkeeping. There are a number of portfolio management programs listed below, ranging from a simple program that lists stock holdings all the way to sophisticated programs that give portfolio weightings for a portfolio that might include stocks, bonds, options, money market funds, CDs, and government-backed mortgage securities such as Ginnie Maes, Freddy Macs, and Fannie Maes. (None are available as yet to calculate hard assets, although there are programs that help you keep track of real estate portfolios.)

In addition to being able to doublecheck all of the work your brokers do for you, a portfolio management program—kept up to date—can allow you to stop and survey your entire portfolio at any time and make some changes if you think the portfolio is losing sight of your original goals. Many of the portfolio management programs listed below contain portfolio analysis modules that allow you to rank your holdings by income, P/E, risk/reward, and other variables ranked either against the market as a whole or against some idealized portfolio.

Most of these systems can gather information from the Dow Jones News/Retrieval Service so you can update the prices on your holdings without inputting price data from the keyboard. This can be very helpful for large portfolios or for an individual who is managing numerous portfolios. However, in the case of a small investor, once again, you must do the cost/benefit analysis of the added cost of modem, membership fee for the pricing service, and telephone time charges.

Just the Facts, Please

At its simplest level a portfolio management system should mimic on the screen what you would do on paper to keep your records. You should look for a program that either sets up its records most like the way you want or one that gives you the flexibility to look at the books in a way that is most familiar to you. You may want a system that arranges the portfolio in a number of different ways so you can have a different perspective every now and again.

Every portfolio program will be set up differently in terms of how you prepare the data for input, but every one should ask for at least the following basic information: the date you made the purchase or sale, the amount of shares, cost per share, and commission. From this information, once you update the stock price with a new quote, any portfolio program will calculate your open position. This does not do much for you except keep track of each stock you own and your total portfolio, just as you would with paper and pencil. The value so far is that you do not need a calculator and/or scratchpad.

If that was all portfolio management software did, it would be pretty dismal. The majority of programs have a number of the following important features, and you should look for the program that does the most for the least money in the format you are most comfortable reading.

Does the program account for stock splits, dividends, fractional shares, and variable commissions? If a stock splits two for one you own more stock worth less per share in your cost analysis. For instance, if you own 100 shares of a $10 stock, and that stocks splits two for one, you now own 200 shares of a $5 stock. For purposes of figuring your cost per share and at what point you have a taxable gain, you need a program that accounts for this split and will adjust your cost-per-share as such. If the program does not automatically do this, you need to do away with the original entry and reenter the material after the stock is split, doing all the division and multiplicatin by hand (or by calculator).

A good program should allow you to keep track of dividends collected and should print out a summary report of all dividends that either can be attached to your IRS 1040 in lieu of schedule D or can be used to fill out schedule D.

If you reinvest your dividends in shares of stock you will still have to pay taxes on them (unless the company is an electric utility company qualified to give tax-deferred dividends to investors who reinvest the dividends). In addition, however, the dividends purchasing new shares are not always equivalent to a round number of shares, and you may be buying fractions of shares. Since the stock price changes from quarter to quarter, each new set of shares purchased with reinvested dividends will have a share, you may end up having to recompute the figures by hand when it comes time to pay capital gains taxes or compute a capital loss when the total block of shares is sold.

If you use more than one broker, you will be paying different commissions. Therefore the program should not assume that each purchase of a stock is made at the same commission. The program should allow for a commission to be stated with each purchase, not just at the beginning of the screen for each stock. You may buy 100 shares from a full-service broker who turned you on to a stock, then purchase additional shares later from a discount broker. Shares purchased through dividend reinvestment programs or direct purchase from the company via a shareholder's plan could be made with no commissions. Again, since commissions are expenses calculated *before* tax is calculated, you may have to recompute if the program does not do it for you.

Does the program show you the annual dividend rate and income generated from the investment? This is a good tool for evaluating your portfolio and a good way to weight your portfolio. You should know how much income you are generating so that you can adjust your portfolio as your needs and investment goals change.

Does the program do "tax lot accounting?" This is one of the most important features of good programs, and one that many programs neglect. If you have bought blocks of the same stock at different times, when you go to sell that stock, you can designate which block you want to sell. If you do not designate, the IRS will assume that you sold the first block you bought—so-called FIFO or first-in-first-out accounting.

This can have major tax consequences. Here is an example: We have already discussed tax lot accounting, but it is worth reinforcing the idea. You buy 100 shares of XYZ company on Jan. 10, 1983, at $10 per share. In April, with the price hovering at $9.50, you assume the company is ready to go and buy another 300 shares. In July, the company has started to get big sales and you figure it is a buy at $13.50, so you buy 300 more shares. In November, you take your Christmas bonus and buy another 100 shares at $15. The next April, you need a quick $2,000 to pay your Federal income taxes, so you decide to sell 100 shares of XYZ, which is selling for $21.50. Which 100 shares do you want to sell? Some long-term shares, obviously, so you pay the long-term capital gain rather than the short-term. But you want to pay the least tax, so you sell the shares bought in January of the previous year for $10 per share.

If, however, the price of XYZ in April 1984 when you needed the $2,000 had been $13, you probably would have sold the 100 shares you bought in November at $15 and 100 of the shares you bought in July at $13.50. That way you would have realized a short-term loss and held your long-term gain for another day.

This must all be recorded in your portfolio records, and a good program will do this. In addition, a good program will be constantly averaging your cost so that if you sell your entire holding in a company at once, you will know the cost basis for computing your taxes.

Does the program weight your portfolio? A good program should take your entire portfolio value and break it down by type of investment—stocks, bonds, options, CDs and other cash equivalents, and possibly other categories. That way, if you have decided that you want 20 percent of your portfolio in cash, 20 percent in income stocks, 20 percent in growth stocks and 40 percent in bonds, you will get a look at how each new investment changes your portfolio and what kinds of sales you will have to make to offset your purchase and keep your balance. If the program also has a ranking system within each category, you can identify the best possible sale.

Does the program "flag" investments that are about to go long-term or options that are about to expire? These can be very important points. With a large portfolio or multiple portfolios, an investor can't always keep track of when each investment is about to go long-term. (Neither can a broker—who must keep track of this for *dozens* of clients—unless he has good software, but more on that later.) As we have seen in our tax discussions, this is the time in the life of an investment when decisions must be made. At each turning point, an investor must think about whether the investment is meeting its goals and whether the short-term loss would be more advantageous than giving it more time, or whether the long-term gain is worth waiting for rather than taking the cash and investing it in something more profitable or just taking a fast profit and running with a stock that has moved rapidly. The program should have some way of "flagging" these investments—a "days to long-term" column of some kind, an "investments long-term this week" warning, or possibly even a flashing cursor next to each investment that will turn long within 10 trading days.

The same is true of options. If an option expires it is worthless. With investors who trade a lot of options it is sometimes difficult to remember what comes due when, especially when trying to time exercising the option to wring every dollar out of it. Warrants acquired either from working for a company or from buying "units"—shares and warrants—often have long lives and can be forgotten. Unfortunately, they are not like Grandpa's 1,000 shares of "railroad" that can be dusted off and cashed in a generation later if they have expired. Again, a flag helps.

Does the program handle multiple accounts on one data diskette and does it cross-reference? Not only the broker needs to keep track of a number of accounts these days, because the brokerage account is no longer Dad's sole purview. Many households will have an account for Dad, one for Mom, a joint account, another one for Mom (the lawyer) for her personal corporation pension trust, another one for Dad (the engineering consultant) and his Keogh Plan, a custodial account for each of the three kids, and a trust for Grandma that is paying her bills now and will keep her estate out of probate court when she dies. It is convenient if you can keep all these records on one data diskette and can cross-check investments.

If Grandpa owned a chunk of one of those wonderful old utilities and left it to Grandma, she might want to sell it now that it is in hot nuclear water. In addition, she might have spread it around to the grandchildren for birthday presents or high school graduations. It would be nice if the account maintainer could flick a command and ask the computer to fish up all the holdings of "Power and Light" and see who has how much and what to do with it. Grandma might want to sell it off, since it is 20 percent of her holdings and she really needs a little more stability to sleep well at night. The college student children might love the 17 percent dividend and think the stodgy old investment now has little sex appeal—it might even be worth reading the business section to watch it move.

Programs that update via the telephone lines often update holdings in all portfolios automatically if they are on the same data diskette.

Analysis

Once you have all the accounting taken care of in the manner with which you are most comfortable, you may want to do some analysis beyond the rudiments of how well the portfolio is weighted. A number of programs have different analytical tools attached to them that help you to determine how your portfolio measures up against others.

Some allow you to compare portfolios against each other in terms of income, total growth per year, or some measure of value or volatility. You can construct "what-if" portfolios as a way of adding another dimension to your tracking of potential investments, or you can see how your own holdings do against a model portfolio designed by a brokerage house or an investment service.

But it is important to realize that your portfolio should accomplish what *you* want it to, not necessarily what the market or a broker thinks you *ought* to want your portfolio to accomplish. The computer can help you accomplish this by doing the donkey work and giving you more time to think.

Programs

Advisor (K-Wave Financial Services, P.O. Box 1675, Sausalito CA 94965, 413-332-9434) runs on the IBM PC and CP/M operating system computers. The program is designed for the professional user and can handle in excess of 800 portfolios. It does cross-referenced reports, income and year-end tax reports, and other accounting. Updating is manual or via the Dow Jones News/Retrieval Service.

Andromeda Stock Trader and Calculator (Spiral Enterprises, 308 Crown Rd., Willow Park TX 76086) runs on the TRS-80 model I and costs $35.50. The program is geared toward the individual who invests only in stocks. It keeps track of purchase date, total amount paid, quotes and dividends—current year and total—and will print attachments to Schedule D.

Blue Chip Portfolio Manager (Xor Corporation, 5421 Opportunity Court, Minnetonka, MN 55343, 612-938-0005) runs on the IBM PC and costs $79.95. The program handles splits and dividends and computes tax consequences of each transaction as it occurs, and changes, parameters to do "what-if" analysis.

Casette Portfolio (Radio Shack, 1500 One Tandy Center, Fort Worth TX 76102, 817-390-3155) runs on the TRS-80 models I and III with cassette drive. This is one of the Radio Shack in-house investment programs. It provides transaction records and analysis of yield, market value and unrealized gains or losses.

Tandy has another much more sophisticated portfolio management program. Electronic Broker ($995 for the TRS-80 model II). This program is aimed at the professional money manager or broker and does portfolio management for numerous portfolios with a number of securities and transactions.

Certified Personal Investor (Sundex Software Corporation, Inc., 3000 Pearl St., Boulder CO 80301, 303-440-3600) runs on the IBM PC and costs $149.95. The program is menu-driven and keeps track of the standard long and short-term capital gains and losses, dividends, reinvestments, splits, and individual lots. It does preparation of IRS schedules B and D.

Fundfile (Parsons Software, 118 Woodshire Dr., Parkersburg WV 26101) runs on the TRS-80 color computer with extended color BASIC and a printer and costs $29.95 (available only in diskette). This program can handle 900 transactions and up to 50 securities. It reports value and realized and unrealized gains or losses.

Futures Trading Support System (Investment Support Systems, Inc., 41 Vreeland Ave., Totowa NJ 07512, 201-890-0940) runs on the IBM PC and PC XT and is custom-designed and priced. The program is designed for serious commodities traders or brokers and does full commodity portfolio management, including updates, break-even prices, profit or loss calculations, margin accounting, and pairing contracts on FIFO or other tax basis. It can accommodate 100 trades outstanding.

High Yield (Hourglass Systems, P.O. Box 312, Glen Ellyn IL 60137, 312-690-1855) runs on the IBM PC, Apple with 80-column card, Osborne, Northstar, and most other CP/M operating system computers and costs $75. The program is designed for management of mutual funds, but can be used for other investments. It gives bid and ask price, type of transaction (reinvestment, cash dividend), and other information.

The Holding Page (Compubyte Inc. P.O. Box 1825, Cape Coral FL 33910, 813-793-1656) runs on the IBM PC and costs $399. The program is primarily designed for brokers and handles up to 500 accounts with a maximum of 3,500 open transactions. It records all transactions and includes a "tickler" file for important dates. This file can be programmed to read out option expiration dates or "going long" dates.

The Intelligent Investor (Robert Gentry and Associates, 810 Camelview Plaza, 6900 E. Camelback Rd., Scottsdale AZ 85251, 602-941-5212) runs on the IBM PC, Apple II, TRS-80 models with 48K and two disk drives, and NEC-PC 8000. Series II requires a 132-column printer. Series I costs $75; Series II $130. The Series I program keeps cash and securities records, valuation, dividends and interest, brokerage commissions, and margin expenses. It also does portfolio performance evaluations. Series II does the same and adds performance evaluation in interim time periods and printouts.

Investor System (Macson Inc., 40 Sunset Dr., Seekonk MA 02771, 617-399-7130) runs on the TRS-80 Model I and is priced on application. The program has three related segments. The first records weekly position in value, risks, and expectations, and builds an audit trail for later tracing and year-end records. The second segment is a decision system that works on principles of timing. The third segment allows for maintenance of up to 99 portfolios.

Investment Manager (International Microcomputer Software, Inc., 633 Fifth Avenue, San Rafael CA 94901, 415-454-7107) runs on the IBM PC and CP/M operating system computers. The program does the standard computations for long and short-term gain and loss, interest, and dividends, and analyzes the portfolio's performance using a compounded rate of return, an adjusted return, and a portfolio impact statement that uses beta and weighted average beta to project long-term return for a portfolio based on stock volatility.

Investment Master PC (Alro Computer Software Services, 3100 E. High St., P.O. Box 927, Jackson MI 49204, 517-787-2204) runs on the IBM PC and costs $199. The program handles up to 2,000 transactions, does portfolio value, capital gains and losses and dividends received. It follows IRS guidelines for reports.

Investment Trades Manager (Ellenbogen Associates Inc., 2 Greenlea Court, Westport CT 06883, 203-226-9280) runs on the IBM PC and costs $595. The program handles stocks, bonds, government securities, mutual funds, warrants, rights, options, commodities, and futures. It can be updated from Dow Jones News/Retrieval Service, and does valuation, long and short-term gain and loss statements, and more.

Investment Transaction Analyzer (Mikel Systems, Inc., P.O. Box 33679, Tampa FL 33679, 813-837-4270) runs on the TRS-80 Model III and costs $100 for a manual entry system and $1,000 for automated data retrieval system. In addition to doing portfolio management—keeping track of gains and losses, taxes and dividends—this program allows the user to return on investment analysis for the portfolio as well as options analysis for individual options purchases.

Market Manager (Dow Jones and Co., P.O. Box 300, Princeton NJ 08540, 609-452-2000) runs on the IBM PC, Apple II, and Apple III. This is part of the Dow Jones package (Market Analyzer for technical analysis and Market Microscope for fundamental analysis). It handles stocks, bonds, options, mutual funds, and government securities, and uses the News/Retrieval for updated information. It handles realized and unrealized gains and losses.

PEAR Systems (Remote Computing Corporation, 1044 Northern Blvd., Roslyn NY 11576, 800-645-3120 or 212-895-3810) runs on the IBM PC and Apple II and costs $600 to $695. A professionally oriented program, PEAR handles multiple portfolios and cross-references portfolios by securities held as well as cross-referencing securities by how many portfolios hold them. Updating is via telephone or manually; accounting is by IRS standards. It handles fractional shares from splits and reinvested dividends.

Permanent Portfolio Analyzer and Inflation Proofer Tutor (C.R. Hunter & Associates, Inc., 1527 Northwood Dr., Cincinnati OH 45237, 513-761-9322) both run on the IBM PC, the Apple II+, *IIe* and III. Permanent Portfolio Analyzer costs $295 and Inflation Proofer Tutor costs $25. The analyzer uses the theory of purchasing power to value any given portfolio. The program produces both a balance sheet with current net worth and unrealized gains or losses as well as a 10-year projection analysis that tracks the portfolio's purchasing power through a number of inflation scenarios. The "tutor" program teaches the concepts of inflation-proofing a long-term portfolio, explaining how projections of long-term purchasing power are made, then goes through portfolio analysis exercises.

The Personal Invester (PBL Corporation, P.O. Box 559, Wayzata MN 55391, 612-473-8998) runs on the IBM PC ($195) and the Apple II ($145). The program uses the Dow Jones News-Retrieval Service to get quotes as well as news and information that can be displayed. The portfolio management section accommodates 300 stocks, 700 purchases, and 500 sales per data diskette. It handles stocks, bonds, mutual funds, options, and other financial instruments.

Personal Portfolio Manager (Dynacomp, Inc. 1427 Monroe Ave., Rochester NY 14618) is available for most computer models and costs $69.95. The program shows open positions, as well as realized gains and losses, and does point and figure chart of portfolio value. It has manual input.

Personal Portfolio Manager (Embassy Computer Products, Inc., P.O. Box 88, Little Neck NY 11363, 212-961-9806) runs on the VIC-20 and the Commodore 64 and costs $49.95 for diskette and $44.95 for tape. The program determines the current value of stock, bond and mutual fund investments and computes portfolio value at any time or changes over time.

Portfolio and Client Management System (Reveal Software Inc., 6 Chelmsford Dr., Muttontown NY 11545, 516-626-1166) runs on the IBM PC, Apple II, and Apple III, and costs $1,250 to $1,550. The program is designed for brokers and money managers. It is menu-driven and gives brokers a large calendar file to help them manage their client accounts. The program tracks transactions for clients and generates dividend, gain and loss, and tax reports.

Portfolio Management (Dogwood Software, 3905 Dogwood Dr., Greensboro NC 27410) runs on the TRS-80 models I, III, and IV and the Lobo Max 80 and costs $40. The program can handle two portfolios including 35 stocks on each diskette. It can analyze both portfolios at once with simple entries, and shows a 13-week moving index of portfolio value.

Portfolio Management (Hewlett Packard, 3000 Hanover St., Palo Alto CA 94304, 503-757-2000) runs on the HP-85 and the HP-86B and costs $250. The program uses the Dow Jones News/Retrieval Service for updates. Investments are classified when the portfolio is created. Eleven classes, 50 standard subclasses, and 50 customized subclasses are available. It has built-in graphics for pie charts; up to 35 portfolios are stored per diskette.

Portfolio Management (Project Techniques Ltd., Box 658, Richmond, Ontario, Canada KOA 2Z0, 613-836-5161) runs on the Apple II + and *IIe* and costs $50 for screen output only and $75 for printer output version. The program handles up to 300 accounts with 300 different stocks and 2500 transactions at any one time, keeps track of stocks and options, cross-references accounts by holdings or which have options due in any particular month, and does average costs of shares for all shares traded.

Portfolio Management System (Applications Systems Group Inc., 276 Fifth Ave. Suite 901, New York NY 10001, 212-684-6631) runs on the IBM PC and PC XT and a number of minicomputers and costs from $2,000 to $25,000, depending on configuration. This is a brokers' program that provides account maintenance for multiple clients and generates reports. It does cross-referencing, industry analysis, and commission analysis.

Portfolio Master PC (Techland Systems Inc., 25 Waterside Plaza, New York NY 10010, 212-684-7788) runs on the IBM PC; it costs $195 for the individual investor versions and $390 for the professional version. The program generates valuation, distribution of capital, tax reports, and income calendars. Updating is via Dow Jones or manually. It handles margin accounts and broker's commissions.

Portfolio Master 3.1 (Investors Software, P.O. Box 2605, San Francisco CA 94126) runs on the Apple II and costs $195. This is manual or via Dow Jones (the program gives you a discount on a Dow Jones password). It reports current value, long- and short-term realized and unrealized gains and losses, Dow tax-lot accounting, and flags options.

A professional model, Professional Portfolio Master, also runs on the Apple II and costs $495. It cross-references portfolios by security held and updates all portfolios automatically with one call to Dow Jones News/Retrieval Service. A timer will also delay the call to Dow Jones to take advantage of cheaper night rates.

Portfolio Pro (Personal Micro Services, 1758 Deerpath Ct., Suite 1018, Naperville, IL 60565, 312-420-7108) runs on the Apple II series and costs $69.95. The program keeps track of stocks, bonds, metals, and other securities and generates IRS tax schedules B and D. It handles splits.

Portfolio Valuation System (Computer Aided Decisions, Inc., 31 Milk St., Boston MA 02109, 617-542-6181) runs on the IBM PC and Apple II and costs $1,100. The program analyzes and appraises portfolios using either the CompuServe or Valport pricing services. PVS segregates securities into investment categories and subcategories, then cross-references portfolios by security holding.

Portware (Portware Inc., 5724 Tucker Ln., Edina MN 55436, 612-935-6226) runs on the Apple II and costs $650 for the total package. Portware is a portfolio management program in six modules. Portrac does portfolio accounting. Portrate analyzes portfolios against each other or model portfolios. Portrend compares measures of portfolio return against market indexes. IRS (Income Record for Securities) records dividends and interest for IRS schedule B. Portcom is the communications module that allows updating via Dow Jones, and MP/Cross is a multiple portfolio cross-referencing module for professionals and multi-portfolio managers.

Stock Manager (Omni Software Systems, Inc., 146 N. Broad St., Griffith IN 46319, 219-924-3522) runs on the IBM PC and North Star and costs $150. The program does long and short-term gains and losses, calculates average cost per share of each stock, average price per share of all stocks owned, total costs, total costs of reinvested dividends, and generates reports including income tax Schedules B and D. It flags investments that will go long-term in next 30 days.

Stock Portfolio Reporter (Micro Investment Systems, Inc., P.O. Box 8599, Atlanta GA 30306, 404-892-3194) runs on the IBM PC and costs $179. The program updates via Dow Jones and reports stock price, dividend yield, cost, gains and losses, P/E multiples, and relative strength to do portfolio analysis while also doing portfolio management. It handles up to 100 stocks.

Stock Portfolio Management System (Atlantic City Computer Corporation, 19 Bryant Rd., Turnersville NJ 08012, 609-228-3131) runs on the IBM PC and the TRS-80 models I, II, and III (no price available). The program handles multiple portfolios, computes standard short and long-term realized and unrealized gains and losses. It also keeps a running year-to-date record of gains and losses in each portfolio, does IRS schedule D, and has cross-referencing by portfolios holding particular stocks, profitability potential of writing a covered call, and bond yield to maturity.

Stock Portfolio System (Smith Micro Software, P.O. Box 604, Sunset Beach CA 90742, 213-592-1032) runs on the IBM PC, Apple II and Apple III, and costs $185. The program reports portfolio status, profit and loss, dividends and interest, and expenses. It flags securities going long-term, dividends or bond interest due, and options expirations. Up to three margin accounts can be tracked.

Telebroker (Teleware, Inc., P.O. Box 729, Pine Brook NJ 07058, 800-225-0076) runs on the IBM PC and PC XT and the Apple III. Cost is $495 for the PC and $595 for the PC XT and Apple III. The program can accommodate up to 400 accounts, 1,000 securities, 20,000 open positions, and 30,000 records. It does automatic portfolio valuation, realized and unrealized gain and loss reports, and can interact with word processing programs to generate reports and letters.

The $2 Broker (Brokersoft, Inc., P.O. Box 1762, Wilmington NC 28402, 800-334-0693) runs on the IBM PC and the Apple II+. Its cost varies from $100 to $750 depending on computer and number of client files available.

The program can accommodate up to 2,500 clients and 30,000 transactions and does all the standard portfolio management tasks and reports. It has a "tickler" file for important dates and a client call list for professionals.

Following are a number of programs that combine aspects of fundamental and technical analysis and, in some cases, portfolio management.

Complete Financial Packages (E & H Electronics, 2699 E. 28th St., Suite 416, Signal Hill CA 90806, 213-426-3327) runs on all personal computers and costs $1,000 as is. Customization runs between $2,000 and $20,000. It is a full set of investment software that does stock market, option, cash flow, and portfolio analysis. It uses Dow Jones News/Retrieval Service for updating, and can be modified for corporate use along with payroll, accounting, inventory, and mailing lists.

The Computing Investor (The Computing Investor, 29 Estancia, Marana AZ 85238) runs on the Apple II+. Prices vary depending on "program package" purchased. The program comes as a package of modules such as Quickfolio, a sample portfolio evaluator; Chartpro, a price/volume chart generator; Transactor, a portfolio management program; and Vector-S, a predictive trading model.

Investpak (McGraw-Hill Book Co., 1221 Avenue of the Americas, 27th FL., New York NY 10020) runs on the Apple II+ and the TRS-80 models I and III and costs $200. This is a series of 25 programs that handle such problems as risk/return, commissions, margins, tax computations, stock and bond analysis, convertible bond analysis, and options. The program comes with *A Guide to Computer-Assisted Investment Analysis,* a book of do-it-yourself programming for investment analysis.

SMART System (Software Resources, Inc., 186 Alewife Brook Pkwy, Cambridge MA 02138, 617-497-5900) runs on the Apple II and III and costs $1,950 ($2,450 for hard disk). The program is a package of technical analysis and portfolio analysis and record-keeping tools. In addition to a number of standard technical studies, user-determined studies can be performed. Statistical studies include covariance analysis and multivariate regression analysis. Its portfolio accounting system includes reports of realized and unrealized gains and losses and tax accounting. The program can be used in conjunction with VisiCalc and will accept Compu Trac formatted files. Its communications software will allow access to time-sharing systems.

The Stock Manager (Analytical Service Associates, 21 Hollis Rd., Lynn MA 01904, 617-593-2404) runs on the IBM PC and Apple II + and costs $125. This is a package of nine programs that do stock evaluation, internal rate of return analysis, compound interest and annuity. Portfolio management portions do standard long and short-term gains and losses. Taxes and commissions are considered in analysis.

The Stock Market Analysis Package (Computronics, 50 N. Pascack Rd., Spring Valley NY 10977, 800-431-2818) runs on the IBM PC, Apple II, TRS-80 models I, II, and III, and CP/M operating system computers; it costs $99.95. The program is a collection of small programs that analyze potential stock, bond, convertible, options, and annuity investments and do portfolio accounting. Taxes and commissions are taken into account.

Stock Market Series (Claud E. Cleeton, 122 109th Ave. S.E., Bellevue WA 98004) runs on the TRS-80 models I and III (cassette) and PET computers and costs $15. This series of programs uses the mathematical formulas laid out by Cleeton in a series of investment books. Studies include price analysis, moving averages, frequency analysis, option volatility and normal values, and options strategy tables.

Wall Street Window (R & D Associates, Box 2727, Reston VA 22090, 703-476-6597) runs on the IBM PC and costs $395. The program combines a number of stock analysis techniques such as moving averages, volume comparisons, trendline analysis, and price/volume with a portfolio management program that automatically calculates taxes and commissions. Up to 112 stocks, each with over one year's historical data, can be downloaded from the Dow Jones News/Retrieval Service and stored on each diskette.

Chapter 12

Brokers and Money Managers

The computer revolution not only affects what individuals can do to keep their own investment records and make their own investment decisions, but it has profound implications for the roles of brokers and money managers.

It was the mainframe computer that first gave money managers and brokers the memory power to gather information on all the companies they wanted to follow. Now the personal computer has made that power available to brokers and money managers in a more timely fashion and at far less expense. No longer do they have to worry about the cost of having the time-sharing service make another run through the data. The more the software is used, the faster it is amortized.

Not only can the broker or money manager use many of the same programs that we have looked at for use by personal investors, but he or she has a whole range of other programs from which to choose.

The computer revolution in investing can cause investors to go one of several ways in their use of computers and their use of human services to assist in their investing. One investor will want to strip off all human interference with his trading, buy the computer software to do the kind of analysis he or she wants to do, open an account with a discount broker, and go from there.

Another investor may want to allow the money manager to use all the new tools available and hope that the human understanding and the increased memory and computational power of the computer can lead the money manager to make good decisions for him—if not better than before, then at least as good. Since the money manager is able to do more of the mundane work faster, he might be able to manage more portfolios and—it could be argued—would then be willing and able to charge less per customer for managing the account.

A third investor may decide that if brokerage houses are using all of this computer software (and possibly even individual brokers), then he might as well just take more brokerage house recommendations and pay the full service charge. You can pay a lot of commissions for the price of a computer, or even the price of a few software packages. After all, why should an investor spend $400 for a good portfolio package if his broker can prepare the same high-class reports as part of the commission fee.

In addition to opening the door for some innovative ways of delivering services to customers, the computer can serve as the impetus for some changes in the broker/client relationship that are potentially harmful as well as some out-and-out abuses by brokers.

To understand a little better how the computer revolution is changing and could in the future change the relationship between brokers or money managers and their clients, we have to understand a little bit about how these people operate.

Money Managers

The role of a money manager is rather straightforward. For a fee—usually a percentage of your portfolio based on the size of your portfolio or a percentage of the net increase in your portfolio based on the manager's performance each year (but never on a commission basis)—the money manager is responsible for managing your investment portfolio.

Investors entrust different amounts of their portfolio to their money managers. Some entrust money managers with virtually all their investments beyond the household checking account. Others purchase their own life insurance, keep some money in one form or another of liquid savings, and ask their money managers to invest their portfolio in areas with which they are less familiar. Managers usually have either complete or nearly complete discretion over the investment decisions.

When looking for a money manager, most people visit a number of them and check out prices and method of pricing and get some general ideas about how the manager would structure a portfolio. But after the decision has been made about whom to use, the work of determining the structure of a portfolio begins. Once a plan has been drawn up, the investor often just sits back and waits for the yearly reports of how his or her funds have progressed. This is by far the easiest and most personally tailored way to invest. Most money managers work by themselves or in small groups.

Money managers receive favorable commission treatment by trading in large blocks and parcelling out the investment into the individual accounts of the investors they represent. Most money managers try to handle "institutional money," mostly corporate pension funds. Sometimes a big money manager will not be the right person to handle a small personal account since he might not have enough time to devote to the small account because of commitments to larger institutional clients. Some money managers do their trading through discount brokers while others use full service brokers, receiving the brokerage research at the institutional level.

The idea of the mutual fund is similar in that it is a pool of funds from a number of investors and the money is managed professionally. In a mutual fund, however, the individual investor does not have a chance to tailor the investment program to his or her needs but must find a fund that most closely allies itself with the investor's goals.

Brokers: Selling is the Name of the Game

A broker, unlike a money manager, earns his or her living by *selling.* Theoretically, the broker does not care if your investment goes up or down because he or she makes the commission on the purchase and the sale no matter what. In fact, some people might argue that brokers like to sell a few bombs because it guarantees them a healthy number of sales. This might be a somewhat cynical view of the brokerage industry, but probably less cynical than a lot of other ideas about brokers.

The psychology of investing on a broker's advice is quite arcane. Investors are constantly complaining that their broker "touted" them to a stock that took a beating. But no matter how badly broker-inspired investments do, investors have tended to come back for more because, obviously, they like playing "the Game"—and because in the past there has really been little or no other source of information for the small investor.

The less cynical view of a broker, however, would hold that if he screwed too many clients, then no one would come back to invest more money with him. The broker would eventually have to get out of the business and sell shoes.

The relationship between individual brokers and brokerage houses is different from most other employer-employee relationships. An individual broker works on a commission for everything he sells. That commission is a percentage of the commission the brokerage house earns on the sale. Clients tend to follow brokers more than they follow brokerage houses, and brokers tend to go where they get a better deal. If a broker brings in $250,000 in commissions, about $150,000 of that will go to the firm. But if one firm offers him the opportunity to keep an extra two percent, that broker might be gone—with his client list—in a matter of days.

In the opposite way, if a broker is only bringing in $60,000 or $80,000 a year, the firm may not think he is bringing in enough after his cut to pay for the ancillary services they are providing—desk, telephone, secretarial services, his share of the research department salaries, etc. During the 1970s, the industry lost a large percentage of its brokers because business was slow and they could not bring in their keep.

This can have a profound impact on how brokers and brokerage houses determine what kind of computer assistance to use. In the past, brokerage houses have used quote vendors who deliver information about prices. The quote vendors have been hooked into the New York Stock Exchange, the American Stock Exchange, and, more recently, the National Association of Security Dealers Automatic Quote (NASDAQ) system that delivers prices about consolidated over-the-counter trading.

Brokers kept individual records in a cursory manner about their clients' accounts and the full trading records were kept either on the company's mainframe or a time-sharing computer (used by small brokerage houses). Clients were put on a brokerage-wide mailing list to receive certain types of investment reports and brokers sent out other information on request.

Now, with personal computers, brokers can do a lot of the recordkeeping that previously could only be done by the mainframe. But with that ability comes the question of control and supervision. Brokerage houses are now in the process of determining if they should allow brokers to have their own personal computers in the office. If the answer is yes, the houses are asking, should we standardize on one particular type of computer? What are the possibilities for networking? How do we control the use of software?

With business picking up, will the number of brokers increase or will the number of brokers out there handle the increased client load using computers? In addition, will brokerage houses, like banks, try to shuttle their smaller clients to automated brokers—computers—to do their trading? Will brokerage houses let any of their clients who want to trade over the telephone through a computer system? These are some of the questions that will be answered by the end of this decade and could cause major change in the brokerage industry.

Reason would tell us that brokers would fight these trends, and—because of the delicate relationship between an individual broker and his or her parent company— they might win although the firm could do better financially by automating as much of its front office trading (there is no doubt that the *back* office work will be automated) as soon as possible.

"I've Got a Stock . . ."

But before we talk about the brokerage house of the future, let us talk a little bit about a broker's day and the computer tools that are making his life easier. If these tools work out, the broker should be able to meet both his goals—servicing more accounts and generating more commissions—and his clients' goals—better servicing of their accounts—at the same time.

In addition to knowing what his clients have in their portfolios, a broker must know what his clients' goals are and what kind of investments they are looking for.

Current software for brokers allows them to keep all their own client portfolio records as well as records of the kinds of investments in which their clients would be interested. At the push of a button, a broker can cross-reference his files and pull out the names of all clients who might be interested in purchasing a position in the company's latest oil and gas leasing tax shelter, or the latest issue of a tax-exempt municipal bond unit trust. And if adverse news comes to his attention about an investment a lot of his clients are in on, he can get a list in seconds and start making calls to see if anybody wants to sell out.

In addition, much of this software allows the broker to use the database management module to set up lists of likely clients for future "prospecting," and to generate letters to both clients and prospects with his word-processing software.

While the personal computer can be a boon to broker-client communications, it also can open a Pandora's box of possible violations by the broker of SEC regulations—either by design or by accident.

The SEC has already ruled on a case—and barred a broker for one year—involving personal computer misuse. According to the SEC, a broker in the Chicago office of Paine Webber defrauded four investors by sending them personal computer printouts showing that their accounts were making money when they were actually losing money. The broker apparently convinced the clients that the personal computer records were more accurate than the records kept by the back office, which at the time was involved in the tedious task of combining its records with those of Blyth Eastman Dillion, a brokerage house Paine Webber had just acquired.

This kind of obvious fraud is only the most blatant example of what could happen given larcenous or merely overzealous brokers. What would happen if:

- ☐ A broker, after reading the in-house research report at home over the weekend, thought a particular new issue coming out the following Thursday looked good. Having his computer at home, he dashed off letters to 10 clients he knew (from looking at his client lists) were interested in the new issues market. The official-looking letters are mailed out on Saturday without being looked over by the branch manager or another supervisor. In addition, the letters do not have the standard disclaimer that, basically, nothing is certain in the world of investing.

- ☐ A broker forgot to back up his diskette, and, not having a manual bookkeeping system anymore, lost the records of 10 clients' portfolios.
- ☐ A broker, knowing that a few of his clients are particularly interested in technical analysis, bought some software programs and began doing a special research report for these clients. Then, after having some success with his technical modeling, he begins using his success and his model as a sales pitch when making "prospecting" calls. To compound his problem, he uses the pitch not only with friends of those who follow his technical commentary, but all those in his prospecting database.

These are just some of the possible indiscretions brokers may perform that are giving brokerage industry management a whole new set of ulcers. Some companies are dealing with the issues by setting up personal computer policy while others are playing it by ear. And the SEC has admitted that it has not spent much time as of yet dealing with personal computers and compliance.

One company that has set up a policy is Smith Barney. All brokers who purchase computers must register the hardware and software with the Smith Barney compliance office. The broker must keep a backup set of records by hand and must clear all work done on the computer with the compliance office. All information stored on the computer is company property. The computer cannot be used in any sales pitch and no broker-generated investment analysis can be done and sent out without compliance office clearance.

These problems may be circumvented to some extent when brokerage houses settle on a uniform personal computer system—or a system of terminals tied to linked minicomputers via terminals, as is being proposed by a number of the current quote vending companies. In this kind of a networking system, compliance will be easier to monitor since material for external consumption will be generated only from a few centrally located printing facilities.

If brokerage companies use their computer facilities well in the coming years, they may produce a series of form letters that will contain the necessary disclaimers and hedging language so that brokers could just pop in the particulars and command the computer to call up the portion of his client or prospect file to whom he would like to send the letter.

The Future: Robot Brokers and Teleresearch

As has been mentioned, the E.F. Hutton brokerage firm has recently come out with Huttonline, an on-line research service for its brokerage customers. No doubt this will be the first of many such research services offered by full-service brokerage firms.

In addition, brokerage firms are selling software on a so-called "soft-money" basis—that is, the software is sold by the brokerage firm on the condition that the user do a certain amount of business with the brokerage. There can be no doubt that in the future, brokerage firms will be offering lines of software to customers. Either the software will be shipped from the developer through the brokerage firm to the user for the user to do the work with or, in some cases, the brokerage house will do the work and ship the completed studies as a "value added" service to its customers.

In this scenario, there may no longer be any distinction between a full-service and a discount broker. Brokerage houses may offer a full range of pricing options.

For the investor who wants to do his own computer homework, there will be a purely discount brokerage service—no doubt with an invest-by-phone system—where the user computer, entering a user code, issues buy and sell orders directly over the telephone lines to the brokerage house's back-room computer system. Already there are four firms that offer invest-by-computer services: the Fidelity brokerage company of Boston, the San Francisco firm of C.D. Anderson, North American Investment Co. of East Hartford, and Unified Management Co. of Indianapolis. Each one has a system that is somewhat different technically and keyed in to a different marketing tool the firm uses. Fidelity and C.D. Anderson are using the Trade Plus system of telephone trading, with its mainframe, software and database (although Fidelity says it has made major enhancements). NAICO/NET, the North American system, and the Unified Micro Computer account are handled on in-house systems using proprietary software designed by those firms.

The key benefits to consumers of these systems is convenience more than speed. SEC regulations say that all trading by "unsophisticated" traders must be monitored, so when a customer orders a trade on one of these systems, it does not go right from his fingertips to the trading floor. Instead, it is screened by the brokerage firm to make sure it fits in with the general type of trading the customer said he would be doing when he filled out the account application form. Fidelity, Anderson, and Unified all said they can screen and retransmit a trade by computer faster than one where the customer calls the broker. North American said that it can do a computer trade in less than two minutes if the trade is executed during the market day.

Since speed isn't the main factor, it is the ability for consumers to do their stock trading off-hours, evenings and weekends, that is a big selling point of these systems. You can put in an order in the middle of the night and know that it will be executed in the morning when the market opens. "Think of the doctor," says Eric Cobren, marketing manager for Fidelity's system. "When the market opens he might be in the operating room. He can't take a call from his broker."

As of the end of May 1984, the four systems in operation offered basically the same services. In addition, all offer double-security protection—a password to get into the system then a special code for your account. But each provider had ideas about how they were going to grow and expand the services offered. In addition, Rose and Co. and Schwab and Co., two large discount brokers, had plans to offer computer trading by the end of the year.

A Quick Run-Through

By May, the four systems looked like this:

Fidelity charges $195 to get hooked into its system. Time costs are 40 cents per minute of connect time during prime time (8:00 A.M. to 6:00 P.M. Mondays through Fridays) and 10 cents during off hours. The connection is made by local telephone call to the Telenet network. There is a basic monthly time charge of $15. Stock quotes for all exchanges are available on a 15-minute delay. Real-time quotes are available if the customer pays exchange charges. Fidelity provides the software for real-time quotes at no extra cost.

From the main menu, you can get into a number of submenus. Menu 10 allows you to set up a number of stocks and options you want to keep track of for possible trading. You can number them in order of the priority you want to watch them.

Menu 20 is the ordering menu. This is the menu you will use to actually conduct trades. When you choose to buy or sell stocks or buy or sell options, you will get a submenu that takes you step by step through the process. If you don't know all the information asked in the questions in the submenu, you can get those from the information menu, menu 50.

Menu 30 gives you your portfolio information. The Fidelity portfolio is interactive, so that if you have investments you did not acquire through Fidelity, you can enter them from the keyboard into your portfolio and from then on the computer will calculate changes in their value along with the rest of your portfolio.

Menu 40 allows you to list a number of different records, including trades and tax records necessary for the IRS.

Much of the information in the portfolio and records areas are the same that you would have to pay $400-$500 to acquire in a portfolio accounting and analysis system.

Menu 50 is the information menu. If you don't know a stock symbol and have the company name, or if you know the symbol but not the name, you can get it here by cross-referencing what you know against what you don't. If you type in the first few letters of a company, the computer will give you all the possible ways to end what you have written and the stock symbols that coincide with all the various possible company names.

This is also the menu from which you use the electronic mail to communicate with your broker.

The analysis menu allows you to transfer data from one section of the database to another and to analyze options using some software in the Trade Plus system.

Some of the menu selections require that you dip further into the Trade Plus computer's data bank, and for this you pay a premium.

Currently, the C.D. Anderson system offers many of the same options as Fidelity's, since it is based on the same software. However, Cobren says Fidelity has already begun to modify the software and enhance it. By the end of 1984 the company hopes to allow users to buy and sell shares in Fidelity funds through the system and get not only the cash value of a share of the funds on the quotes, but get positions in the funds in the portfolio section, move their money from one fund to another (an extension of telephone transfer), and have access to their cash management accounts. Cobren also hopes that there will be some enhancements to the portfolio to do analysis and reorder the portfolio by performance and some of the other criteria that some portfolio analysis packages do.

The Unified Management Corp.'s system, Microcomputer Account, is keyed to that company's cash management account, UNISAVE. Any UNISAVE account holder can use a PC to get into it. Much of the system is free, such as computer trading, your portfolio, and a running statement of transactions through the account. The portfolio is not interactive, but by using the electronic mail you can have your broker add things you have not purchased through Unified to your portfolio. Unified's research, a proprietary product that is a compilation of P/E data, 260-week adjusted closing prices, balance sheet, and earnings information from 10 quarters, as well as 20-minute delayed quotes, are available for $5 per hour off hours and $10 per hour during peak time. A $5 surcharge is added if you use the national network, which allows you to get on-line with a local call to CompuServe (you don't have to be a CompuServe member).

North American Investment Co.'s system, NAICO-NET, is taking the idea of on-line brokerage a little further than other systems. If you have an account with DELPHI ($49.95), you can use NAICO-NET for no extra charge, or you can bypass DELPHI by paying $19.95 to NAICO-NET and using Timenet, another national telephone network. If you have a DELPHI account you can apply for a NAICO-NET account using the computer, and you can apply to the exchanges using your computer if you want to get real-time quotes. Telephone charges for NAICO-NET are 10 cents non-prime time and 28 cents for prime time.

David Glassman, NAICO-NET's developer and telecommunications expert, envisions the day when customers will "borrow" high-powered analysis software for only the price of time (at some surcharge). Already, NAICO-NET has introduced options software that allows the user to evaluate up to 80 different trading strategies.

All four of the vendors that offer trade-by-computer services at this time are discount brokers. Whether the system ever catches on in full-service houses is doubtful. But if full-service houses unbundle services, they may institute computer trading and set a rate structure for each service rendered.

There will be a separate rate for computer traders, and another for those who like to issue their orders through people and receive back confirmation by word of mouth that the trade has been executed. Another fee schedule may be set up for those who want to receive the company's research and have a steady relationship with a specific broker (similar to today's full-service brokerage).

Those who want the brokerage house to run specific tests for them using the investment models they believe in would pay yet a higher price (possibly on a flat monthly rate) or buy the test generated. This would take Glassman's idea one step further: Not only would the customer be borrowing the software and paying for the time, but he would be borrowing the expertise of those at the brokerage house who conduct and analyze the results of the tests.

For instance, a client may want the brokerage house to send him the latest run of the 60 days out-30 days back model for the Ex Dividend Monitor program on the 10th of each month, or send him a weekly charting of the NYSE moving average and on-balance-volume after the market closes each Friday using Compu Trac.

Political Problems

This will be the easy part. There is, no doubt, a population of hard-core computer users that wants nothing better than to add the computer's speed in order processing to the already large bag of investing tricks they can make their little electronic pets perform.

It will be much more difficult for the brokerage firms to push the computer age. Already we have seen computer banking, touted through the late 1970s and into the first few years of the 1980s, fizzle.

Experiments with banking at home have shown consumers hesitant to use the systems. One reason is security. 1983 was the year that computer security became a big news issue. It also was the year that a lot of banks completed their home banking experiments. Consumers were found to be afraid that their money could vanish into thin air in the middle of a computerized transaction.

In addition, people actually found the computer cumbersome in doing financial transactions. Pay-by-phone was a hit because a person could call up the bank pay-by-phone number and tell the person or tape machine at the other end "pay X hardware $24.95." Getting through three menus to the "pay a bill" level of the bank-at-home programs, then writing in the person to whom the bill was to be paid and the amount, ended up taking more time than writing a check. People also resented the fact that some banks were going to install bank-at-home only on dedicated dumb terminals. Other banks, trying to make the system inexpensive by aiming it at users of home computers, found their customers reluctant to monkey around with the backs of their television sets to plug in the ATARI just to pay the mortgage.

NAICO-NET claims to have about 3,500 users, but C.D. Anderson had only about 400 using the system six months after it had been initiated. Fidelity refused to say how many users it had after two months in business; Unified put its number at 150 for the first 60 days.

From this reaction, it is doubtful that brokerage houses could push users into investing at home. There may be enough hard-core computer users to keep a few of these systems going, but many will have trouble generating any money—at least in the near future. Many brokerage houses may keep them going as loss-leaders, hooking users on that particular brokerage service and hoping for the day when computers will truly become ubiquitous.

Automatic Brokers?

The automatic teller machines, the other aspect of computerized banking that could be carried into the brokerage world, has had more success than banking at home, but it has been limited.

Again, there is a core of people who like the ATM because it gets them out of waiting lines to see tellers for routine transactions. But many banks misjudged the appeal of ATMs. When New York's Citibank ordered in early 1983 that its customers with less than $5,000 in their combined savings and checking accounts had to use ATMs for deposits and withdrawals, the backlash was tremendous. The feeling of people that their bank suddenly did not think their money was good enough because there was not much of it was almost overwhelming, and Citibank was eventually forced to rescind the regulation in New York City, although it was kept in effect—with a higher minimum—at some Long Island branches.

Would people walk into a broker's office, sit down at a computer, and key in an order? Possibly, but as in banking, there are a number of people who feel that an important part of making the transaction is the human contact.

If a brokerage house installed five automatic broker machines and held classes for people on how to use them, they probably would get a number of their clients—especially smaller investors who make somewhat frequent trades—to use them. People would certainly use them to get quotes on their stocks (many brokerage houses allow people to come in and bang away at quote machines today) and to get the positions in their portfolio, but there is doubt about whether any serious trading would be done on them. If a brokerage house were to install the machines and put a sign up saying, "If you are trading less than 500 shares you must use the automatic broker," the firm would probably lose all of their potential walk-in customers and many of its regulars who do not trade in lots that large.

But beyond the customer reaction, the brokerage house would probably have a mass insurrection on its hands by brokers who were afraid the firm was trying to "strip their books" (take away their accounts) for the sake of pocketing the entire commission. After all, there are good institutional brokers and good retail brokers, and retail brokers bring in a good percentage of many firms' business. If brokers could convince their clients that they were really getting more service—and service is the name of the game—by dealing with a human being than with a machine, they could then either force the firm to drop the automatic broker idea or move to another firm, taking with them all their under-500-share clients (who were the potential client base for the automatic brokers) and their over-500-share clients—who were worth a lot to the firm.

Chapter 13

The Future

The computer has only begun to have an impact on the investment world. So far the computer has given smaller investors the ability to do studies previously available only to individuals and firms with large amounts of computing power, time, and money. In addition, we have begun to see personal computers infiltrating the brokerage industry and changing the ways in which brokers and their clients interact.

What can we expect in the future?

First, we can expect the current types of software to proliferate. The consumer market will determine which kinds of software will be most successful but my belief is that programs at the higher and lower ends of the price range will be the ones to capture the consumer's imagination. In addition, I would venture that the most popular software in the near future will be software that combines a number of different functions necessary for maximal investing capability—most notably portfolio management, portfolio valuation, and a few technical analysis studies. The big breakthrough will be when someone finds a way to create out of the database on the Dow Jones News/Retrieval Service a database that one can manipulate with fundamental studies such as Micro/Scan or Value/Screen.

Already Micro/Scan is offering an updating service via modem for users who do not want to wait for the canned database to update their data. But it is still expensive—$50 to $75 per update. When a 1200 baud modem can take the data from Dow Jones in a few minutes, or make a first cut in the database and break out a subset—say, electric utility stocks—that will be a breakthrough.

But this is all refinement. The big question is what will be the next generation of computer investments. A number of people are working on that question and have different answers.

The Thinking Program

One possibility is a truly intelligent investing program, or a so-called "expert system." This falls in the realm of artificial intelligence or cybernetics.

Raden Research Group has been working on an Artificial Intelligence (AI) program that will study the commodities market. The goal of artificial intelligence researchers—in any field—is to develop computer systems that will not just recognize patterns of past trading and chart them, leaving the human user saying, "Aha, the last time this happened, this kind of pattern developed and in the next few days the market did this," but will actually study variables and "learn" how to make human-like decisions based on all the information it has accumulated.

Cybernetics is a field first conceptualized in the late 1940s by Norbert Weiner, a mathematician. It encompasses not only mathematics but also engineering, machine technology, biology, ecology, and a number of other disciplines. A cybernetic system, Weiner theorized, will have a purpose and self-awareness of its progress toward the goal. The system's components will have complex interaction and the system will be dependent on receiving adequate information from its environment. The system will also adapt to changes in the environment.

The need to develop self-teaching systems—systems that recognize historical patterns and predict future patterns rather than just predicting the next day's market movements—are very important, Aronson argues. Current market trend analysis, he contends, fails primarily because of the human tendency to fit information into a normal curve, to make "laws" out of the simple descriptions of market data. If a set of indicators predicted market movements in 1980, did the same set of indicators signals the same market movement in 1975, or 1970? David Aronson of Raden Research argues that traditional technical methods do not validate tests because they fail to determine what is truly important in a pattern and what is extraneous. The only way to get around this problem is to develop a system that does not use linear or parametric equations to create models out of historic data.

Aronson theorizes that a Cybernetic AI system can be developed to analyze markets. Raden's first attempt at putting together a cybernetic trading system was called Cybernetic Analysis and Prediction (CAP). The newer system is called Pattern Recognition Information Synthesis Modeling (PRISM).

In the case of a Cybernetic trading system, the goal, according to Aronson, is to get the computer to assist with data interpretation rather than merely with data presentation. To do this, the computer's underlying logic must be tapped. And to do that, one would have to develop a computer that would, in effect, bring to life Asimov's idea of psychohistory—a computer that would take into account all human determinants of market movement.

Artificial intelligence programs are termed *heuristic*, —that is, they allow the computer to solve problems using human logic and thought patterns. Heuristic programs solve problems by going through the computer's memory and trying to solve the problem for every variable, just as a person does—unconsciously. For instance, if you want to build a desk and have the top but need the legs, you may search around your basement for material that could be used for desk legs. In your basement you find four garden chairs, a four-foot pile of bricks, two bicycles, and four three-foot-high two-by-four pieces of wood.

Looking at this collection, the solution to your problem is obvious: The two-by-fours, either at their present height or cut down to a more comfortable size, will constitute good legs for a desk.

But suppose you had just landed on the Earth from Mars and had never before seen any of this stuff. You might try putting the desk-top across the two bicycle seats, or four arms of the lawn chairs, or cutting the pile of bricks in half before deciding that a desk top two feet off the floor is not high enough.

This is basically the process that artificial intelligence researchers are trying to program into their computers. In the PRISM system, Raden programmers are trying to get the computer to look at all the variables that go into market fluctuations and separate the ones that are useful from those that are not. In "Artificial Intelligence & Pattern Recognition to Assist the Market Analyst," a two-part article David Aronson wrote for *Financial and Investment Software Review,* he argues that when PRISM is fully operational it will be better able to analyze markets than are human beings.

Humans are limited, Aronson argues, in their ability to do "configural thinking"—that is, the ability to analyze a number of variables and think about how they interrelate, and which ones are important and which are unimportant. People are only able to really focus on three or four variables at a time, Aronson states; cognitive psychologists have shown that when the human system is overloaded with variables, people tend to see patterns where none exist and fail to see patterns that do exist. Market analysis, he contends, is configural in nature.

He extends this argument by saying that those who believe in an efficient market—our friends the Random Walkers—are only right in that all information human beings can assimilate and analyze has been discounted and reflected in current price. However, a heuristic computer program that is able to do configural thinking better than human beings should be able to determine patterns and pick out important variables that humans cannot.

Raden Research is currently trying to develop a PRISM model to predict the next 20 years of stock market activity using over 500 input variables going back to 1963. Aronson says that the model has picked out only a few worthwhile indicators that consistently predict the same movement in the market each time they appear. So far, the model has been programmed on mainframe and minicomputers, but Aronson believes that when 32-bit microcomputers become available, this kind of pattern-recognition model will be available to users of the smallest computers.

Local Area Networks

Another bit of computer technology that could change the way individual investors do their research is the local area network (LAN). Currently, LANs are used within corporations to link a number of personal computers to high-cost, low-use products such as the highest quality printers or hard disks, which have the combined storage capacity of many individual diskettes. Hard disks also afford a firm control over software so that it does not have to be distributed in diskette form. Personal computers at remote sites can also be networked with the home's firm's equipment.

At some point in the future, networking may become a feasible tool by which unaffiliated people can share resources. An investor who wanted to use an expensive program such as Ex Dividend Monitor or who wanted to use a few of the Compu Trac studies could have the programs "downloaded" from a host hard disk to his or her personal computer. The software might be owned by a brokerage firm that made it available on a fee basis, or it might be owned by an association of personal computer owners in the same geographic area. It might even be owned by an investment club. LANs could make for a new generation of investment clubs—which were big in the 1950s and '60s.

There are legal as well as technical problems with LANs. Because of copyright laws, it is illegal to share software. Some software companies are writing special contracts for firms to buy only a few copies of their program and share them, either by handing the diskette around or by storing the software on hard disk and electronically moving it from user to user by way of a LAN. But it will take a number of years before the legal system works out all the quirks of groups of unaffiliated people jointly owning software and sharing it electronically.

Hassles such as these will be worked out, for it is to the software vendors' benefit to distribute goods as widely as possible. There can be no doubt that the twenty-first century investor will live in a different world from the one we inhabit, a world where information will be just a touch away and where he or she will be able to take a look at any market from more angles than ever imagined. It will be a world where personal computers can save and retrieve information never before utilized by smaller investors and where computers, if people like David Aronson are correct, not only remember what happened in the past but learn from it.

If Harry Seldon were creating his field of psychohistory today, chances are he would use it to corner the market.

Appendices

Appendix A
Investment Games

There are a number of personal computer users who may not have enough disposable income to enter the investment fray, but may be so enthralled by the Game aspect of investing that they need an outlet for their energy.

For these people, there is an increasing number of computer games that simulate financial markets. Here is a listing.

Beat the Street (stocks)
MEA Software Associates
P.O. Box 2385
Littleton CO 80161
$49.95
Apple II.

Millionaire (stocks)
Blue Chip Software
19824 Ventura Blvd. Suite 125
Woodland Hills CA 91364
$59.95, $69.95 for 8″ disk format
IBM PC, Apple II, DEC Rainbow, ATARI 800, most MS DOS, CP/M and CP/M operating system computers.

Tycoon (commodities)
Blue Chip Software (above)
Same prices, same computers.

Stocks and Bonds
Microcomputer Games Inc.
Avalon Hill Game Co.
4517 Harford Rd.
Baltimore MD 21214
$25
IBM PC, Apple II, ATARI 400 and 800.

Appendix B
Resources

The list of places to turn to for ongoing information about the computerization of the investing world is currently small but growing. Start with:

American Society of Individual Investors
612 North Michigan Avenue
Chicago IL 60611

The society puts out a bimonthly magazine, *Computerized Investing,* which is available to members at discount.

American Association of Microcomputer Investors
P.O. Box 1384
Princeton NJ 08542

This society's bimonthly is called *The AAMI Journal,* and comes as part of the membership price.

The Boston Computer Society
Investors User Group
One Center Plaza
Boston MA 02108

The group is geared toward individual investors and puts out a monthly bulletin.

The Financial & Investment Software Review
P.O. Box 6
Riverdale NY 10471

An independent quarterly aimed primarily at individual investors.

Wall Street Computer Review
150 Broadway
New York NY 10038

A glossy monthly magazine intended for the investment professional using personal and minicomputers.

Glossary

Glossary

amortize: Technically this means to reduce the principal of a loan by regular payments. But it can also be used to mean using a good or a service enough so that the cost is spread among a large number of individual instances; i.e. to amortize the cost of a computer over 1,000 stock trades means the $5,000 computer cost $5 per trade to purchase.

balance sheet: A financial statement that lists a company's assets on one side and balances the bottom line figure against liabilities and equities on the other side.

Black/Scholes Model: An option valuation model developed by two finance professors to determine the probable value of an option at a time in the future.

bond: A security issued by a corporation or government entity to persons who lend it money. A bondholder has no equity in the company, only the position of lender. Bonds pay a set rate of interest for a given period.

broker: A person who sells securities, commodities, insurance, or other investment vehicles to the public or to institutional investors. There are full service brokers who work out of brokerage houses that offer a number of services including providing research and advice. Discount brokers merely execute trades. Discounters charge as much as 70 percent less than full service brokers, and do not "sell" securities to their customers.

call: An option that allows a buyer to buy 100 shares of a given stock at a set price on a particular date—to call the stock from the person who "writes" the call.

capital gains, capital losses: Gains or losses realized through the sale of capital assets such as securities or real estate.

Short-term gains or losses are realized when the capital good is held less than one year; long-term capital gains or losses when the good is held one year or more.

capital gains taxes: Capital gains are taxed in a unique way. Short-term capital gains are taxed at regular income tax rates (as regular earned income) while long-term capital gains have a 60 percent exclusion; i.e. only 40 percent of the gain is taxed at regular income tax rates. On the other hand, a short-term capital loss may be written off one's taxes at $1 for each $1 lost against capital gains. Long-term capital losses are written off at $1 for every $2 lost. If there are no capital gains to offset the losses, capital losses can be written off against other income up to $3,000.

capitalization: The way a company is structured in terms of its debt, equity, and the type of stocks and bonds it has issued.

commission: The amount paid by the purchaser or seller of a security to the broker for services rendered in buying or selling.

commodity: Also called a *commodity option* or a *commodity future,* this is a contract to buy a given amount of a commodity at a set price on a specified date. It is a vehicle used either for speculation or hedging on the future price of that commodity.

convertible bond: A bond that also has the ability to be converted to shares of common stock. In this way, the bond pays a given rate of interest, and so cannot fall below a "floor" in terms of value. If the common stock should rise, investors can convert their bonds and take advantage of the capital gains potential of the stock. Companies can call the bonds and force investors to convert or liquidate.

database: A large set of information usually stored on a mainframe computer that others can gain access to. There are a number of commercial databases that allow users to connect personal computers to them in order to get information about investing opportunities.

debt: Borrowed money. A bond is debt for the company or government entity that issues it. A home mortgage is debt, as is a personal loan.

debt/equity ratio: The D/E ratio gives some indication of how much money a company owes in relation to its total market value in terms of shares of stock.

dividends: Money paid to investors out of profits. Many stocks pay dividends, especially after a company has become mature and needs to retain less earnings for corporate use. In this way, equity owners share profits. Dividends are usually paid quarterly. Some insurance companies also pay dividends.

earnings per share: EPS, as it is commonly known, is the "bottom line" of a company's profitability—after all the interest on debt is paid, the taxes and all the operating expenses, how much profit did the company make per share of equity? Some of this EPS is kept as "retained earnings" to put back into the business so less borrowing is necessary, while some of it is paid to shareholders in the form of dividends.

equity: The value of an ownership position in real property, such as real estate or securities. For an individual, buying stock is taking an equity position in a company, since stock represents a share of ownership. For the company, the total value of the stock held by all stockholders represents the shareholders equity as opposed to the company's debt.

fundamental analysis: The method by which some analysts look at the underlying "fundamentals" of a company's finances, market, industry, business practices, and other areas to try to determine the true value of the company's stock.

government obligations: Government denotes the Federal Government here. Government obligations are considered the debt instruments issued by the U.S. Treasury to offset the national debt. These are Treasury bonds, bills, and notes and United States Savings Bonds.

income statement: A financial statement that lists all of a company's income, expenses, and the bottom line result, which is *earnings per share.*

interest: The payment made on borrowed money. Banks pay interest on savings accounts (money borrowed from account holders), as do brokers on their money market mutual funds. Corporations also pay interest to bondholders, who are, after all, lenders.

margin: A vehicle used to add leverage to an investment. An investor is allowed to borrow, from a brokerage house, the value of the securities held by the brokerage house in order to buy more securities. In this way, an investor can buy 200 shares of stock by putting up cash for 100 shares and borrowing against the 100 to buy the other 100. However, if the value of the stock goes down, the 100 original shares may not be worth enough to cover the debt, and a *margin call* may ensue, where the brokerage house either gets the investor to put up more cash or securities to collateralize the loan or liquidates all or part of the position to pay off the loan. Margin loans also incur interest.

modem (modulator-demodulator): A telephone link that allows one computer to talk to another over standard telephone lines. A modem translates digital signals from a computer to analog signals for the phone lines and translates the analog signals back to digital at the other end of the "conversation."

mortgage obligation bonds: A number of federal (and some state) agencies guarantee loans made by banks to certain homeowners. These agencies, in effect, buy the loans from the banks that issue them originally. The agencies get the funds to buy the mortgages from investors who buy bonds representing a portion of all of the mortgages purchased. The payments made by homeowners each month, in turn, are used to pay the interest to the investors who purchased the bonds. Some of the agencies and the bonds they issue are the Government National Mortgage Association (Ginnie Mae bonds) and the Federal Home Loan Mortgage Corp. (Freddie Mac bonds).

municipal bonds: Municipals are issued by states, cities, towns, and independent state agencies such as university systems, transit authorities, and housing authorities. They are issued both for general obligations and for specific revenue raising. Interest from municipal bonds are exempt from federal income taxes (capital gains are not exempt) and many states exempt bonds issued by their own state agencies and municipalities from state income taxes.

mutual fund: A mutual fund (sometimes called an investment company) is a pool of funds from a number of investors used to invest in securities—either bonds, stocks, or short-term money market instruments. New investors may enter the fund, old investors may make further contributions or liquidations, and the manager of the fund actively seeks to improve the performance of the fund by buying and selling securities. Mutual funds are sometimes confused with unit investment trusts, which are a limited portfolio of securities (usually bonds) that sell a set number of units, then close. Unit trusts are not actively managed.

option: A contract to either buy or sell 100 shares of stock at a certain date for a specified price. Options are used either to speculate on a rise or fall in the price of a stock or to hedge against such a rise or fall. Options are purchased for a "premium" of a few dollars per share, which makes them highly leveraged.

peripherals: Computer components that add to the central processing unit to enhance the power and usefulness of the computer.

personal computer: A computer that is small and inexpensive enough to be owned by a small businessperson or homeowner; a desktop-sized or smaller computer costing less than $5,000 with peripheral equipment.

portfolio: The group of securities an investor owns. Portfolio management is the maintenance of portfolio records. Portfolio analysis is the analysis of the strengths and weaknesses of the portfolio.

preferred stock/preference stock: Stock issued with a stated dividend payment rather than one determined each quarter (common stock). Preferred and preference stock are considered "senior stocks" and "fixed income securities" like bonds. They are, however, considered equity rather than debt in determining the company D/E Ratio.

price/earnings ratio: The ratio of the price of the stock to the earnings per share of the stock. Theoretically, different industry groups have different average P/E ratios, and stocks within that group that vary can be considered undervalued or overvalued. Earnings per share is one of the components analysts use to determine value.

put: A put allows a purchaser to sell 100 shares of stock at a given time for a specified price—to *put* the stock to another person.

software: The series of instructions that tell a computer what to do and how to do it. For personal computer, these instructions are usually electronic signals on a floppy diskette.

stock: An ownership or equity interest in a company. It represents a portion of the company's value, in terms of the assets it has minus the debts it still owes.

technical analysis: The analysis of securities markets by following past price movements and price movement trends.

yield: The annualized return on an investment. It is usually considered as the interest or dividend as a percentage of the original price of the security or the price an individual paid for it. When the security is sold, any capital gains or losses can be added or subtracted to the dividends or interest paid to get a total yield. Yield is calculated closely in bond purchasing.

Index